Stage Management

THIRD EDITION

Stage Management

A Guidebook of Practical Techniques

LAWRENCE STERN

Allyn and Bacon, Inc.
Boston London Sydney Toronto

The author wishes to acknowledge his gratitude for permission to reprint excerpts from the following sources:

Hildegard Knef, *The Gift Horse*, translated by David Anthony Palastanga. New York: McGraw-Hill Book Company, 1971. English translation copyright © 1971 by Hildegard Knef.

The Son of Any Wednesday, Muriel Resnik. Reprinted by permission of the William Morris Agency, Inc. Copyright © 1965 by Muriel Resnik.

Library of Congress Cataloging-in-Publication Data

Stern, Lawrence, 1935–
  Stage management.

  Includes index.
  1. Stage management.   I. Title.
PN2085.S77 1987   792'.023   86–22192
ISBN 0–205–10287–5

Printed in the United States of America
10 9 8 7 6 5   91 90 89

In memory of Xenia Chekhov

A CHRONOLOGICAL APPROACH AND PRIORITIES

TASK	PAGE	PRIORITY	COORDINATE WITH
BEFORE REHEARSALS BEGIN			
Get things to run smoothly on stage and backstage	1	A	
Gather equipment	54	B,E,F	
Be aware of police, fire, and municipal regulations	218	A	Producer, Tech Dir
Inspect safety conditions	121	A	
Get to know the theater	56	B	
Make a diagram of the stage	56	C	Tech Dir
Check out the fuse boxes	58	C	Tech Dir
Make a diagram of lighting instruments	61	C	Tech Dir, Light Design
Keep a do list	124	B	
Make a prompt script	20	A,B,D	Director
Identify the problems of the script	24	A	Director
Write out plots	25	B,C,G	Dir, Technicians
Make master calendar	35	B,C	Everyone
Schedule staff meetings	39	C	Producer
Distribute rehearsal schedules	39	B,C	Producer, Director
Arrange the callboard	44	C	Producer
Distribute and explain company rules	44	C,G	Producer, Director
Keep a budget and record of your expenses	89	A	Producer
Obtain audition forms	74	B,C	Producer, Director
Prepare staff, crew, cast lists	80	C	Prod, Dir, Staff, Crew
Make gel patterns	156	D	Technicians
Make supply directory	213	E	
Post emergency numbers	47	A	
DURING READINGS AND REHEARSALS			
Prepare audition rooms	67	B,C,D	Producer, Director
Post notes for readings	68	B,C,D,F,G	Prod, Dir, Publicist
Accept résumés	72	E	Director
Control scripts	73	B	Director
Make preset diagrams	97	A	Dir, Tech Dir, Sc Des
Prepare for rehearsals	99	B,D	Director
Post running order	115	B,D	Director
Supervise department heads	137	C	Prod, Dept Heads
Control required forms	78	C	Producer, Director
Conduct deputy election	84	B	Union, Cast
Keep cast on time	131	A,B	Director, Cast
Distribute itineraries	205	C	Producer, Cast
Distribute touring agreement	207	C	Cast
Post duty roster	192	C	Everyone
Make checklists	177	B	
Supervise props	139	A	Property Master, Producer, Director
Distribute scene shift diagrams	169	B,C,D	Scene Designer
Contribute to advance letters	209	C	Producer
Maintain order	112	B,E	Director
Call rehearsal cues	100	A	Director
Take blocking notation	101	B,C,D	Director
Make French scene diagrams	106	E	
Spike set pieces	108	A,C	Tech Dir
Prompt	108	C	Director, Cast
Give rehearsal, publicity, costume calls	112	A	Everyone

KEY: A. I've got to do this first. The quality of the production will be adversely affected if I don't.

B. I've got to do this because if I don't, time and energy of staff and cast will be wasted.

C. Someone else may do this well, but I've got to make sure it gets done.

D. I can assign this task to a subordinate if I make sure it gets done.

TASK	PAGE	PRIORITY	COORDINATE WITH
Warn cast	111	E	Director, Cast
Keep rehearsal log	119	E	
Submit rehearsal reports	119	B,G	Producer
Time rehearsals	117	B,D	Director, House Manager
Post photo calls	113	E	Publicist, Director, Costumer, Cast
Prepare lighting sheet	149	B,C	Light Techs
Work on take-in; brief crew	162	C,D,B	Scene Designer, Tech Dir, Crew
Make shift plot chart	157	C,D	Tech Dir
Supervise arrangement of scene dock	163	C,D	Tech Dir
Supervise technical rehearsal	173	A	Director, Tech Dir
Choreograph scene changes	160	B,D	Tech Dir
Prepare area lighting diagram	155	C	Light Designer
Prepare re-gelling plans	153	C	Light Designer
Post sign-in sheets	132	B,C	
Place curtain call light cues on lighting sheet	183	B	Director, Light Techs
DURING PRODUCTION			
Conduct lighting check	147	A	Light Designer, Light Techs
Post scene shift diagrams	166	B,C,D	Tech Dir
Give calls (prior to curtain)	135	A	Cast
Caution audience	169	C	Producer
Call late actors	131	A	Cast
Coordinate with house manager	187	A	House Manager
Give cues	179	A	Technicians
Check immediate effect of each cue	181	A	
Supervise shifts	157	C,D	Tech Dir
Inspect shifts	165	B,C,D	Tech Dir
Time performances	117	B	Director
Walk the curtain	184	D	Tech Dir
Time curtain calls	183	A	Director
Maintain sets	170	D,C,D	Tech Dir
Be aware of cast morale	197	A	Cast
Keep the show in hand	195	A,C	Director, Cast
Post V.I.P. list	193	F	Producer
Rehearse understudies, block replacements	198	C	Producer, Director, Cast
POST PRODUCTION			
Distribute strike plan	201	B,C,G	Tech Dir
Post changeover schedule	203	C,G	Producer, Tech Dir
Supervise moves	205	A,B,C	Producer
Write letter to next stage manager	225	F	
Write critique	226	D	
Write letters of recommendation, thank-you notes	226	F	
IN GENERAL			
Make contact file	215	E	
Make a theater information packet	63	C,F,G	Producer, Tech Dir
Get acquainted with unions	220	C,E	
Send out résumés	278	A	
Read theater news	211	E	
Keep in contact with theater acquaintances	283	F	
Start a theater library	215	F	

E. I'll do it if I have time, and it would help, but we'll survive without it.

F. A luxury; I'll leave it for last.

G. This might be helpful for another show, but will be useless here.

Contents

Foreword

The best way to introduce this book is to speak well and perfectly about the Author. For you can't expect a stage manager like Lawrence Stern to stand up front and blow his own horn. Someone who knows him must do it for him, and I gladly assume the task.

Now there are all sorts of virtues a stage manager must have. You will find them listed and profusely described in the pages of this book. But the supreme virtue among many is: The stage manager must arrive before everyone and leave long after everyone else is gone.

Of course that is the essence of creativity in any field you may want to mention. Those who love writing stay up until dawn to finish a story. Those who love painting work around the clock until they drop dead in their tracks. Stage managers . . . ?

Lawrence Stern is one of those superb men who quietly go about their business, keep charts, arrive two hours early and, long after the play has closed or collapsed, or both, can be found carrying out the trash, cleaning up the lobby, filling in the final forms, or holding the flashlight while the author of the play crawls around on the floor of the ladies' room helping some poor blind thing find her lost contact lens.

All this Lawrence Stern has done, and more. His passions may be quiet, but they are there. Instead of your usual slob, found all too frequently in our unhappy society these days, Lawrence Stern is one of those who gives you 150 percent of himself. I know that sounds impossible, but I have seen him do it. And this book, with its incredible amount of detail and huge compilation of firsthand knowledge is proof of all that I say.

Frankly, I don't know how your average stage manager ever got along without this book, just as my own Pandemonium Theatre Company was never the same once Lawrence Stern moved on to other fields.

There you have it: some sort of idea of the man who wrote this book. But you needn't take my word for it. Just leaf through the book swiftly, checking chapters, pages, paragraphs. You'll soon find that a subtitle of the book could well be More Than You Ever Wanted To Know About Stage Managing. Except of course, that would be foolish: you can never know enough.

Let Lawrence Stern be the best teacher you ever had. He's here. *Listen* to him!

Ray Bradbury
Los Angeles

Preface to the Third Edition

A great reward of having written this book has been hearing from so many readers. In this third edition, Allyn and Bacon has allowed me to print some of their comments.

One comment on cuing challenges the tradition of the theater that I was taught and accepted without question. I point this out because I feel that everyone who works in theater wants to improve production techniques. We ought to keep our minds open. We ought to try new techniques to see if they will work.

Looking forward to the fourth edition, I'm hoping that more readers will contribute suggestions. If, after reading this guidebook, you find that there is information missing that would be useful to stage managers, please let me know. Many readers will work in staging environments unfamiliar to me: theme parks, ballet, dinner theaters, ice shows, lounge acts, festivals, etc. If you look back on your experience and say, "I wish I had read that in *Stage Management*," please let me know.

On page 317 you'll find a reader's comment form with my address. Thanks for your help.

L.S.
Hollywood, 1986

Preface to the First Edition

In the many levels of live theater—educational, children's, community, showcase, and professional—there are few provisions for training in stage management. It is often assumed that anyone can do the job reasonably well who has a mind to, without previous training or experience, and the result of this is a great deal of trial and an enormous amount of error. A new stage manager typically makes his or her own kind of improvised performance, trying to carry out the functions of stage management without ever being able to find out for sure what those functions are, except by trial and error. Unfortunately, there are few places where anyone can find any written summary of useful principles or primary needs of stage management, and what they do find by gleaning from texts on directing, stagecraft, or the like, is not usually appropriate to any one person's theater situation, much less to a reliable or professional standard for this kind of work. Most managers solve their problems with whatever organizational skill and inventiveness they possess—but at an unwarranted cost in time, effort, and uncertainty.

At the amateur levels of live theater, particularly in educational and community theater, the problems resulting from such a lack of guidelines for stage management are compounded by the fact that often the duties of the producer, director, stage manager, and even business manager are assumed by one person. This individual is frequently a faculty member or volunteer who has had little or no experience in stage management. It is this person who stands to profit most from this book.

However, this guide is written in the hope that it will prove to be a valuable tool for all producers, directors, stage managers, and supervisors of theatrical programs, regardless of theater level or staging environment.

L.S.
Los Angeles, 1973

1

Making Things Run Smoothly

A Point of Departure

The cast, staff, and crew of a live theater work together toward a common goal: a good performance. Thus, theater is necessarily a group effort in professional, amateur, or educational theater. However, it is *never* a group effort of vague fellow committee-members, but of associated autocrats—a playwright, a producer, a director, a stage manager, designers, and above all, actors. Each accommodates the others, and to some extent may overlap others in function when necessary, considering the wide variety of differing conditions for each show and every kind and level of theater. But each autocrat assumes distinct responsibilities and accepts them completely: The *producer* is the general manager who has responsibility for obtaining the personnel and resources to make theater happen. The *actors* must serve as the most essential dramatic media, without whom no theatrical ideas or emotions can be communicated to an audience. The *director* must interpret the playwright's script through the medium of actors and designers. The person who has responsibility for making the entire production run smoothly, on stage and backstage, in pre-rehearsal, rehearsal, performance, and post-performance phases, is the stage manager.

Stage management in general involves more responsibilities and resources than any one manager ever needs to apply to any single production. So with this guidebook I shall describe and give examples of many more methods for stage management than should be applied to any one production, and you will need to use your judgment in determining which will be most effective for you. However, at this point you might also benefit from some overview of these functions to show how the responsibilities of stage management are needed and applied. I can provide this best through a personal anecdote about a situation in which I did not even act as stage manager.

The Care and Feeding of the Amateur
Stage Manager: A True Tale of the Theatre

The North Covina Theater Guild was about to present *Take Me Along*, and I had been asked to direct. Their producer, a housewife, was Mrs. Betty Spelvin (all names changed to protect the very innocent). She had been with the group since its inception, or, to put it another way, she was the inception. She had statuettes on her desk from the Adult Drama Festival and a gavel that proclaimed her "Best Producer" on her bookcase.

My first encounter with my producer concerned the absence of the stage manager. At the production conference prior to rehearsals I asked where he was. When she told me he could not be there for the meeting, I shrugged and assumed that he would appear for the following nights' meetings, since his name appeared on the staff list.

At the first reading I again asked for the stage manager. "Oh," said Betty, "he doesn't come in until production week." Production week was her term for the week of strenuous rehearsals prior to opening night.

"When he does come in, what does he do?"

"Why he gives the actors their calls and pulls the curtain," said Betty.

From my five years as an Equity stage manager I knew there was more to it than giving calls and pulling the curtain. I also knew that I could not function as stage manager if I waited until the week of technical and dress rehearsals to join the company. "Who gives the light and sound cues?" I asked.

"The light and sound men take their own cues. They can see from the booth in back. They're junior high school kids, but very dependable."

"Well, who is supposed to assist me during auditions?"

"You're doing just fine. You're really organized. If you need any help, just yell." And she dashed off before I could.

After the readings I cornered her in the box office to ask who would be taking blocking notation during rehearsals. "The director always does that," she answered.

"Who calls the cues, warns the actors, and sets the furniture and props during rehearsals?"

"We all pitch in," smiled Betty reassuringly, "and it all gets done, so don't you worry."

"Who mimeographs and distributes the rehearsal schedule?"

"The girl in the box office. She's very good. She'll join us in two weeks. Listen, I know this isn't the way you're used to doing things in

Hollywood, but believe me, it all comes together like magic on the night."

(When I was six years old, my seven-year-old neighbor attempted to saw the lady in half using a rusty saw and me as the lady. I don't believe in magic!)

"I must have a stage manager to assist me starting tomorrow night," I said.

"Impossible," she replied. "We just haven't been able to find reliable people to work as stage manager. We have no budget for them. It's always worked out that the director is better off doing it himself."

"Let me put it in this way, Betty. Find me a stage manager or find yourself a new director."

Betty Spelvin, I found out later, had been running little-theater groups in Little Rock, Arkansas; Omaha, Nebraska; Boulder, Colorado; Manila, the Philippines, and a few other places where her husband was stationed. She had been known to sew entire wardrobes overnight, paint complete sets after dress rehearsals, get up on lines in an afternoon to stand in for an ailing actress, and fire, replace, or take over for directors on the spot.

There must have been a short supply of directors in North Covina that week. Also, Betty was moving to a new home and her daughter was about to be married. And Betty was expedient. So the next night I had a stage manager.

Paul Crowell was young and inexperienced but alert, intelligent, and personable. He was anxious to learn and caught on quickly. I gathered examples of work I'd done as a professional stage manager—schedules, promptbook, sign-in sheets, cast lists, scene shift diagrams, etc.—and turned them over to him. I explained to him the only thing I thought essential.

"As stage manager you will have total responsibility for making things run smoothly. As producer, Betty's function is to obtain the personnel and materials to make our production happen. As director, my function is to interpret the script. Both Betty and I are concerned that things run smoothly, but you are the only one on the staff who is totally in charge of smooth running. If there's a minute delay in rehearsal or production, it's your fault, and for every second within the schedule that you can deliver productive rehearsal time, you, personally, will be improving the quality of the group's performances."

Paul had been a class officer in high school. He'd lettered in baseball and football. He was efficient and had a way of getting people to move with him.

The North Covina Theater Guild was immediately responsive to what they assumed were innovations in making theater. The cast and staff had never had complete schedules and cast lists so early. Cast members were surprised when labeled prop boxes and backstage mapped prop tables appeared before they had even set aside their scripts. Most of all, they were shocked when they found rehearsals beginning at the moment called and ending at the time specified. At rehearsals all of the light and sound cues were called by the stage manager. Sound effects were used at rehearsals a week prior to the tech. Costumes were paraded well before dress rehearsals. There were no last-minute rushes. There were no late rehearsals. The tech rehearsals ended at 11 P.M. And was I amused when I overheard cast members talking about "the new method from Hollywood."

A few years have passed since Paul stage-managed his first show in North Covina. A Christmas card from Viet Nam informed me that "tanks are less temperamental than actresses and easier to stage-manage." He is now in law school.

And Betty Spelvin, bless her heart, is still running the North Covina Theater Guild. With her husband retired from the military, she is probably dug in to stay—producing, directing, stage-managing, serving coffee in the lobby at intermission, and selling theater parties.

I know I've mellowed. I certainly realize that stage management is not understood at many amateur theaters.

But I still think it's desirable. So for all of the Betty Spelvins of the world, here are five suggestions for the care and feeding of the amateur stage manager.

Get a Firm Understanding of the Function of the Stage Manager

There is no definitive list of duties of a stage manager that is applicable to all theaters and staging environments. A stage manager for a comedy performed in a theater in the round might carry out specific duties that are totally different from those of a stage manager for a traveling pantomime troupe. But the function is the same. Regardless of specific duties, the stage manager is the individual who accepts responsibility for the smooth running of rehearsals and performances, on stage and backstage. If you understand this function, you can derive the specific duties for your theater. (This book is intended to help you do this.)

Give your stage manager her or his rightful function and the responsibility to carry out that function—not just a list of duties.

In Betty's case, understanding the function of the stage manager might mean sharing some of her responsibility with him or her. Not a bad idea. Betty felt that she had to do everything herself if she wanted it done right. As a result she did everything. If she could get over her I-am-the-savior-of-the-theater complex, perhaps she could devote more of her creative energy to the producer's function of obtaining personnel and materials. Obtaining a proper stage manager would have saved herself and her directors a lot of work.

Get Firmly into Your Mind the Qualities that Make a Good Stage Manager, and Don't Settle for Anything Less

Organizational ability is one of the primary qualities of a good stage manager. Leadership ability is another. The stage manager must be able to influence the staff, cast, and crew. He or she must be a take-charge type and a self-starter and must be the kind of person who has the capacity to accept responsibility. (This book describes and applies most of these qualities in detail.)

As a producer you are expected to control quality in selecting your staff. You should select the stage manager with the same care that you use to select your director, scene designer, and costumer.

Motivate Your Stage Manager

If your stage manager is new to the work, you must make her or him see that everything she or he does contributes to the improvement of the production. It is not enough for the stage manager to understand his or her function and specific duties. Point out, for example, that in setting rehearsal furniture fifteen minutes prior to rehearsal three hours of cast time may be saved, time that can be devoted to rehearsing that will result in a more polished performance.

In short, make sure that your stage manager knows that every bit of work he or she does is desirable, necessary, and appreciated.

Collect the Work of Past Stage Managers as a Reference

It is easier to set up a rehearsal schedule if you have a well-ordered one in your hand. It is easier to improve a rotating duty roster if you have a past example to imitate. It would save a new stage manager considerable time and energy in making a shift plot chart if she or he had an old form to work from.

Collect such materials in a loose-leaf notebook arranged in the general order of their use: pre-rehearsal materials, rehearsal materials, production materials, post-production materials. (The material in this book provides a start in this direction.)

Reward Your Stage Manager

Cast members are generally rewarded by the response and applause of the audience. Directors clip their reviews. Producers count the money at the box office. But in most amateur theaters the stage manager is forgotten.

Kind words and letters of praise would be a good start. But why not let your stage manager in on the rewards available to other cast and staff members? Give her or his name prominence in the program. Publish her or his biographical sketch along with those of the cast. At the annual banquet when your theater group gives out its awards for best actress, best director, etc., why not select a best stage manager, too? Could you put a plaque that records the name of the outstanding stage manager of each year in the lobby? Find other ways to honor your stage manager— and he or she might come back for another production.

A new director who finds a stage manager who has been through several productions with a group on hand inherits an experience level that can get the director off to a flying start.

Well, Betty, that's the way it should be. But, if as in so many amateur theater groups, you want to continue to distribute the stage manager's duties while holding on to the function—if you want to continue to bring in people at the last minute to pull the curtain and give the actors their calls, and call them stage managers—if you want to continue to paint scenery and sew costumes at the last minute because you haven't done your work of obtaining a stage manager who could schedule work calls— if you want to continue to make amateur theater amateurish—then that's your problem.

2

Characteristics of a Good Stage Manager

I have since learned what a stage manager does. Everything. In production he is master of all details, liaison with Actors' Equity and the hairdresser, maker of appointments and planner of time for the cast, assistant to the director, rehearser of understudies and replacements, supervisor of all moves in and out of theaters, confidant and hand holder of cast, director, and author. Once the play opens he's the man who runs the show, attends every performance and is responsible for the condition and upkeep of the set and costumes, the temperature of the theatre, as well as the cast, and is responsible for the level of performances. He's Big Daddy. And Porter (stage manager for *Any Wednesday*), unobtrusively but meticulously organized, highly efficient, funny, warm and caring, was perfect casting.*

In the quotation above, playwright Muriel Resnik praises her stage manager as, "Unobtrusively but meticulously organized, highly efficient, funny, warm, caring." Are these the highest attributes? Let's examine some of the qualities of a good stage manager.

Proposition 1

Good stage managers assume responsibility.

They say to themselves, "I am the one who must make things run smoothly on stage and backstage. Beyond me the buck does not pass." This is an active role, not passive. It is not merely coordination. It is not merely doing what one is told. It is not merely the sum total of the myriad little duties. It is taking charge. It is accepting responsibility.

---

*From the book by Muriel Resnik, *The Son of Any Wednesday*. Reprinted by permission of Muriel Resnik. Copyright © 1965 by Muriel Resnik.

Professional Attitude

The significant difference between professional and nonprofessional stage managers is not whether they are paid or are members of a union. The significant difference is whether or not they are willing and able to accept responsibility for making the production run smoothly on stage and backstage in pre-rehearsal, rehearsal, performance, and post-performance phases.

Your professionalism will make a significant difference in your relationship to the theater staff. The producer, director, technical director, and other staff members are also concerned that things run smoothly. But they have higher priority responsibilities. You are the only one on the staff for whom this is the primary responsibility.

If you can and will accept this responsibility, you are an equal of the producer and director on the team that makes theater. If you do not accept this responsibility, and simply carry out a number of assigned tasks (pulling the curtain, giving the actors their calls, etc.), then you are a subordinate of the producer and director. Which are you?

Proposition 2

Good stage managers keep their cool.

Can you exercise emotional self-control during all phases of production?

You will be working with excitable, conceited, self-centered, temperamental, volatile, sensitive, nervous, explosive people. But you will serve them best by not becoming emotionally involved in their arguments, controversies, or displays of temper.

If the leading lady stalks out screaming and crying, hand her a tissue to show her you care, but don't tell her or the director who was right or wrong in their dispute. It's none of your business. They will resolve their problems without your help.

If the producer asks for the cooperation of the cast in nonacting chores (cleaning the dressing rooms, selling tickets, publicity, etc), don't give a noncooperative cast member a five-minute harangue or diatribe on his or her responsibilities. It is your job to insure that cast members know what the director and producer expect of them—the time, the place. You may post a duty roster. You may hand out written memos. You may phone them to remind them. You may explain. But you may not lose your temper with a cast member for any reason at all.

If a cast member is late for half hour call, even habitually late, and fails to call the theater, you may remind, you may explain, you may plead, you may cajole, but thou shalt not lose thy cool.

In general, don't raise your voice to cast members. Reply to raised voices in calm, steady, controlled tones.

If a director or producer should reprimand you, privately or before the company, for your prompting technique (as an example) or anything else, don't sulk. Get on with the job the way she or he wants it done.

If you blow a cue, don't get upset. Concentrate on getting the next one right.

Know your own panic response. Then control it. You have reacted to crises in the past. You know you can survive the next one. In time of panic there must be only one question in your mind: "Is there any action I can take to alleviate this situation?" If so, do it. If not, keep your cool. Don't get swept up in the panic. Errors tend to compound.

Example:

During a performance a telephone bell failed to sound. The actors started to ad-lib thinking that the cue was simply late. The stage manager in the booth realized that it was not late, but a mechanical failure. There was absolutely no way for the stage manager to get the bell to ring. There was no way to inform the cast on stage that the bell was not about to ring. The cast continued to ad-lib until one actor picked up the phone saying, "Thought I heard it ring."

What should the stage manager have done?

Answer: nothing

The stage manager in this case panicked, left the control booth, and ran backstage to repair the bell—even though it was not to be used again during the performance. As a result, the next two sound cues were omitted. The error was compounded.

It is terribly uncomfortable to watch a cast ad-lib around a mechanical failure. But that's the price of insufficient preparation.

1. Did the stage manager test the bell during the pre-curtain routine?
2. Did he make sure that the bell wire was out from under the feet of backstage actors and crew?
3. Did he check to see that all connections were soldered?
4. Did he have a separate emergency bell wired in? (Do you think this is going too far?)

A week later during a performance of the same play, the bell failed again. It was unquestionable negligence on the part of the stage manager. But a bell was heard. A cast member had brought an emergency bell to ring offstage because she didn't want a repeat of that incident. (Apparently the cast member didn't think an emergency bell was going too far!)

Stage Manager, if a cast member has to ring your bell for you, it's time to hang up your clipboard.

Keeping one's cool means never appearing harassed, belligerent, insecure, apologetic, or imposed upon. It's not enough to be doing your job well. You've go to let the cast know by your deportment and the relaxed smile on your face that everything is under control. This gives the cast confidence. In this way, your cool may often be a positive contributing factor to the overall quality of the production.

Proposition 3

Good stage managers keep their mouths shut and their eyes and ears open.

Do you tend to be quiet and observant? If what you say always has to do with the immediate improvement of the rehearsal or production, cast members, crew, and staff will listen to you. If you run off at the mouth endlessly, you will have to struggle to gain attention when you have something significant to contribute. Where between these two extremes are you?

If you have a choice between shouting across the stage to a subordinate to change some gel frames, and crossing the stage yourself to deliver quiet instructions, choose the latter. The cast, staff, and crew will come to appreciate the fact that you are the great mover without the vocal display.

Don't waste your own time promoting yourself. Efficient work is hard to hide so you need not explain how efficient you are to staff members.

Be alert to what is going on around you. During breaks, stick with the director. In casual conversation with actors and staff she or he will agree to changes in lines, props, cues, or design. You should make these changes, or cause them to be made, without further instruction.

Example:

During a break, an actor approaches the director and asks if he may omit a line that's been troubling him. She agrees to the omission. You were getting a cup of coffee instead of staying at the director's side. At the next rehearsal of the scene the actor omits the line. You prompt. The actor breaks character to advise you that the line was cut. You turn to the director for confirmation. The director doesn't remember since it has been three days since this scene was last run. The actor and director discuss it. They agree to omit the line, or the director decides at this time she wants the line delivered. The rehearsal resumes. But there has been a delay that you might have avoided if you had stuck with the director and kept your ears open.

There are no breaks for stage managers. If you must have refreshments, bring a thermos and pack a sandwich or snack in your kit.

Don't gossip with the cast. You will often be privileged to know things that are going on at the administrative level, or between the producer and the director, or between the conductor and the harp player, or about closing date, casting history, salaries, etc. Keep it to yourself.

If a cast member should ask you what you think of the director, staff, crew, or another cast member, try the following delivered by rote in a loud if not sincere voice: " 'X' is the best director (producer, scene designer, publicist, actor, actress, etc.) I've ever had the pleasure of working with." When you are no longer associated with that production you can say what you really think, but until then, a complete, beguiling display of "I-know-how-to-play-this-game" is the most effective way to fly.

Don't align yourself with any clique of actors within a cast. The stage manager is a friend to the whole cast. If you choose to go out after the show with one group habitually, make it clear to the others in the cast that you would also like to be with them. Invite them to come along some time.

Proposition 4

Good stage managers think ahead.

Don't just sit there, anticipate!

What is the company going to be doing later today? Tomorrow? Next week? Does everyone know about it? Is everything ready? You have made a master calendar, schedules, do-lists, duty rosters, a prompt script, and checklists. All of these are instruments to help you think ahead. But there is no substitute for constant vigilance.

If something is changed suddenly, what future effects will the changes have? What other changes must be made as a result of that change? Who must be notified?

One of your greatest contributions to the performance quality is making the most of every minute between first reading and final curtain. If there is any delay in rehearsal or production, it's your fault.

Stage-managing may be compared to flying a high-performance aircraft. Once you're in the air, you can't make repairs. Once the curtain goes up you can't stop the performance to make changes in the location of set pieces and discovered props. Pilots and stage managers both have extensive preflight checklists for these reasons.

To land a high-performance aircraft you must take several steps prior to entering the landing pattern because the aircraft moves so fast there is not time to accomplish everything once in the pattern. To carry out a tight sequence of light changes and sound effects, the stage manger must also take several steps in advance, like insuring that tapes are cued, that dimmer board presets are cranked in and patches made, and that all hands are rehearsed in the execution of that sequence and understand their cues because once the sequence starts, there is no time to do all of the things that must be done in advance if the sequence is to be brought off successfully.

Although the comparison might be extended, the point is clear: pilots and stage managers must have the same think-ahead discipline in order to be effective.

Serious emergencies call for both keeping cool and thinking ahead.

A fire should be expected momentarily (see Figure 15–1). Do you have a fire extinguisher in the control booth? Do you have another one backstage? Do you have a phone in the booth? If it's a pay phone, do you have emergency dimes taped nearby? Do you know the number to call? Is there a clear unblocked space for you to get out from behind your equipment? Can you give calm instructions to your audience in a tone of voice that will convince them to leave the theater in an orderly fashion? In a huge theater do you have a working microphone in the booth that will allow you to reach the entire audience via the public address system? Do you know how to drop the fire curtain (the asbestos curtain that hangs immediately in front of the main curtain and seals off the stage from the audience in the event of fire)? Are all of the exit aisles, doors, and alleys unblocked? Will the emergency exits open? Is your scenery flameproofed in accordance with city ordinances? Is all electrical equipment wired safely?

If the answer to any question above is no, the stage manager and the producer are derelict in their responsibility for the safety of the audience and the cast.

Stage managers must force themselves out of the rut of thinking that it can't happen here. It can happen here, and everyone in your theater will be safer if you will just assume that it is going to happen here within the next thirty seconds.

Plan ahead for the worst possible type of medical emergency. Assume that a member of the cast or crew will suffer a severe injury or heart attack in the course of mounting, rehearsing, or presenting.

Do you have a company doctor? Is her or his office or home near the theater? Do you know the location of an all-night clinic? Have you driven there on a test run from the theater? (It is maddening to find that the clinic entrance is located on a one-way street and you will have to drive three extra blocks because you didn't make the right approach—while your passenger is losing blood!)

During such emergencies keeping your cool and thinking ahead become traits of paramount importance.

Proposition 5

Good stage managers are considerate.

Do you have that quality of selfless caring that prompts a man to give a woman his jacket when he knows he'll be cold? Can you put the comfort of every cast member before your own comfort?

Is the theater warm enough? Can you get there a little earlier to turn on the heat so that cast members don't walk into a cold theater? Can you turn on the lights so cast members won't have to enter dark dressing rooms?

Is the backstage area too drafty? Can you close some doors or make some baffles out of extra flats?

Do the actresses have to walk to their cars from the theater along a dimly lit street? Can you walk them to their cars or ask other cast members to do so? If it's raining, can you provide an umbrella?

Is there drinking water backstage and in the dressing rooms? Can you arrange for water service or provide pitchers and cups?

Did you dust the rehearsal furniture before the cast sat down?

Do you really listen when cast members speak to you?

Can you offer your cast a natural affection?

Backstage in Hollywood theaters I found the lavish affection and terms of endearment that pass between casual acquaintances to be quite surprising. It did not seem very natural to me. But insecurity seems to be a very common trait among theater people, and they find warmth and affection reassuring. This display of warmth does not come naturally to all people. It is certainly not recommended if it must be forced. But if you can display a natural affection for your cast, as if they were all dear old warm friends or members of your family, why not?

Are you considerate with respect to the creativity of others? Can you offer constructive criticism effectively without stamping out creative instinct? It's very difficult to do.

Many of the creative people—the scene designers, costume designers, choral directors, choreographers, and directors—carry their gifts wrapped preciously within thin skin. Yet, in the theater situation no creator can work alone. He or she must communicate with and gain the cooperation of all the others on the staff to see his or her own creativity come to fruition. The stage manager, unfortunately, is frequently placed in the position of coordinating the creative efforts of the supersensitive. It requires a great deal of patience and tact.

Example:

Set construction is running behind schedule. The technical director complains to you that the scene designer has no concept of economy in design, that he tries to present in total rather than suggesting. She complains that the designer is overburdening the shop with an unconscionable amount of work.

The scene designer complains to you that the technical director has ruined more scenery than a termite on a showboat, that inefficient methods are being used in the shop, and that for two nights running one of his ornamental set pieces has not been placed on stage because it is waiting to be repaired and that this ruins the entire aesthetic balance of the set.

Your chief concern as stage manager is to have the set for the next production ready for the take-in one night hence.

This is the type of situation that requires tactful soothing, and massive doses of consideration. If you try to fix the blame at this point, you are likely to find your next production hung up. Cool them off separately. Commiserate with each, separately. Tell them what an incredibly good job they've been doing up to this point. Praise their strong points. Overlook their weaknesses. Sympathize with their problems. Pep them up and send them back to work. They'll get the scenery finished.

Proposition 6

Good stage managers keep their sense of humor.

Making theater should be a happy experience for all concerned. Unfortunately, delays, deadlines, economic pressures, personality conflicts, and other factors sometimes make the process grim.

Don't contribute to the grimness. Leave your personal problems at home. Come to work with a resolve to stay happy.

"I find that most people are just as happy as they make up their minds to be," said Abraham Lincoln. Lincoln considered humor a "labor-saving device" and a "multiple-purpose tool."

"A sense of humor is part of the art of leadership, of getting along with people, of getting things done," said Dwight D. Eisenhower.

Try to keep a smile on your face, and have a good reason for its being there.

A cheerful stage manager can be a great asset to any theater group. Sometimes a cheerful word can get the whole company over a rough spot.

Knowing jokes is not a substitute for having a sense of humor. There are occasions, however, when a good theater story will put the company at ease. A successful director with whom I worked greeted each new cast with a story; it seemed to break the ice and to be very effective for him. The appendix contains a few of my favorite stories.

A corollary of Proposition 6 is that *good stage managers do not have personality conflicts with anyone*. Holding grudges or showing hostility toward any member of the company cannot be a part of your behavior. Go home and kick your cat, but don't let any member of the cast, staff, or crew feel that you dislike her or him. It simply does not expedite production.

Proposition 7

Good stage managers are organized and efficient.

Throughout the chapters that follow the emphasis will be on organization and efficiency, so no further comment should be needed here.

Proposition 8

Good stage managers are punctual and dependable.

If you are not there on time or early, or cannot be depended on, you simply cannot be a stage manager.

In summary, good stage managers

accept responsibility,
keep their cool,
keep their mouths shut, eyes, ears open,
think ahead,
are considerate,
keep their sense of humor,
are organized and efficient,
are punctual and dependable.

How do you compare?

In her mystery novel, *The G-string Murders*, Gypsy Rose Lee writes, "As stage managers go, Sammy was about average, but that isn't saying much for him. I've worked for a lot of them and I haven't found one yet that didn't think he owned the theater and everybody in it."* What an unfortunate fictional portrait. I ask all of my student stage managers to read your book. I feel it encourages them to be efficient without being offensive or despotic.

> Billy C. Creamer
> Theater Director
> Rolling Hills High School
> Rolling Hills Estates, CA

*From the book by Gypsy Rose Lee, *The G-string Murders*.

3

Getting the Play
and Understanding It

During the readings, rehearsals, and production, you must have a copy of the script and a thorough understanding of it. In order to expedite readings and rehearsals, you should check to make sure that there are enough scripts on hand for actors and staff.

Usually copies of the script are ordered when the rights of production are obtained from the play service (Samuel French, Tams-Witmark, etc., see below).

If, however, you are going into production with one copy of the script, or a vague memory of it, one of the first things you must do is make sure you have on hand an adequate number of scripts. This may possibly be limited to determining how many are necessary, or it may mean actually going to pick them up.

It is desirable to have for reference the catalog of at least the major play services. A postcard will get them from:

Anchorage Press
Box 8067
New Orleans, LA 70182

Baker's Plays
100 Chauncy St.
Boston, MA 02111

I. E. Clark
Box 246
Schulenburg, TX 78956

Drama Book Publishers
821 Broadway
New York, NY 10003

Dramatic Publishing Co.
4150 N. Milwaukee Ave.
Chicago, Il 60641

Dramatists Play Service, Inc.
440 Park Avenue South
New York, NY 10016

Eldridge Publishing Company
Franklin, OH 45005

EMA Plays
280 Riviera Dr.
Harvey Cedars, NJ 08008

The Heuer Publishing Co.
P. O. Box 248
Cedar Rapids, IA 52406

McKay's Contest Plays
David McKay Company, Inc.
2 Park Ave.
New York, NY 10016

Music Theatre International
49 E. 52 Street
New York, NY 10022

Performance Publishing Co.
978 N. McLean Blvd.
Elgin, IL 60120

Pioneer Drama Service
2171 S. Colorado Blvd., Box 22555
Denver, CO 80222

Readers Theatre Script Service
P.O. Box 178333
San Diego, CA 92117

The Rogers and Hammerstein
   Library
598 Madison Ave.
New York, NY 10022

Samuel French, Inc.
45 W. 25th St.
New York, NY 10010

(or)

7623 Sunset Blvd.
Hollywood CA 90046

Tams-Witmark Music Library, Inc.
560 Lexington Ave.
New York, NY 10022

Check with your post office to determine the type of mail service that you must have to insure that the scripts get to you on time. It is usually worth the cost of specifying airmail, special delivery, or at least first class, rather than the less expensive book rate, to make sure that your scripts won't be delayed in the mail.

In determining the number of scripts you will need, consider:

1. Will all speaking parts need scripts? Check your visual display of characters on stage (discussed later in this chapter) to see whether a few pages of one script can be removed for one or two other speaking parts.
2. Will the costume designer, scene designer, property master, or any other staff member need a script? The publicity person can often make good use of a script.
3. Will a lonesome follow-spot operator or any other crew member need one?
4. Will understudies or replacements need them?
5. Can the budget allow for a few extra copies?
6. Do you have copying equipment?

It is not legal to reproduce any part of a published script unless the copyrights have expired. But in the event that you are working on an original, unpublished play, you would want to have the address and phone number of a copying service in your contact file. Perhaps you will want to use a mimeograph or spirit duplicator to make additional scripts or sides yourself. Hectofax masters for a spirit duplicator, which can be made on a Thermofax machine, can save a lot of typing, assuming that you do not have access to even more sophisticated copying equipment.

Sides, a part of a script giving only one character's lines, each pre-, ceded by the cue for the line, may be typed or hand-copied by apprentices or the actors, if necessary.

When script shipments arrive, you should immediately check the content against the invoice or manifest. It is quite possible to find the score of *South Pacific,* scripts for *Oklahoma,* and sides for *Flower Drum Song* in a shipment sent out for a production of *The King and I.* Such errors must be called to the attention of the play service as soon as possible in the hope of obtaining the correct materials in time. You may have to resort to long-distance phone calls.

Lock up your scripts and let them out only on a sign-out basis. Otherwise, they will disappear. It's not usually criminal intent. It may be the chorus girl who wants to read for a principal part in the next week's production who loses her script on a cast picnic. This does not mean to imply that she should not be permitted to see a script in advance of readings, but she should have to sign it out.

All scripts and sides should be signed out when issued to cast members and staff. Lock up the sign-out sheet in the same cupboard as the scripts. Scripts, sides, and scores are usually due back from cast, staff, and musicians on the day preceding or coinciding with the close of the show. (This is payday in professional companies; the cost of lost materials can then be deducted on the spot.) Post a notice to this effect and a price list on the call board. Note your intent in the company rules.

Frequently a cast member with just a few lines will elect to copy them rather than sign out a skimpy side, thus avoiding the possibility of losing it. You would be wise to encourage this.

Normally in musical stock and musical comedy the scores, scripts, and sides are packaged and returned within a week after the close of the production in order to decrease rental costs. This task is usually assigned to an apprentice or the company "gopher" (a production assistant sent to "go fer" things). If a closing night review of the past year or season is to be presented, you may want to retain one score and one script from each of the shows.

On straight playbook shows you may allow the actors to keep the scripts, or you may ask that they return or pay for them. Determine your policy and relay it to the cast.

All too frequently you may be held responsible for missing scripts and asked to pay for them. So it is a good idea to mark each script with a number so that each may be accounted for.

Scripts sometimes get tied up for unusual reasons.

Example:

In casting a big-name show, an actor may be sent a script even though there is no intent to cast that actor. You may even be called upon to deliver the script to the actor's home. The script is never seen again until a few weeks after opening, when it comes back through the mail with a hard-to-read note, "Not my cup of tea," and the big-name actor's initials.

Agents for professional actors often beg directors or managers for scripts, and receive them, even though there is no intent to cast the agents' clients. The agents feel that showing the scripts to their clients is tangible proof that they are working and that their clients are being considered.

When a script is issued for any unusual reason, don't count on its being returned in time to meet your needs. It is best to replace that script immediately if you have on hand only the necessary minimum with which to begin rehearsals.

Although your responsibility for scripts may be very limited, you should know how to get, replace, reproduce, lock up, control, and re-trieve scripts as part of your work in expediting auditions and rehearsals.

Of even greater concern is the processing of your own script—making it into a working tool.

The Prompt Script

Turning a script into a prompt script increases the size of the margins (see Figure 3-1). This allows you to make all of your cues and warns (warning alerts) large and clear. It gives you adequate room to make clear blocking notations and diagrams. It also gives you sufficient room to make production notes.

To make a promptbook, cut or "unbind" the pages of a script and mount each page on a standard size (8½ × 11) loose-leaf sheet (unruled) so that both sides of the script can be seen (see Figure 3-2).

If you are willing to use two printed scripts to produce one prompt script, this is by far the fastest method: you simply paste alternate printed pages to opposite sides of each loose-leaf 8½ × 11 page.

Whether your prompt script is made from two scripts, or by the "economy" one-script method, you need to consider the best placement of loose-leaf page space around the printed script, and Figure 3-2 shows the alternatives. Note that for the one-script cutout method with loose-leaf page pasted around printed script edges, pattern 1 calls for ce-menting, taping, or gluing four sides of every page while patterns 3 and 4 require that only two sides of each page be attached. I feel that pattern 2, which requires that three sides be attached, gives me the most de-sirable distribution of additional space.

If you cannot spare an extra printed script and must paste loose-leaf around printed pages to show both sides of each printed sheet, then start by making a heavy cardboard template cut to show all the printed area of each script page (see Figure 3-2). With a single-edged or mounted razor, you can then cut about five loose-leaf sheets at a time to the

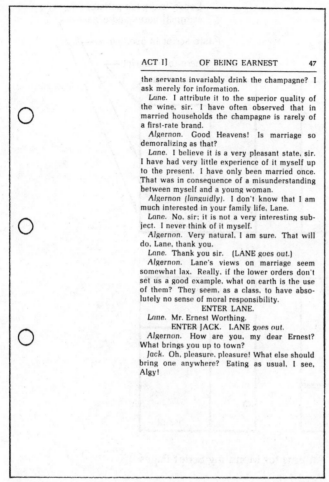

ACT I]   OF BEING EARNEST   47

the servants invariably drink the champagne? I ask merely for information.

Lane. I attribute it to the superior quality of the wine, sir. I have often observed that in married households the champagne is rarely of a first-rate brand.

Algernon. Good Heavens! Is marriage so demoralizing as that?

Lane. I believe it is a very pleasant state, sir. I have had very little experience of it myself up to the present. I have only been married once. That was in consequence of a misunderstanding between myself and a young woman.

Algernon (languidly). I don't know that I am much interested in your family life, Lane.

Lane. No, sir; it is not a very interesting subject. I never think of it myself.

Algernon. Very natural, I am sure. That will do, Lane, thank you.

Lane. Thank you sir. (LANE goes out.)

Algernon. Lane's views on marriage seem somewhat lax. Really, if the lower orders don't set us a good example, what on earth is the use of them? They seem, as a class, to have absolutely no sense of moral responsibility.

              ENTER LANE.

Lane. Mr. Ernest Worthing.

         ENTER JACK. LANE goes out.

Algernon. How are you, my dear Ernest? What brings you up to town?

Jack. Oh, pleasure, pleasure! What else should bring one anywhere? Eating as usual, I see, Algy!

Figure 3-1   A Promptbook Page with Script Page Numbers Visible

correct size, making one loose-leaf cutout page for each two-page leaf of printed script.

Use Scotch Magic Transparent Tape, a crayon-shaped glue stick, or rubber cement to attach script pages to the cutout loose-leaf sheets. Rubber cement is the most forgiving. Errors can be corrected without cutting as rubber-cemented pages can be pulled apart and restuck without damage to the pages. Glue sticks are faster and more convenient. I have found the Pritt Glue stick to be excellent. Some liquid glue sticks wrinkle the paper when dry. It is best to experiment and find the right glue stick before pasting up your entire script.

With the help of a few apprentices, using assembly-line methods, you can assemble an "economy model" prompt script in less than one

Figure 3-2   Four Patterns for Mounting Script Pages

hour. Allow several hours if you are making your first script by yourself, and five hours with a hangover following a cast party.

Next, you should make tabs for each scene so that you can quickly turn to any scene without thumbing through the script. You may purchase tabs at a stationery store or you can make your own, using tape. Each tab should be labeled (see Figure 3-3). Place the scene tabs on the last page of the previous scene, not the first or second page of the scene, so that the tab will open your script properly, with the desired scene immediately displayed.

Rehearsal schedule, pronunciation guide, plots, set sketches, and cast lists should also be tabbed so that you can turn immediately to whatever information you need during a rehearsal without wasting time by shuffling through a lot of paper.

A neat, well-made promptbook is an asset, but no critic will ever review your promptbook. Great paperwork does not necessarily make

Figure 3-3 Page Tabs for Rapid Reference in a Prompt Script. Note that the tabs are in alphabetical order so that the stage manager has extremely easy access to any information that he needs during rehearsal or production.

great theater. It might be possible for some people to keep all of their blocking notation in their heads and make sound-and-light cue notations in the margins of uncut scripts, but most managers could not work this way, and most wouldn't feel secure or comfortable. I advise you to do whatever works best for you, but I would suggest that super-organization of your promptbook is a great system.

Keeping the Prompt Script in a Safe Place

Once a skilled stage manager has worked on a prompt script it becomes a valuable tool and should therefore be safeguarded.

There are two possible ways to do this. The first is that the prompt script is *always* with the stage manager. It goes home with the stage manager. If anyone needs information from the prompt script in the middle of the night, he or she calls the stage manager. The stage manager is so prompt and so reliable that there is never any question in anyone's mind that the prompt script would be missing when needed.

The other possibility is that the prompt script is kept in a secure place in the theater—locked up when the stage manager is not using it during rehearsals. The idea here is that if something should happen to the stage manager, someone else could pick up the prompt script and run the rehearsal or show.

You will have to decide which of these two possibilities is best for your theater.

Access

Anyone who needs information from the prompt script should ask the stage manager for that information. The prompt script is the stage manager's tool, and as a courtesy to the stage manager, no one should go into the prompt script without the stage manager's permission.

Key or Code

In educational theater the stage manager is often advised to set up the prompt script so that anyone can read and understand all the cues and notes, as well as the blocking notation. The stage manager is instructed to make a key for abbreviations and symbols on the front page of the prompt script. Couldn't hurt.

Understanding the Script

You must understand the script. You must understand it well before casting and before rehearsals begin if you are to be effective. To understand it you must analyze it and identify its problems. The word "problem" is used to mean anything that must be done to run the show.

Try to allow a quiet time of intense concentration for your first reading. It can pay off in the accomplishment of a lot of work. And all of this pre-rehearsal work can pay great dividends in time-saving during rehearsals.

As you read, use light pencil in the margins of your script to identify all possible light cues, sound cues, special effects, costume changes, or peculiarities, properties, entrances, exits, and pronunciation questions.

You might want to use the following code:

L — Light cue
S — Sound cue
Ef — Special effect

P — Property
E — Entrance or exit
? — Pronunciation question

Of course, any code that works for you is fine.

For every light, sound, and special effect, using a ruler and working in light pencil, you should draw a horizontal line closest to the line of dialogue preceding an oral cue, or under the description of a visual cue. This line should cross the entire promptbook page so that you can see it quite easily during rehearsals.

About a half page preceding the line, draw another horizontal line marked "warn lights" or "warn sound." In the case of two light cues and a sound cue in a tight sequence, you need put in only one warn line before the sequence, but it should be marked "warn light/sound series" (see Figure 3-4).

It is too early to number these cues or to write them in ink, since there may well be changes during rehearsals. You will use the penciled lines to call the light and sound cues during rehearsals.

Plots

As you identify the problems and put in your light pencil lines, you might also wish to list the problems. A list of problems is a *plot*. A functional plot is one that allows your associates to obtain a complete grasp of the problems in their areas without having to refer to the script. In other words, *plots allow you to digest the script for others.*

In deciding whether making plots will be of practical value, ask yourself this question: "If I were the sound technician on this production, would it help if I were handed a sound plot?" In productions where the technical people come in just a few days before opening, having plots ready is particularly valuable.

Copies of your plots should be given to all staff members concerned. Your copy should be kept in your promptbook, properly tabbed, to be changed in rehearsals as necessary.

If, as you read, you listed problems on separate sheets of paper headed "Light plot," "Sound plot," "Special effects," "Properties," and "Pronunciation," then you now have rough plots ready.

Some acting editions of plays contain costume and property plots. They do not always contain all of the information you will need, but you will be able to modify them easily (see Figure 3–5).

In general you will want to cite on each plot for each entry the following information: the page, the act and scene, and a complete description of what happens.

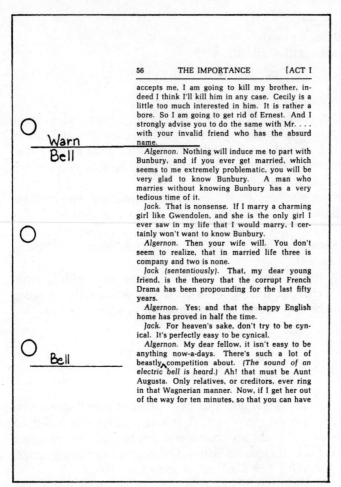

56   THE IMPORTANCE   [ACT I

accepts me, I am going to kill my brother, indeed I think I'll kill him in any case. Cecily is a
little too much interested in him. It is rather a
bore. So I am going to get rid of Ernest. And I
strongly advise you to do the same with Mr. . . .
with your invalid friend who has the absurd
name.

Algernon. Nothing will induce me to part with
Bunbury, and if you ever get married, which
seems to me extremely problematic, you will be
very glad to know Bunbury. A man who
marries without knowing Bunbury has a very
tedious time of it.

Jack. That is nonsense. If I marry a charming
girl like Gwendolen, and she is the only girl I
ever saw in my life that I would marry, I certainly won't want to know Bunbury.

Algernon. Then your wife will. You don't
seem to realize, that in married life three is
company and two is none.

Jack (sententiously). That, my dear young
friend, is the theory that the corrupt French
Drama has been propounding for the last fifty
years.

Algernon. Yes; and that the happy English
home has proved in half the time.

Jack. For heaven's sake, don't try to be cynical. It's perfectly easy to be cynical.

Algernon. My dear fellow, it isn't easy to be
anything now-a-days. There's such a lot of
beastly competition about. *(The sound of an
electric bell is heard.)* Ah! that must be Aunt
Augusta. Only relatives, or creditors, ever ring
in that Wagnerian manner. Now, if I get her out
of the way for ten minutes, so that you can have

Figure 3-4   Lightly Penciled Cues and Warns for Use during
Rehearsals

Light Plot

Leave plenty of room between entries (see Figure 3-6). The director may
add lighting effects not called for in the script and may add many dim-
mings and brightenings of areas during rehearsals.

Sound Plot

Frequently at sound recording sessions, the sound technician and staff
members, each holding a copy of the sound plot (see Figure 3-7), work
at selecting and rerecording, or creating and recording sound effects.
At such sessions you will insure that all the needed sounds are recorded,
in proper order, and of appropriate length.

COSTUME PLOT	Actor Provides	Borrow	Rent	Purchase	Responsibe; Date
MRS. JONES:					
Green and white silk polka dot dress					
White shoes					
Long white gloves					
White bracelets and earrings					
Pink silk fringe dress and stole					
Pink shoes and white beaded evening bag					
FRED:					
Light blue shirt					
Grey flannel pants					
Dark red tie					
Black shoes					
Red wool school jacket (Monroe High School)					
FATHER:					
Pajamas, orange and white stripe cotton					
Black shoes					
Grey suit					
Print shirt					
White shirt					
Soft grey hat					
JANE:					
Green jumper and white blouse					
White low heel shoes					
White bag					
White dress					
Light blue suit					
White gloves					
White high heel shoes					
HENRY:					
Dark blue and white stripe shirt					
Print shirt					
White shirt					
Blue dungarees					
Grey sneakers					
Grey socks					
Brown socks					
Tan shoes					
Light brown double breasted suit					
Blue apron					
JEEVES:					
Black double-breasted tuxedo					

Figure 3-5 Costume Plot as Modified from the Script

Costume Plot

Besides giving some indication of the clothes to be worn (see Figure 3-5), you should also identify quick changes that will require change booths in the wings or at the tops of aisles and/or series of changes that will require that an actor be assisted.

The costume plot published in the actor's edition of a contemporary non-costume play in which each cast member wears one costume throughout might require only the director's approval. But in a musical like *Little Me*, in which the lead plays several roles and is forever making quick changes, you will need to write a meticulous plot with cues for costume assistants and presets for costumes.

page	lt. effect	cue	cue #	instr dmmrs	int	tmg
114/64	Shop up	after Fore-man's entrance				
114/70	Shop out	David: "Whee" and Marvin's exit				
115/71	Dressing room in	following David's exit				
115/78	Dressing room out	David: "No, he's a hard-ware salesman!"				
116/78	Stage and Stage Mana-ger's area (Now the foots!) (But no worklight!)	after entrance of cast				
116/82	Stage and Stage Mana-ger's area out	David: "I am your older brother! By a former mar-riage!"				
117/82	Stage to general with worklight, no foots	when cast in place				
117/83	Stage down to effect of single work-light	Mother: "A very nice young man." & her exit				
117/84	Worklight out	David: "I trust I haven't kept you waiting to long."				
	Curtain calls lighting					
	Curtain lights out					
	House in					

Figure 3-6 Light Plot, Listing Cues. Note that cue numbers will not be established until the technical rehearsal. The columns left blank for "instruments/dimmers," "intensity," and "timing" will normally be filled out by the light technician working with the SM.

Properties

Note whether the prop is discovered or carried on—if discovered, where, and if carried on, by whom (see Figure 3-8). During rehearsals, note whether the prop enters stage left or stage right, so that if there are two or more prop tables backstage, you will know where to preset that prop.

Property control is discussed at greater length in Chapter Ten.

ACT SCENE PAGE	SOUND CUE SHEET	VOLUME	TONE	SPKR SLCTN	TIME	OTHER
1. Intro music		30 min prior to curtain in time	4	balance	1,2,3	30 min	fade out Gently
2. Fade out intro		to cue up 3rd cue (on "places")	—				
3. Roar of airplane	I-1	just prior to curtain	8		1	20 SEC	
4. Thunder, lightning, heavy rain	I-1	"You won't be needing your raincoat."	7		2	90 sec	
5. Bells and light rain	I-2	"Hold on to my hand."	5	Treble	2	20 sec	
6. Car approach motor sick	I-6	"I don't hear anything."	6	balance	3	20 sec	
7. Motor strangles, car door slams	I-6	"...His usual cheerful self."	8		2	10 sec	
8. Bicycles (like loud crickets)	I-10	"We'll meet you there." & ad libs (as they exit)	4-9 (fadeup Gently)		2	90 sec	

Figure 3-7 Sound Plot, Listing Cues. Space should be left between cues so that additional cues may be entered. The last five columns are set through coordination of director, stage manager, and sound technician during rehearsals.

Entrances and Exits

List each character, the scenes he or she is in, and the pages on which he or she enters and exits, in the following way:
Irene:

I–1, 16–24; I–2, 26–30, 50–53;

II–1, 57–73, 78–83; II–2, 84–112
Constance:

I–1, 5–19; I–2, 26–45; etc.

(In Act I, Scene 1, Irene enters on page 16 and exits on page 24. In Scene 2 of Act 1, she enters on page 26 and exits on page 30, then reenters on page 50 and exits again on page 53.)

You may wish to post your list of entrances and exits prior to a casting call so that actors may easily find lines to read for their parts.

You may also want to put in light pencil-line warns for entrances of actors, about a page preceding each entrance. It is not a stage manager's function to warn actors for their entrances during performance, but you will find that warning them during rehearsals is helpful. This aspect of rehearsal procedure is discussed in Chapter Eight.

Long strips of paper rather than penciled lines may be used for entrance warns. The marker warns are harder to miss than the light lines and may be completely removed from the prompt script prior to opening night. The marker may also be handed silently to an assistant to summon the actor. (See Figure 3-9).

THE BEAUTY PART

Stage Right Prop Table

Act I Scene 4

PROP/SET PIECE	person'l	preset	WHO/WHERE	work	SOURCE	final
coffee cup, white take-out	X		Quagmeyer	X		X
attache case	X		Hubris	X	Bill	X
script	X		Hubris/in attache	X	Lawrence	X
artist's smock	X		Hubris/in attache	X	Maria	
April Monkhood's picture	X		Hubris	X	Lawrence	X
phone, old beat up		X	on table	X		
radio, old beat up		X	on table	X		X
vase to hold brushes		X	on table	X		X
brushes		X	in vase	X	Dinah	X
small white paper bag		X	on table	x		X
push broom		X	behind easel	X		X
oil paintings		X	on chair	X		
abstract of woman		X	on easel			
bottle of whiskey in white bag		X	Quagmeyer	X		
easel, paint smeared						
table, beat up, paint smeared						
2 beat up, non matching chairs						

Figure 3-8   Property Plot (May Double as Control Form)

From your notations of entrances and exits you may now make up a visual display of characters on stage, a graph that shows at a glance which actors work together on what script pages (see Figure 3-10). This device will be invaluable to you in planning rehearsal schedules, finding appropriate pages for readings, double casting, and removing script pages to serve as sides for a minor role. The visual display should be placed in your prompt script as a reference tool.

Actors and Their Entrance Cues

During performances actors are responsible for making all of their entrances on cue. They alone have this responsibility. This arises out of very understandable circumstances: during the performance the stage manager can only be in one place—the work area—where she or he is busy following the book and cuing sound, lights, and curtain. Cues sometimes coincide with an actor's entrance, i.e., doorbell rings prior to the entrance or the director calls for a subtle increase of light intensity

Figure 3-9 Actor Warn in Prompt Script for Quick Access during Rehearsal

Figure 3-10 A Visual Display of Characters on Stage. Numbers denote script page numbers. Note that the "blocked" line allows you to see what scenes have yet to be blocked, and who's in them. The "v" denotes voice only.

on the door area as the actor enters. So the stage manager cannot be in two places at once, cuing and pushing the actor on stage. There might be several actors entering from more than one entrance. So out of very practical considerations it is necessary that each actor be responsible for her or his own entrance. In professional theater the union insists on this.

There are some exceptions: The stage manager is responsible for actors being in place when they are discovered at the rise of the curtain, and when they are offstage about to enter within the first few seconds after the curtain. After calling "Places, please," the stage manager checks that all discovered cast members are in their appropriate blocked positions. The procedure for checking this, in a theater-in-the-round example, is discussed in Chapter Twelve under "Shift Inspection."

And there are even some exceptional exceptions: Occasionally a producer or director overrides normal procedure and asks that the stage manager "supervise" the entrance and exits of an actor who has particular difficulties. Such an exception is discussed as an example under "Calls" in Chapter Nine.

During rehearsals the situation is different. In the role of expeditor of rehearsals, the stage manager should closely supervise the entrances of cast members. In many theaters there is no monitor system that broadcasts the rehearsals to offstage areas where the actors may wander for fittings or to run lines. So the stage manager warns them of their entrances, following the procedures described under "Warning" in Chapter Eight.

Pronunciation Questions

You may wish to make a list of all words in the script about which there is a question of pronunciation. Give the pronunciation of all proper names in the script which might be pronounced in two ways.

Example:

Middle of the Night by Paddy Chayefsky—"Mrs. Nieman." Obviously, all members of the cast should pronounce this name the same way. Should it be pronounced *Nē-man* or *Nī-man*?

List foreign words and phrases and give both the pronunciation and meaning.

Example:

A Majority of One by Leonard Spigelgass—"mashugina"; *ma-shoog-i-na,* Yiddish meaning "crazy."

List unusual and uncommon words and give pronunciation and meaning.

Example:

The Emperor by Hermann Gressieker—"trīreme"; *trī-rēm*, an ancient Roman galley with three banks of oars on each side.

Example:

The Cherry Orchard by Anton Chekhov—"Epihodov"; *"Ep-(i)-hóe-doff*, a clerk who proposes to Dunyasha.

Cast members aren't expected to be Russian scholars but should be provided with correct pronunciations of characters' names.

This list may be posted as early as the readings for the benefit of those trying out for parts. But it is especially beneficial to you, since you must pronounce the words correctly while prompting. You should keep a copy in your prompt script.

Special Effects

If there is only one special effect in a play, there is obviously no need for writing a plot. But if you are doing a play that calls for many, you will want to list them for consideration by the scene designer and technical director. Such a list might include a heavy fog, walls shaking and dishes falling off shelves, a trapdoor disappearance accompanied by a flash of smoke, a sliding panel, firing of weapons, etc.

Making plots and lists seems far removed from making theater happen. It is not recommended unless you can clearly see that it will expedite your production.

However, hard work in analyzing the script and identifying its problems before rehearsals begin pays off—your work becomes easier with every day that passes. Lack of preparation before rehearsals begin results in a terribly overworked and panicked feeling as opening night approaches. I've always preferred the former.

I feel that two or three weeks of work on material before rehearsals start is a must, depending on how fast you can type and organize.

Curtiss Marlowe
Stage Manager
Liberty Theatre
North Hollywood, CA

4

Scheduling and Company Rules

The Master Calendar

Time, management of time, and the coordination of the cast, crew, and staff are very important to every theater. In order to keep everyone on time and their efforts meshing smoothly, it is desirable to post a master calendar—and only one master calendar—in a convenient place so that it is available to everyone on the staff. The master calendar can be your most effective tool for coordinating the staff.

The master calendar (see Figure 4-1) should be large enough so that several lines may be written legibly in the space allotted for each day. It should, of course, be developed after consultation regarding the needs of producer or management, department heads in various phases of production, and above all, after conferring with the director, with whom you work in a direct supporting role. The calendar should list many of the following kinds of events, but not necessarily all of them, and not necessarily in the following order:

Deadline for set drawings/line drawings (see Chapter Eight)
Deadline for lighting plans (see Chapter Eleven)
Deadline for cleaning/repairing lighting instruments (see Chapter Eleven)
Deadline for obtaining sufficient copies of the script (Chapter Three)
Readings/auditions (Chapter Six)
Deadline for complete casting (Chapter Six)
Understudy casting (Chapters Six and Sixteen)
First rehearsal (Chapter Eight)
All subsequent rehearsals (Chapter Eight)
Work calls (Chapters Four and Twelve)

Sunday	Monday	Tuesday	Wednesday
		1 10 STAFF CONF.	**2** 7:30 Readings 9:30
6	**7** 1ST DAY THTr. AVAILAble 10AM 1ST Rehrsal (contracts) 2:00 Pub. Photos	**8** 10AM Rehearsal 11:30 STaff Conf.	**9** 10:00 STAff conf. 10:30 REHEARSAL
13 10:00 WORK CALL	**14** 10:00 rehearsal	**15** 10:00 REhearsal	**16** 10:00 Staff Confer. 10:30 REHEARSAL
20 10:00 WORK CALL	**21** CAST DAY OFF 8:00 TAPE ALL SOUND CUES MUSIC	**22** 10:00 AM REhearsal 10:30 STaff MEET.	**23** REHRSL 10AM Staff conf. deadline: Reserve opening night & invitations
27 9:00 Work call SET COMPLETE 8:00 Rehearsal Run Through	**28** cast day off 10:00 Focus lghts 2:00 Flameproof sets	**29** 10:00 STAFF CONf. 8:00 Tech Rehearsal	**30** DEADLINE: All COSTUME COMPLETE 8:00 Tech Rehearsal

Figure 4-1   A Master Calendar

Staff conferences (Chapters Four and Eight)
Deadline for memorization of lines (by act) (Chapter Eight)
Deadline for obtaining all rehearsal props (Chapters Eight and Ten)
Take-in day (see Chapter Twelve)
Deadline for completion of sets (Chapter Thirteen)
Deadline for completion of sound effects (Chapter Thirteen)
Focus lights (Chapter Thirteen)
Fittings of costumes (Chapters Eight and Thirteen)
Publicity picture calls (Chapter Eight)
Publicity interviews (Chapter Eight)
Deadline for reservation of opening night tickets
Deadline for obtaining all final props (Chapter Ten)
Integration of sound effects into rehearsals (Chapter Thirteen)
Integration of film effects into rehearsals (Chapter Thirteen)
Costume parade (Chapters Eight and Thirteen)
Special costume rehearsal

Thursday	Friday	Saturday	**NOTES**
3 2:00 – Readings 4:00 6:00 *readings* 7:30	**4** 2:00 Readings 5:30	**5** DEADLINE: SET DESIGN LINE DWGS.	
10 10 AM REHEARSAL 2:00 COSTUME FITTINGS	**11** 10:00 Rehearsal	**12** CAST DAY OFF 10:00 WORK CALL	
17 *Deadline: Live sound effects obtained* 10 AM Rehearsal	**18** DEADLINE ALL REHEARSAL PROPS 10:00 rehrsal.	**19** *Cast day off* 10:00 WORK CALL	
24 11:30 Rehearsal DEADLINE: All props final	**25** DeadLine: All lines memorized 10 Rehearsal INTEGRATE SOUND	**26** *Take-in Day:* 10 work call 8:00 REHEARSAL RUN THROUGH	

Figure 4-1   *(Continued)*

First rehearsal with musicians
No-actor tech/all set changes (Chapter Thirteen)
First technical rehearsal (Chapter Thirteen)
Second tech (Chapter Thirteen)
First dress rehearsal (Chapter Eight)
Second dress
Invitational dress/previews
Flameproofing of set (Chapters Eight, Fifteen, and Eighteen)
Fire inspection (Chapter Eighteen)
Opening night (Chapter Eighteen)
All performances (Chapters Fourteen and Sixteen)
Understudy rehearsals (Chapter Sixteen)
Closing night (Chapter Seventeen)
Strike (Chapter Seventeen)
Take-out day/sets and props returned (Chapter Seventeen)
All other use of the stage (Chapter Seventeen)

If you plan to have every aspect of the production in final shape all at the same time, you are likely to have problems. But by spacing deadlines for various aspects of the production, you may check on, and overcome, small crises rather than have to face (and hopefully surmount) total panic.

Example:

If you wait until the technical rehearsal ("tech," Chapter Thirteen) to check on the progress of your sound effects, you may find that the tape is not ready and the source records that the sound technician expected to tape at the last minute are missing. At the second tech the sound technician finds that wires to a backstage speaker are missing and there is no spare wire in the theater. So you may get your sound effects working by dress rehearsal, if then.

But if you put your sound tape completion deadline two days before your target date for sound integration at a rehearsal, and put the date of integration two days before your technical rehearsal is scheduled to run, you can afford to slip one day, even two or three, and still be ready for tech with all sound ready for plug-in. Similarly, you must try to plan checkpoints in other areas and get your coworkers to try to meet these checkpoints so that everything shapes up neatly for the first technical rehearsal.

Some deadline dates must naturally fall before others. "Take-in" day, for instance, must come before "focus lights" day, since focusing of instruments is dependent on placement and shape of set pieces. Rehearsal props deadline (Chapter Ten) should precede line memorization deadline so that actors may pick up their props (or substitutes for them) as they set down their scripts.

If all staff members are required to post their requirements for use of cast members and stage and rehearsal space on the master calendar, conflicts will be avoided.

Example:

The crew arrives for a work call and finds the cast on stage for an extra rehearsal. After it is determined whose needs are greater, cast or crew depart, losing time. If all of the stage requirements had been posted on the master calendar, this situation would have been avoided.

The master calendar should not be placed on the callboard or made available to the cast under normal circumstances. It is kept away from cast members so that actors do not become confused about their rehearsal schedule or concerned about technical deadlines. All information that cast members need from the master calendar should be made available to them by other means, particularly the rehearsal schedule (see below).

Staff Meetings

Some theaters have regularly scheduled staff conferences. Most do not. If conferences have not been held in the past, you should initiate them. Getting everyone on the staff to sit down at once to discuss problems and progress can save a lot of time and grief.

At staff meetings you should ask intelligent questions that will urge your coworkers to reveal specifics about what they are doing. "Everything is going just fine and on schedule," is not a satisfactory contribution to a staff meeting from any department head. It should be show-and-tell time, with every member showing diagrams and drawings and discussing the specifics. (For examples of typical situations, see Chapter Ten on Properties.)

Example:

At dress rehearsal it is found that the leading lady's costume blends perfectly into the set designer's flats to the point where all but her face and hands disappear when she stands against them. Something has to be changed at the last minute. This problem would have been avoided if the set designer and costume designer had talked it out at a staff meeting.

A full review of the master calendar is a good way to start the first staff meeting.

Rehearsal Schedules

Carefully oversee the preparation, posting, and distribution of the rehearsal schedule. If possible, the schedule should be posted at the very first reading and distributed before the first rehearsal.

This takes a lot of coordination with everyone in a supervisory position. If you are working with amateurs who are not expected to be at the total disposition of the rehearsal schedule, you will have to coordinate the schedule with the cast as well. If you are working with professionals who are at the total disposal of union restrictions, you will have to crank into the schedule the exact union requirements, specifying days off as well as required coffee breaks on more complicated schedules.

Once content is determined, clarity should be your chief concern in writing the schedule (see Figure 4-2). Make sure that for each entry you give the time, date, place, and scenes to be rehearsed. It is not enough

THEATER TWENTY

5060 Fountain Avenue
phone 666 9059

Numbers You Need
(clip for wallet or purse)

Coordination (Jackie)	383	2171
or	461	2028
Stage Manager (Frank)	272	9887
Theater	666	9059
Reservations	938	1142
Rehearsal hall	274	4301
Fire emergency	274	5421
Police emergency	274	7171
Ambulance	274	0126
Chicken Delight	274	0253

REHEARSAL

SCHEDULE

Act I Sc 1: Rita, Arlene, Sandy
     Sc 2: Jonas, Terry, Sylvia, JoAnne
     Sc 3: Arlene, Jonas
Act II Sc 1: Sandy, Dee, Norma, Rita, Arlene, Jonas
     Sc 2: Jonas, Arlene
     Sc 3: JoAnne, Terry, Dave, Jonas
Act III Sc 1: Arlene, Larry, Rita, Sandy
     Sc 2: Terry, Jonas, Arlene

DATE	TIME	PLACE	SCENES
Sunday, Dec. 8	1-5 PM	Nursery 5	III-1
Tuesday, Dec. 10	7:30-10 PM	Nursery 5	I-3, II-2
	(all lines must be memorized by this date)		
Thursday, Dec. 12	7:30-10 PM	Room 203	I-2, III-2
*Saturday, Dec. 14	1-5 PM	Nursery 5	II-3
Sunday, Dec. 15	1-5 PM	Nursery 5	I-1, II-1
*Monday, Dec. 16	7:30-10 PM	Auditorium	runthrough
	(all costumes must be worn; make all changes)		
Tuesday, Dec. 17	7:30-10 PM	Auditorium	runthrough
Thursday, Dec. 19	7:30-10 PM	Auditorium	First Tech
Friday, Dec. 20	7:30-10 PM	Auditorium	Second Tech
†Saturday, Dec. 21	1-5 PM	Auditorium	First Dress
Sunday, Dec. 22	1-5 PM	Auditorium	Second Dress
Monday, Dec. 23	8 PM Call		Opening Night
Tuesday, Dec. 24	2 PM Call		Second performance
Thursday, Dec. 26	2 PM Call		Third performance
Friday, Dec. 27	2 PM Call		Fourth performance
Monday, Dec. 30	2 PM Call		Fifth performance

*On Saturdays, entrance to the building is by way of parking
lot only.

Open dates are not necessarily off. Stay flexible for extra
calls.

†Director wishes to see all costumes work on stage long
before dress rehearsal. If your costume is approved, you
need not wear it again until dress rehearsal.

Figure 4-2 A Rehearsal Schedule

to identify the act (Roman numeral) and scene (Arabic numeral) i.e.,
II-1, III-2. You must list the names of the cast members involved. Do not
assume that cast members will know which scenes they are in. Assume
the worst, that cast members will find ways to misinterpret the schedule.
Take the time to make reading and understanding the schedule easy for
cast members. This is not done out of contempt for actors, but out of
respect: If you can free them from the mechanics of production you may
allow them greater concentration on their primary function.

Your schedule might also include a wallet-sized area with important
telephone numbers that can be clipped for the cast member's wallet or
purse. Numbers to be listed are (1) a coordination number or numbers
that cast members can call to leave messages when supervisory personnel cannot be reached directly, (2) your home phone number, (3) the

home phone numbers of any other staff or supervisory personnel whose assistance may be required by members of the theater group, (4) the theater number, (5) rehearsal hall number (if different from theater number), (6) police emergency, (7) fire emergency, (8) ambulance emergency, (9) food service, (10) ticket reservations (if different from theater number), and (11) any other numbers that might be helpful as quick reference to the cast.

The rehearsal schedule need not (and probably should not) include any of the technical deadlines for staff members posted on the master calendar. This might be confusing to cast members. But line memorization deadlines should be included and dress rehearsals noted. Notes on parking, access to the theater and rehearsal areas, and other helpful information would also be appreciated by cast members.

If you are unable to fill the entire rehearsal schedule with specifics, it is best to get out a tentative schedule, so labeled, with dates and blank spaces for the unknown variables, so that cast members may fill in the blanks (see Figure 4-3).

Sometimes it is effective to staple a second copy of the rehearsal schedule into each cast member's script on the premise that the script is less likely to be lost than a single sheet of paper.

It may be desirable for you to print the following lines at the bottom of your schedule: "Open dates are not off! They haven't been set yet. Please keep your personal schedule open for additional rehearsals as called." Keep in mind, when first making up the rehearsal schedule, that to include extra "safety" rehearsals initially, and then cancel them when they are determined to be unnecessary, is easier than to call extra non-scheduled rehearsals as opening night looms larger.

In some amateur theaters the cast may be told halfway into rehearsals that they will have to come to previously unscheduled work calls if they want to have scenery. There is much unhappiness. To avoid this, stage managers in amateur situations should plan work calls before rehearsals begin and put them on the schedule with a note that cast members will be expected to attend in work clothes.

When rehearsing a musical in one week, it becomes necessary to juggle principals, chorus, dancers, and extras between five or more different areas and still retain one's sanity. This calls for extremely careful planning of a more sophisticated schedule (see Figure 4-4), and the determination of all concerned to meet the schedule.

The worst problem in keeping to such a complicated schedule, where work periods are broken down to the hour and even half-hour, is that the staff members—musical director, chorus director, choreographer, and costume designer—are unwilling to release the cast members they are working with at the end of the specified time period. They are always in the middle of something very important and need five minutes more. It becomes difficult to cajole these creative people into keeping to the schedule.

```
TENTATIVE REHEARSAL SCHEDULE          The Chapel Theatre
                                      2222 Lomita Blvd.
                                      373 3636
```

```
Tuesday    Aug   4    Readings
Wednesday  Aug   5    Call backs
Friday     Aug   7    1st rehearsal    All rehearsals are at
Monday     Aug   10                    7:30 pm sharp!
Wednesday  Aug   12
Friday     Aug   14
Monday     Aug   17
Wednesday  Aug   19
Friday     Aug   21
Sunday     Aug   23
Monday     Aug   24
Wednesday  Aug   26
Friday     Aug   28
Sunday     Aug   30
Monday     Aug   31
Wednesday  Sept  2
Friday     Sept  4
Sunday     Sept  6    Deadline:  All Act I lines
Monday     Sept  7
Wednesday  Sept. 9
Friday     Sept.11
Sunday     Sept  13   Deadline:  All Act II lines.
Monday     Sept  14
Wednesday  Sept.16
Friday     Sept  18
Saturday   Sept  19
Sunday     Sept  20   Hold this day open for rehearsal.
Monday     Sept  21   1st Tech
Tuesday    Sept  22   2nd Tech
Wednesday  Sept.23    1st Dress
Thursday   Sept  24   2nd Dress
Friday     Sept  25   Opening Night
```

1. Everyone in the cast must be available for all rehearsals
Please note in accepting roles that you are accepting a four
night per week schedule and that starting Sept. 18, you are
committed for 10 nights in a row without one night off!!!!!!!!
Please do not accept roles unless you are willing to give
this amount of time.

2. Dancers: Additional rehearsals, not on the schedule, may
be called.

3. Performances: Six consecutive weekends, Sept. 25 – Oct.
31, Friday and Saturday nights with some additional performances on Thursday and Sunday nights, depending on group
sales. (Pickup rehearsals: Wednesday or Thursday nights preceding first performance of the week.)

      DAMN YANKEES DAMN YANKEES DAMN YANKEES

Figure 4-3   A Tentative Rehearsal Schedule

A second problem is that a lot of cast time is lost in shepherding
members between rehearsal areas.

With many work areas and short work periods a certain amount of
confusion and delay cannot be avoided, but clear and careful scheduling
can help to minimize it.

Is it desirable to mimeograph or duplicate schedules? Yes, it is. It is
one of the ways in which you can assist the cast beyond the minimum
requirements of announcing the next call. It saves the cast the trouble
of individually copying the schedule.

Sometimes it is not enough to distribute the schedule, staple a duplicate in each script, post a copy on the callboard, and announce the
next call at each rehearsal. You must "mother-hen" the schedule even

REHEARSAL SCHEDULE

TUESDAY - JULY 14

TIME	AUDITORIUM	TENT	CHORUS ROOM	MUSIC ROOM	COSTUME SHOP
10:00		Frank			
10:30		II-5		Julie	Ravenal
11:00		II-5	Girl Sing. Dancers	Ravenal	Male Danc.
11:30	Frank, Karen	Ravenal Magnolia	Girl Sing. Dancers Male Danc.	Julie	Andy
12:00	I-1	(Lunch)	Girl Sing (All Danc. to lunch)	(Lunch)	(Lunch)
12:30	I-2	(Lunch)	" "	(Lunch)	Parthy
1:00	(Lunch)	All Danc.	(Lunch)	Joe	Magnolia
1:30	(Lunch)	" "	(Lunch)	Andy, Parthy	Steve
2:00	I-3	" "	Girl Sing	Ravenal	Joe, Frank
2:30	I-3	Male Danc.	" "	Queenie	Girl Danc.
3:00	I-4	All Danc., Girl Sing.		Ellie, Frank	Julie
3:30	Andy	" "		Magnolia	Queenie, Ellie
4:00	Pict. Call				
4:30					
5:00		I-2			
5:30					Local Chorus
6:00	Joe, Queenie		Local Chorus		
6:30	Ellie, Frank	" "			

Notes: Today is day off for Male Singing Ensemble.
Picture Call: 4 p.m. Aud. - Check sep. picture call sheet to see if you are needed. Report to costume shop, then aud.

Figure 4-4 A Single Day Rehearsal Schedule

beyond this. If a cast member is late, you must check to find out why, in the hope of eliminating future tardiness. If a cast member is absent, you must call to make sure that the actor knows the next call.

If there is any change in the schedule, it is your responsibility to see that every person concerned is informed of the change.

Keep several extra copies of the rehearsal schedule in your prompt script, always ready to hand one to a cast member who has misplaced his or hers, one to the upholsterer who wants to know when the stage will be free so that she or he can recover the sofa, one to the lady who lives above the theater and wants to know when not to play her TV, and more to all others concerned, ad infinitum. Of course, every staff member should be on your initial distribution.

Company Rules

A handout of company rules is a helpful device to let cast, staff, and crew know what is expected of them (see Figure 4-5).
Categories of rules that you will want to include are:

A. Backstage behavior, noise, and cleanliness,
B. Tardiness,
C. Guests backstage and complimentary tickets,
D. Costume upkeep.

When the rules are approved, distribute them to all concerned, preferably at the initial meeting of the company. Post a copy on the callboard.
Just as you want to know what is expected of you, actors want to know what is expected of them. Take time at the first company meeting to review the rules and explain the reasons for them.

Example:

Tent theater rule: "Cast members must sit in the last two rows of the theater when not on stage during rehearsals." This brief rule alone seemed unjustifiable; after all, the emply seats in front were a much more convenient waiting place. The rule could have been explained in just a few lines: the asphalt surface of the center of the tent became so hot during rehearsal hours that the chair legs sank into and destroyed the surface. The back rows were not surfaced and were thus practically indestructible.
If there are good reasons for rules, try to make the reasons clear to cast members. This will result in greater cooperation on their part. Reasons for rules that seem obvious to you are not always so obvious to cast members—like the fire hazard of smoking backstage. Be patient in explaining.

The Callboard

The callboard has already been mentioned as the place to post the rehearsal schedule and company rules. Let us take a closer look at it.
The callboard is a backstage bulletin board for cast, crew, and staff (see Figure 4-6). It is usually located near the stage door where cast members can't miss it when they arrive and depart.
The basic items that every member of the company must be able to find are:

Player's Ring Gallery
8325 Santa Monica Blvd.
December 13, 1964

The Company of
ONE FLEW OVER THE CUCKOO'S NEST

1. You must sign in each night. Never sign in for another actor.

2. Please call 555-2424 if you expect to be late for half hour call.

3. Please use the stage door, not the front door.

4. Please open and close the stage door quietly.

5. Please stay backstage after 8 pm (7:30 pm Sat.).

6. Cast members are not allowed in the box office.

7. Extremely important and emergency messages can get to you by calling 650 6920 during performance, and only that number.

8. Please leave costume laundry with st. manager on Sunday night after performance. You must fill out laundry slip.

9. Please stay out of the light booth.

10. Please do not speak to st. manager during light cues, sound cues, and set changes.

11. All cast members must take curtain call in complete cost.

12. Please smoke behind theater, & not in the backstage hlwys.

13. No visitors are allowed in dressing rooms during perf.

14. Please be alert to the monitors for your cues. The st. manager is responsible for warns only before acts, not before individual cues once the act has begun. (See your Equity rules.)

15. Please do not talk during perf. while backstage. If you must communicate, please whisper. The wall between aud. and dressing rooms is not sound proof.

16. Keep theater doors closed because of air conditioning.

17. Please do not congregate with aud. during intermission.

18. Please wear appropriate clothing backstage.

19. Please do not use the pay ph. during perf. because of noise.

20. Please help in Saturday night buffet cleanup.

21. Please stay out of the entrance areas during entrances & exits of other actors & during crew shifts. You can be seen by the audience.

22. Please do not use the men's room during perf. It is noisy and near an entrance. Both men and women may use the women's room during perf., but please wait until the water has stopped running before opening door, and hold door closed to prevent slamming.

23. Use good judgment about not using the water fountain during silent moments of performance.

THANK YOU IN ADVANCE FOR YOUR HELP AND COOPERATION!

Laurence S.
stage manager

Figure 4-5   An Example of Company Rules

A. Emergency phone numbers (see Figure 4-7),
B. The next call (see Chapter Eight),
C. The rehearsal schedule (described above),
D. The sign-in sheet (see Chapter Nine),

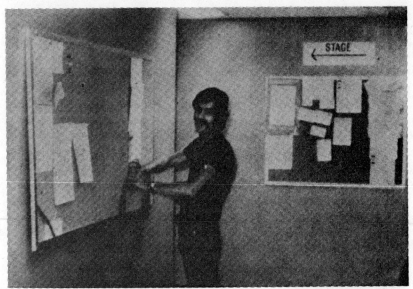

Figure 4-6 A View of a Well-Organized Callboard. Frank Marino, stage manager for the touring company of *Grease*, posts a letter on the callboard at the Shubert Theater in Los Angeles. Note that the callboard is spacious, well lit, and ideally located—at the stage door. Ushers' callboard is seen in background.

    E. Closing notice (see Chapters Thirteen and Seventeen),
    F. Company rules (described above).

Some other items that you might wish to post are:

    A. Helpful phone numbers (cab service, food service, and nearby restaurants and hotels if cast members are from out of town),
    B. Cast list (see Chapter Six),
    C. Favorable reviews (if favorable to *all* cast members),
    D. Invitations to other theaters,
    E. Advertisements of lessons and services of special interest to cast members,
    F. Telegrams and letters to the cast,
    G. Duty roster (see Chapter Fifteen),
    H. Curtain call order (see Chapter Fourteen),
    I. VIP list (see Chapter Fifteen).

Take down the notes for readings (see Chapter Six) when casting is complete. Remove all items that are no longer timely from the callboard. Bring your organizational skill and artistic ability to the arrangement

EMERGENCY

FIRE   555-2419

POLICE   555-4711

AMBULANCE   555-3210

ALL NIGHT CLINIC and how to get there 555 3699

White Memorial Medical Center
414 North Boyle
  (West on Brooklyn past Soto to Boyle
   turn left on Boyle)

DIAL-A-PRAYER for producer's use only 555 2783

courtesy Lawrence Stern, stage manager 555 3179

Figure 4-7   Emergency Phone Numbers for Callboard
Display

of items on the callboard so that cast members can find what they want quickly. It might be advisable to divide the callboard into three areas: permanent, temporary, and urgent.

The callboard should be large enough to accommodate all of the bulletins that must be posted without having them overlap. Make sure that extra pins are available to put up additional material, and attach a pencil to your callboard so that cast members may initial bulletins and the sign-in sheet, as well as make notes for themselves, without having to search for a pencil.

With your master calendar discussed and posted, staff meetings arranged, rehearsal schedules coordinated and distributed, company rules determined and explained, and the callboard made orderly, you have made a good start at making things run smoothly.

5

Getting into
Your Theater

Who Reports to Whom?

The stage manager should know who reports to whom in *her* or *his* theater. The stage manager should know not only to whom she or he is responsible, but also to whom everyone else on the staff is responsible. In the role of personnel coordinator this information is important.

The easiest way to find this out is to talk to people on the staff. If still uncertain, you should bring up the question at the earliest staff meeting. Even in theaters in which the distribution of tasks has been codified over the years, time may be taken at the first production meeting of a season to review and adjust for current staffing, personal preferences and capabilities of staff, and staff members' available time.

Figure 5-1 shows an idealized organizational chart for a hypothetical theater. I can readily guess that it does not apply to your theater. There are so many variations in staff organization that it would be impossible to provide charts for every theater here. Several factors causing variation are discussed below.

Designing an organizational chart for your theater might be desirable if you have a high turnover in personnel and you need to brief incoming personnel quickly. The more your organizational chart differs from what might normally be expected, the more your theater needs an organizational chart.

The chart is not as important as is knowing who does what. Authority in the theater generally stems from function. The authority of the lighting designer over the lighting technician stems from their relative functions. The function of the lighting technician is to repair, gel, hang, wire, and focus lighting instruments. Obviously, the lighting technician takes orders from, and is responsible to, the lighting designer.

Figure 5-1 Organizational Chart. This chart represents an idealized hypothetical theater and most probably does not represent the organization at your theater. There are an infinite number of variations in the organization of a theater's staff. Some of the causes of variation are discussed in the text. This chart shows primary lines of responsibility only. The stage manager, for example, reports to the production stage manager and to the producer, as well as to the director. Also, the organization shifts *when the curtain goes up.* Actors who reported to the director now report to the stage manager, and light and sound technicians who reported to designers now report to the stage manager.

As succinctly as possible, here are the functions of the theater staff:

The *producer* is to obtain the personnel and materials to make theater.

The *director* is to interpret the script through the use of actors and designers.

The *stage manager* is to insure that everything runs smoothly backstage and onstage.

The *actor* is to deliver the playwright's words, actions, and characterization, as interpreted by the director, to the audience.

The *technical director* is to execute scene designs and staging devices. (Confusion about the role of the technical director is discussed below. If you as stage manager have any doubts about your working relationship with the technical director, talk it out with him or her. If unable to resolve the conflict, talk with the producer.)

The *theater manager* is to insure the safe, efficient, and clean operation of the theater. (This includes care of the physical plant, box office operations, rest rooms, garbage disposal, gas, electricity, water services, and compliance with city regulations concerning the health and safety of the audience. It may include parking lot operations.)

The *house manager* is to greet and to seat the audience and to attend to the audience's comfort.

The *designer* (costumes, lighting, scene, sound, or makeup) is to plan turning the director's and playwright's concepts into the realities that make stage illusion.

The *technicians* (master carpenter, master electrician, stage hand, etc.) are to turn designs into reality and to run the show.

The *company manager* is to supervise the transportation and housing of the company.

There may be several other titles, real or honorary, on your staff. If you are uncertain about what they do, ask them.

The title of production stage manager may take on different meanings. In some theaters it is simply an honorary title for the stage manager. Sometimes this title is assigned only when there is more than one show being rehearsed and presented in the same theater or theater complex. In this case the function of the production stage manage is to coordinate and supervise the use of the theater's facilities, crews, and subordinate stage managers.

Sometimes the title of production stage manager is assigned to the producer's assistant. In this case, the production stage manager has no specific duties relevant to any one show but troubleshoots and supervises, reporting only to the producer.

Sometimes the production stage manager and stage manager divide duties. The stage manager works rehearsals and turns the prompt script over to the production stage manager at tech rehearsal; then, the production stage manager calls the show, while the stage manager runs the stage crew. Or, in some theaters the production stage manager runs rehearsals and then turns the prompt script over to the stage manager who runs the show; the assistant stage manager supervises the crew and the production stage manager sits in the audience and gives notes to the cast after each performance. This sharing of duties is common in musical theater and opera.

There is no single correct distribution of duties between the production stage manager and stage manager, or between the stage manager and assistant stage manger.

I have stage-managed four more shows now. I finally know the first prerequisite for finding an assistant stage manager: confidence. You must be able to trust this person. When you can trust your ASM, a great weight is lifted from your shoulders. Then it seems logical as to what duties you can assign.

Violet E. Horvath
Stage Manager
Arrow Rock, MO

Some of the factors that determine the distribution are the same factors that might influence the distribution of duties between the technical director and the stage manager:

1. Will of the producer or director,
2. Tradition of the particular theater,
3. Number of people available,
4. Layout of the theater,
5. Personality of individuals filling the slots.

Again, the stage manager gets an understanding of who reports to whom by talking with coworkers. She or he tries to avoid problems by anticipating work that will have to be done and insuring that everyone involved knows his or her specific duties in getting that work done.

Some general principles to keep in mind:

1. Treat everyone on the staff with respect for his or her function.
2. Many hands make light work.
3. If you have subordinates, one of your responsibilities is to insure that they are not overworked. (Sometimes a stage manager feels that since she or he served as assistant stage manager and got the work done, she or he can now lean on the assistant stage manager. If you are the assistant stage manager, you have to

appeal to the stage manager's ego: Explain that you are not the same terrific, outstanding, well-organized, industrious assistant stage manager that he or she was, and that you need help.)

Example Problems:

1. The technical director (TD) tells you that he is in charge of the lighting designer, the sound designer, the shop foreman, the makeup crew, as well as the stage manager. He states that he runs the crew during performances and that you (SM) call the cues. He says that you will report to him for work in the shop on scenery construction prior to rehearsals.

Could be. In some educational and community theaters the TD has extensive responsibility. If you feel that a different system would improve the operation of your theater, speak to the producer. If you feel that you are being overworked and/or need help (an ASM or gopher), speak to the TD and/or the producer.

2. The production stage manager (PSM) tells you that your first duty as the new ASM is to help build a fence around the theater.

Probably. Your duties are what the PSM says they are, even if those duties don't fit your mental picture of the job. If you are a member of a union, you might complain to your union rep. Will building the fence interfere with your other duties? If so, you need to make that clear to the PSM.

3. The director's secretary tells you, the new SM, that he will be holding book (prompting) during rehearsals and will also supervise understudy rehearsals.

How do you feel about it? Do you feel that you have lost some of the authority that goes with your title, or do you welcome the help? Or do you have mixed feelings? Perhaps you welcome the help at rehearsals yet feel that the director's secretary is not as capable of supervising understudy rehearsals as you are. Perhaps you feel that you really need to hold book during rehearsals in order to prepare yourself for running the show successfully.

This is a typical problem of the distribution of tasks among a theater's staff. The same type of problem might occur between the PSM and SM, or between the SM and ASM, or between the TD and SM. There is no correct answer for all theaters. What will work best for your theater?

Talk to the director's secretary about your feelings and discuss what is best for getting the show on most efficiently. If you fail to resolve the conflict, speak to the director and/or producer, and then abide by their judgment.

In all of the problems cited above, you will generally find that as the stage manger gains experience and reputation, more responsibility is given to him or her. As the stage manager moves on to other theaters, experience, reputation, and clout carry along, and the stage manager knows enough to stipulate in advance what specific duties he or she will not surrender to, or take from, others on the staff.

Personal Equipment for Stage Managers

Besides your prompt script, what else do you keep handy? Actually, there is no end of little things to keep on hand to keep the show going, and it is amazing to see how the absence of a small thing at the crucial time can create havoc.

For instance, it hardly seems possible that responsible people would allow a shortage of pencils to delay a rehearsal. But it happens time and again in amateur as well as professional productions.

Consider Hildegard Knef's comments on the rehearsal of the 1954 Broadway musical *Silk Stockings*:

> Today was the first reading. The whole cast sat in a half-circle on the stage with their manuscripts in their hands, a paper cup of coffee beside each chair. . . . Nobody had a pencil. Unbelievable that actors never have pencils at first readings. Henry, the stage manager, lent his and it went from hand to hand until finally Cy Feuer's temper snapped. "I'm well aware that you don't get paid till the opening but you could at least buy one little pencil. . . . We've wasted hours already." . . . I'd love to be able to invite a German student of Theatrical Science to attend rehearsals.*

Let us consider some items of personal equipment you are likely to need in running the rehearsal and the show.

Over a period of time you will find that you might be able to use one or two items in the mounting of one play and one or two items in mounting another. It is not mandatory that you own or buy these items. It is simply handy to collect things.

As the items accumulate with each successive play they'll overflow from your pockets and briefcase. You'll want a kit—a cardboard carton, tool box, or tackle box—to keep everything conveniently near you in the rehearsal area.

The items listed below are, for the most part, self-explanatory. Some of their uses have been mentioned already, and you are invited to imagine a likely use for the others:

Paraffin (When a tooth filling is suddenly lost, a small piece of paraffin may allow an actor to complete a rehearsal.)

---

*From *The Gift Horse* by Hildegard Knef, translated by David Anthony Palastanga (McGraw-Hill Book Company: New York, 1971) English translation. Copyright © 1971 by Hildegard Knef.

Lighter flints and fluid
Matches
Paper clips
Sewing needles
Thread, black and white
Razor blade, single edge
Masking tape, two widths
Electric tape
Two-sided tape
Scotch mending tape
Safety pins
Straight pins
Hair pins
Carpet tacks
Tacks
One-inch brads
Chalk
Pencils, *many*, #2
Pencil sharpener
Large eraser, art gum
Flashlight
Candle
Black ballpoint pen
Marking pens
Luminous paint and brush
Luminous paint solvent
Tape label maker
Graphite lock lubricant
Electric extension cord
Stop watch
Sixty-minute timer
Ruler, 12"
Measuring tape, 50'
Architect's ruler, 1/2" = 1' scale
Tailor's measuring tape
Note cards, 3 × 5"
Oil, small can
Working bell and buzzer
Whistle
First-aid kit
Change, $5 in nickles, dimes, and quarters
Duplicate keys to everything
Rubber cement
Plastic cement
Plasti-tak
Rubber bands

Magnifying glass
AC-DC current tester
Asbestos welding gloves (great for handling hot instruments)
Gel books
Cough drops
Throat lozenges and troches
Aspirin
Aspergum
Can opener
Salt, sugar, tea, coffee, powdered cream, bouillon, packaged soup,
honey, hot chocolate
Wash 'n Dri Towelettes
Paper towels
Paper cups
Nail file
Kleenex
Toothbrush and paste
Toothpicks
Dental floss
Comb
Mouthwash
Water heating element
Gummed reinforcements
Telephone extension
Dust cloth
Tweezers

You will enjoy those moments when you can dip into your kit and
save someone, particularly yourself, a long walk.

Stage Diagrams

If you are starting to work in a new theater, you will want to check out
the plant, record the information, be able to analyze and apply this to
your production needs, and pass on that information in a convenient,
usable form. The easiest way to do this is by making a series of diagrams.

Of course, if you've already done a show in this house, you should
have all the information where it can be referred to quickly.

How big is your stage? Where are the sight lines? How high is the
proscenium? Is there fly space and flying equipment? These are but a
few of the questions that your *stage diagram* should answer.

Usually the stage wings and significant surrounding space—apron,
stairs leading to the stage, backstage area, etc.—are drawn to scale. The
scale of 1/2″ = 1′ is recommended, but any scale that is serviceable will
do (see Figure 5-2).

THEATRE
RAPPORT
Scale ½" = 1'

width: 22'
depth: 12'
height: 8'8"
access: 6'6" - 2'6" - 7'

Figure 5-2 Stage Diagram Drawn to Scale

When you have finished your drawing, list at the bottom the significant dimensions:

A. What is the width of the stage?
B. What is the depth (curtain line to back wall)?
C. What is the height of the proscenium arch?
D. What are the height, width, and diagonal measurements of the largest door through which scenery may pass to get from an outside street onto the stage, or in from the scene shop to the stage?

This last measurement is significant because it limits the size of scenery and set pieces. Obviously, you can't use a set piece or section of scenery if you can't carry it onto the stage.

This diagram and list of important dimensions should be filed in your prompt script.

Some Applications:

A. The set designer is on a tight schedule and won't be in town until the second week of rehearsals. The director has planned essential entranceways and windows so that she could start blocking. Now the director asks you to send the set designer information that will allow him to start his plans without actually seeing the stage.

Figure 5-3 Reproduced Complete Stage Diagram

Typical Problems:

   A. One of the cast members, without asking permission, brings in an electric heater to warm up the dressing room. Soon all of the lights and the heater are out. You are called on to restore current. Where, if anywhere, can the electric heater be replugged?

CYCLORAMA

3rd LIGHT PIPE

2nd LIGHT PIPE

BORDER

1st LIGHT PIPE

GRAND DRAPE

FIRE CURTAIN

LIGHT TREE

LIGHT BEAM

PRODUCTION:_____

DRAMATIST _____

DESIGNER _____

DATE _____

FLOOR PLAN
MORGAN THEATER
2627 PICO BOULEVARD
SANTA MONICA, CALIFORNIA

SCALE 1/4" = 1'-0"

Figure 5-3 *(Continued)*

B. The lighting designer has completed her work and left for another production. The director now decides that he needs another lighting effect. The dimmer source line is loaded to capacity, yet another small dimmer will now be needed. Is there another circuit in the building with enough capacity to supply another dimmer?

C. The sound technician can't get the buzzer to work. A lamp is working from the same outlet. Can you help?

B. You go to a warehouse to pick up set pieces. The furniture dealer offers you one of several rugs that may not be cut. What size will you need? Of course you have that information with you and will not have to make another trip.

C. The set designer of a theater in the round presents his watercolor sketches for the next week's production at staff meeting. You ask how tall the boxy set pieces are. The set designer explains that they are 12 feet tall and that he knows they will fit through the entrances to the tent because he has measured them. You point out that they may fit through the 12 1/2 foot entrances which you have also measured, but since the men who carry them can't very easily hold them a mere six inches off the ground, getting them in and offstage may be clumsy and therefore slow down the scene changes. You also point out that you will have to raise the microphones that hang at the aisle positions since they are only 10 feet off the ground.

The height of hanging microphones was in this case a significant dimension that you should have noted. The demands of a production sometimes determine which dimensions are most significant. If you are doing *Madwoman of Chaillot*, the stage trap dimensions become significant.

Note in example C above that both you and the set designer were anticipating problems on the basis of sketches and diagrams rather than waiting for set pieces to be built to see if they worked.

If your theater expects to be in operation for many years, you will want to make sure that many copies of more detailed stage plans are on hand for the use of transient set designers and technical directors (see Figure 5-3).

Fuse Boxes

Check the fuse box of your theater. Is there a diagram explaining what lines each fuse monitors? Are the fuses labeled in some way to show what's on them? If not, make a diagram or label them. Write on masking tape or use a tape tool. Is each fuse socket labeled with the size and type of fuse it should contain? It is important that this information be readily available. The diagram should therefore be posted near the fuse box if not on it.

Spare fuses of the correct size should be on hand.

Take the time to check all of the outlets in your theater. A current tester is a very inexpensive and handy tool to keep in your kit, (e.g., Circuit Master 90-550 Volt, AC & DC; Fordham Mfg. Co. No. 101).

1st pipe

1-4 Lekos	750 watt, medium prefocus bases, all in good condition
5-6 PCs	400 watt, medium screw bases, #5 lense cracked, #6 focusing pin missing
7-15 Fresnels	500 watt, medium prefocus bases, all in good condition except #11 (#11 seems to have internal wiring problem)

Notes: No spare lamps for any instruments on hand! Only four twofers on hand as indicated.

Ten cables run directly to board. No ceiling plugging locations.

Figure 5-4   Diagram of Lighting Instruments

You are not expected to be a qualified electrician. Yet you should be comfortable with basic principles of electricity. A source that will answer many questions on gauge of wire needed to conduct various loads, and methods of figuring ohm, watt, and volt relationships is H. P. Richter's *Practical Electric Wiring*, McGraw-Hill, 1960. Tuck a copy into your kit.

Don't forget your contact file when you run into problems beyond your experience. Call the lighting designer of the last show on which you worked and ask how the problem might be solved.

Diagram of Lighting Instruments

Next you will want to make a diagram of the lighting instruments currently in place—type, watt, gel frame size, and condition (see Figure 5-4). Indicate space available and outlets available for plugging in additional instruments (see Figure 5-5).

A plastic template of various types of instruments is available from Lighting Associates, 7817 S. Phillips Ave., Chicago, Ill. 60614. You can make your own out of cardboard (see Figure 5-6) to assist in making rapid diagrams of available equipment and its placement in production (see Chapter Eleven).

While making your diagrams you should check on the condition of the lighting equipment (Chapter Eleven). Is it serviceable or will it need repair? Obviously, if the theater owner has rented your company sixty instruments and ten are not working, or if three out of ten dimmers do not work, this must be brought to the producer's or management's attention. If you discover the limitations of your lighting equipment immediately, you will have time to repair, improvise, rent, or buy ad-

Figure 5-5   Diagram of Plugging Locations

ditional equipment. Don't wait until the tech rehearsal to find that in-struments are out of order.

If the lighting designer and technicians are on hand, checking the equipment is their responsibility (see Chapter Eleven). But if they are not, as is frequently the case, you can save the staff and crew a lot of grief by checking out the equipment as soon as possible.

Figure 5-6   Cardboard Template of Lighting Instruments, Scale ¼″ = 1′

Information Packets

If your theater hosts, or has the desire to host, outside productions, you may hope to find on hand a "theater information packet" (see Figure 5-7). Or if you are helping to manage your theater, you may be asked to help develop such a packet.

This packet should include measurements of the stage, details of the technical capability, and other information of value to an incoming company.

The purpose of such an information packet is to allow touring companies and other production companies to determine whether or how they can use the theater. It also allows the stage manager and staff of an incoming production to solve many technical problems before ever setting foot in the theater.

The following pages show sample information sheets with typical detailed specifications on the capability of the theater for any company that might use it for a production. Along with the physical dimension specifications of the stage would be included some scaled stage diagrams such as the one shown in Figure 5–3, as well as diagrams of the rest of the theater building, and diagrams showing the draw-curtain plan or any other special feature of the theater. Along with the description of electrical capabilities might be a series of electrical diagrams if these show distinctive capabilities. A complete information packet would then go on to describe many of the accessory services available from related professionals who are likely to be part of production work in this theater. The accessory services described might include these:

—The availability of stage crew and help, whether regular theater staff or contracted from local area contacts, as well as standard pay scales for them.

—The availability of wardrobe assistants, costume people, laundry and cleaning facilities, dressing room space and equipment, and sanitary facilities.

—Information about customary curtain hours and customary audience preferences in attending matinees, weekday evening performances, etc.

—Contacts for news and media in the area to ease the publicizing process.

—Transportation facilities, local and interstate, passenger and freight.

—Hotel and restaurant services that have proven useful to theater companies.

—Information on ushers and house managerial services, ticket takers, etc.

The packet should also include full information on the seating capacity of each section of the theater, and a detailed account of parking facilities available.

Figure 5-7   Typical Theater Information Packet Material

Theatre: LINDY OPERA HSE.   Date of inf.: March 1, 1965
City: LOS ANGELES   Source of inf.: HSE. CARPENTER
Tot. seat. cap.: 1330   B. off. phone: WE 7 3500
Year constr.: APPROX: 1936   Owner: Mr. SIDNEY LINDEN
Address: 5215 WILSHIRE BLVD   Manager: WILLIAM A. McDONALD

STAGE SPECIFICATIONS

Proscenium height 50 ft.   Maximum trim height 58 feet.
Minimum trim height 68 ft.   Width 42 feet.
There are no unique sight line problems.

Depth: Curtain line to back wall is 24 feet.
Foots to curtain line is 4 feet 4 inches.
The apron is curved with a depth of 7 feet.
The distance from the center of the stage to the stage right wall is 56 feet.
The distance from the center of the stage to the stage left wall is 39 feet.
Describe obstructions, clearance, and/or stacking problems created by any of the following:
Picture screen   NONE   Radiators   NONE
Speakers   NONE   House switchboard   NONE
Columns or pilasters NONE   Legs and borders   NONE
There is no permanent band shell.
The location of the pinrail is on the floor on stage right.
HEIGHT:
    Floor to grid is 59 feet 3 inches.
    Above grid is 8 feet.

HEIGHT:
Floor to weight loading floor is 31 feet.

The total no. of line sets is 41 counterweight.
The no. of line sets available for use is 41.
The no. of lines per set is 5 on 10 foot centers on grid.
The pull lines are 5/8 inch.

The arbors will take from 300 to 350 lbs. in weight.

The type of rigging used is 1 - 1 RATIO.

The length of battens/pipes is 50 ft., & there are 42 available.

The distance from curtain line to last set of usable lines is 23 feet 6 inches.

The distance from curtain line to first available set of lines is 6 inches.

*ENCLOSED IS A LINE PLOT OF STAGE

The stage floor is hardwood and laid on concrete and will take screws;
The stage floor is not raked.

DESCRIPTION OF DROPS AND LEGS AVAILABLE
Full set of beige -- full set of blacks -- 3 pr. legs, 28 feet high
3 borders, 8 feet high -- 1 drop - 28 x 50

Rigging of house curtain: a. Drop - operates from st. right
                             b. Traveler - operates from st. left

The house curtain is not motorized.

The house switchboard is located on stage right.
Roadshow boards may locate either on stage right or left.

The power available for portable switchboards is 500 amps., 120 volts AC. An additional power of 1000 amps. can be brought in.

The electric service is 3 wire, 220 phase - single - AC.

HOUSE SWITCHBOARD:
The type of control is auto transformer.
The number of dimmer circuits is 9.
The wattage per circuit is 6000.
The number of non-dim circuits is 2.
The wattage per circuit is 3000.

A roadshow can play off the houseboard.

Figure 5-7 (Continued)

LOADING:
The loading door is located on stage left - the rear wall of
the stage.
The width of the loading door is 8 feet.
The height of the loading door is 12 feet.
The door is truck level and two trucks can unload at one time.
The distance from the loading door to the stage floor is 2 ft.

A truck can back up to the door.
There are no parking problems.
The truck approach to the loading door is by the street.

*ATTACHED IS A LOCAL STREET MAP WHICH IS MARKED WITH THE
LOCATION OF THE THEATRE.

LOCAL TRANSFER COMPANIES

Atlantic Transfer
10053 International Road
Los Angeles, California
776-1870

Local loaders are required. Rates are $25.00 per truck.

ORCHESTRA FACILITIES:
The maximum amount that the orchestra pit will accomodate is
40.

HEIGHT:
Pit floor to the house floor is 2 feet 8 inches.
Pit floor to the stage floor is 6 feet 3 inches.
Width from side to side is 41 feet 6 inches.
Depth from front to back is 12 feet 3 inches.

There are 40 music stands with light on hand.
The piano on hand is a Baldwin - Concert - 9 foot Grand.

There is a rehearsal room -- 50 feet x 30 feet - adjoining
stage.
The orchestra room is located on stage left.

MUSICIANS:
Minimum requirements for musical shows are as set by local
scales for individual types of presentations.
All men must be A.F. of M.
Local scale for performances is as set by local scales for
individual types of presentations.

House lighting equipment can play off show switchboard.

A first balcony rail may be hung.
The distance to stage is 48 feet.
A second balcony rail cannot be hung.

Box booms can be placed in the house.
The distance to stage is 30 feet.

There is a spot booth and an area for a follow spot (s).
There are 4 power lines available - 30 amps. - AC.
The area will accomodate 4 follow spots.
The distance to stage is 112 feet.

The connectors are straight male bubble.

The number of stage floor pockets is 5 - amps. - 20 - location 2L - 2R 1 USC.

Houselights are controlled from backstage and light booth.
They are on the dimmer.

The nearest available theatrical equipment rental service is
10 miles.

SOUND:
The house acoustics are excellent.
A sound system has not been necessary in the past.
Our theatre will permit a roadshow to use its own sound
system.
Our theatre has its own sound system which is of monnoral type.
The number of mikes is 10.
The type of mikes is Altec.
The gain is controlled from the aud. booth - auditorium left.
Our theatre has a standby amplifier and it also has a pre-
amplifier.

There is a sound technician available at the theatre.

The roadshow's tape deck can be operated through our system.
The number of inputs - 8.
The impedance is for high and low impedance mikes.

We have an intercom from the:
a. stage manager to switchbds.
b. stage manager to stage left
c. stage manager to stage right
d. stage manager to fly floor
e. stage manager to follow spots
f. stage manager to front house
g. stage manager to dressing rooms

The stage manager can work from stage right.

Figure 5-7 (Continued)

6

Expediting Auditions and Readings

In the process of auditioning actors for roles in plays it is desirable to make the actors comfortable and to move them quickly through an interview-audition procedure. In general, two areas are set up, one in which the actors may gather and wait, and a second in which the director, and sometimes producer, musical director, choreographer, and other staff members may interview and audition the performer.

To expedite the procedure you should insure that both areas are properly set up. There should be adequate light to read by and comfortable seating. Access to restrooms should be provided for actors who wish to find a mirror and freshen up. If possible, it is a nice touch to set up a coffee/tea table to show hospitality and consideration for those who are trying out.

Since this may be a difficult time for many actors, you should make attempts to be a cheerful receptionist. You are usually the first person in the company that the actor is exposed to, and the actor starts to form an opinion of the company by the way you deport yourself. You should offer the same warm, friendly welcome that you would want to receive if you were the auditioning actor.

You will want to write down the actors' names as they arrive so that you can audition them on a first come, first served basis.

Working with Actors

You can't make theater without actors. The actor is the central ingredient in making theater happen. Audiences may come to theaters to see the work of stage managers, directors, and producers, but the only people who can communicate any of this to audiences, through ideas and emotions, are the actors. They are the only ones who can communicate this by themselves, and if necessary, they can get along without you. But you can't make theater without the actor.

So, regardless of your personal opinion of individual actors, you have to maintain a healthy respect for the function of the actor. And this healthy respect should be the bedrock of your relationship with cast members. As stage manager, yours is a support function. You are there to help actors, to help them get more out of rehearsal time, to help them concentrate on their task by having everything so well organized and running so smoothly that there is nothing to distract them from their work.

On the other hand, as the producer's foreman and the director's principal assistant, you are a supervisor of the actor's time and whereabouts. When a stage manager posts a schedule or announces a picture call, she or he must expect the actor to be there, just as a military commander who had given a direct order would. When a stage manager has to move backstage, to supervise a shift or for any other reason, cast members are expected to yield the right of way. During performances cast members are expected not to speak to the stage manager unless they are spoken to (with the exception of informing the stage manager of a fire or some other imminent threat to life or safety or the continuation of the performance). Cast members should know that the stage manager is responsible for the smooth running of the performance, and out of respect for that function they should do their utmost to cooperate.

So the actor-stage manager relationship should be one of mutual respect and mutual cooperation. As in all human relationships, this may be difficult to codify further. However, in practice, I've found that it works out quite easily. Early in rehearsals actors realize that you are concerned with their welfare and comfort, that you are anxious to get the show on efficiently, and that you are quite obviously helping them. They see that what you're doing is all for the common goal of a better performance. And so they are willing and anxious to cooperate with you when you exert your authority.

Some comments on the stage manager's relationship with cast members were already made in Chapter Two.

Posting Notes for Readings

During casting calls most actors will ask the "person with the clipboard" for information. You should be able to refer everyone to the notes you have posted.

If you were an actor showing up for a casting call, what would you like to know about the production?

First, is there a part in it for you? Who's putting this play on? Why? Who's directing? What's the rehearsal schedule like? Where can you get

                                        THE EMPEROR COMPANY
                                            December 30

FACT SHEET

What/   A three act play about Nero, notoriously
               cruel and depraved Roman emperor (37 A.D. -
               68 A.D.)

Who/   Hermann Gressieker - author
               George White - translator and adapter
               Lou Rifkin - producer
               Charles Rome Smith - director
               Lawrence Stern - production stage manager
               Norman Houle - set designer
               Hellene Heigh - publicist

Where/   Cahuenga Playhouse, 3333 Cahuenga Blvd. West
               (Barham exit of Hollywood Freeway) HO7 3936

When/   Opens February 7, to run on weekends, four
               week minimum. (See posted rehearsal schedule.)

Why/   To present the highly original and well-
               received German playwright to Los Angeles
               audiences and to showcase local talent.
               This is an Equity production under the
               Hollywood Area Contract.

Figure 6-1 Production Fact Sheet for Auditioning Actors

a script? On what pages does the character you're right for appear? What pages will you be asked to read?

Try to anticipate what the actors would like to know and post that information in the lobby or waiting area where actors can read it before filling out audition forms.

Fact Sheet

Coordinate with the producer and publicist to get the basic facts up for the actors: who, what, when, where, and why. If possible, note on the fact sheet where the actors may obtain scripts (see Figure 6-1).

Character Descriptions

How old are the characters? How much do they age during the course of the play? Who played the part on Broadway? How does the author describe the character? How does the director see the character? Many actors do not have time or opportunity to read scripts and study them before they come to readings. Sometimes the scripts are simply not available to the actor until ten minutes before a reading. You can help the actors adjust to this situation by lining up this information from script and director and posting much of the information the actors will need (see Figure 6-2).

THE RIGHT HONORABLE GENTLEMAN

CHARACTER DESCRIPTIONS

Sir Charles Dilke mid 40's, air of distinc- tion, natural command, enigmatic	pp. 1-14, 16-21, 29-43; 47-50, 55-67; 77-90.
Mrs. Ashton Dilke early 30's, kindhearted busybody, Dilke's sister- in-law	pp. 1-7, 38-42; 55-57; 83-85.
Mrs. Emilia Pattison (later Lady Dilke) mature, ele- gant, charming, quiet integrity & warmth	pp. 7-14, 29-40; 81-90.
Mr. Joseph Chamberlain Statesman of Dilke's stature, at least mid 40's	pp. 10-19, 42-43; 49-54; 77-90.
Mrs. Virginia Crawford (Nia) Vital, restless, intelli- gent, waspish, challenging manner, 22	pp. 14-40; 50-54; 77-85.
Mr. Donald Crawford Late 40's, stiff, inhi- bited, slight Scottish accent, formal & pedantic	pp. 21-27; 81-85.
Sir James Russel Distinguished, incisive, jurist, dry, mid 50's.	pp. 32-41; 50-53.
Sarah Gray Handsome woman, reserved, Mid 30's, a decided cut above her station	pp. 39-44.
Mrs. Rossiter (Lila) Mother of Nia, Maye, & Helen.	pp. 51-56; 81-83.

Figure 6-2   Character Descriptions for Auditioning Actors

Equity Paid Parts

Under some contracts, Actors' Equity Association, the union for actors, determines which parts will be paid or not paid. Under other contracts, Equity allows producers to pay chorus members small additional fees to handle small roles. Post the paid parts list if applicable (see Figure 6-3).

Suggested Readings

You may wish to post a list of readings from the play with which the actors may audition. It sometimes expedites casting calls if actors can

SHOW BOAT

Principals	$5 Parts
Gaylord Ravenal	Rubberface
Julie	Jake
Captain Andy	Guitar Player
Queenie	Backwoods Men
Pete	Piano Player
Landlady	Barker
Old Lady	Carrie
Ellie	Jim
Magnolia	Dancer-Charleston
Vallon	Fatima
Windy	Mother Superior
Dahoney King	Jeb
Parthy Ann Hawkes	
Joe	
Steve	
Frank	
Kim (child)	

Should a production be sufficiently changed, either by cutting, re-writing or re-choreographing, to make questionable the category in which a particular part belongs, please consult with Equity immediately for a determination.

Figure 6-3 Equity Paid Parts Listing

read in pairs, or even three at a time. Otherwise you may be called upon to read with the actors (see Figure 6-4).

Rehearsal Schedule

If the rehearsal schedule is ready, post it. Otherwise you might add a paragraph to the fact sheet indicating the anticipated pattern of rehearsals ("We will be rehearsing for four weeks, afternoons and evenings, Monday through Friday." "We expect to rehearse week nights from 7:30 to 10:30 P.M.")

Audition Form Format

If preprinted audition forms (see Figure 6-8) are not available, you should post a format and examples of the information that the company requires (see Figure 6-9).

Callback Schedule

If many actors are called back to read for several parts, you may want to set up a schedule so that actors may read in groups, showing how they play to one another. The callback schedule would not normally be posted for actors, as it is not necessary for them to know who else is being considered for the part they want. It is helpful for you so that you can manage the callback period carefully (see Figure 6-5).

Thorough preparation for casting calls shows cast members from

THE EMPEROR COMPANY
December 30

SUGGESTED READINGS

Seneca	monologue I 1-2
	w/Nero III 8-11
	w/Burrus II 9
	w/Nero, Agrippina II 6-8

Nero	w/Actis I 11-18
	w/Poppaea II 10-15
	w/Seneca III 8-11
	w/Seneca, Agrippina II 6-8

| Agrippina | w/Nero I 2-4 & 19-21 |
| | w/Seneca, Burrus II 6-8 |

| Burrus | w/Seneca II 9 |
| | w/Seneca, Agrippina I 10-11 |

| Actis | w/Nero I 11-18 |

| Poppaea | w/Nero II 10-15 |
| | w/Nero, Seneca II 16-21 |

| Messenger | w/Seneca, Nero II 25 |

| Paulus | w/Seneca, Nero III 1-7 |

| Thrasea | w/Lucanus, Seneca III 12-14 |

| Lucanus | w/Thrasea, Seneca III 12-14 |

Figure 6-4   Suggested Readings for Auditioning Actors

THE EMPEROR COMPANY
January 4

CALLBACK SCHEDULE

Time	Nero	Actis	Seneca	Poppaea	Paulus
4:00	Nathan Hanek	Betty Ray	Earl Olsen	Liz Victor	Ronald Penny
4:15	John Heyman	Linda Mock		G. Merriman	Ed Marko
4:30	Barton Carton			G. Quentin	
4:45	Bill Cannon	Liz Bullard	Br. Matthews	Dol. MacRae	
5:00	Glen Colmar	Anita Morrel	Ray Anderson	Jean Scott	Mike Delgado
5:15	Erik Douglas	Darlene Gainsborough	John Hammond	A. Shelton	H. Feinberg
5:30	Richard Presby	Manuela Keeney		Abig. Perry	

Figure 6-5   Callback Schedule (Not Normally Posted)

the outset that you are in total command of the situation, anticipating everything.

Accepting Résumés

In the course of casting calls, especially in professional theater, many actors and actresses will submit their résumés. These résumés generally consist of a picture or several pictures in various costumes and poses (composites), and written information giving physical measurements, credits in features, TV, and on the stage; and agent's name and phone number (see Figures 6-6 and 6-7).

The purpose of a résumé is to help the director recall and contact the actor after the reading. In a production involving amateur actors, it is wise for a manager to secure information comparable to the résumé coverage, and keep those notes in convenient form to help the director recall the actors in tryouts.

When you accept a résumé, look it over carefully. For amateur actors, try to secure basic résumé information. For professionals, ask the actor if she or he still has the same agent, and if she or he can still be reached at the same numbers. Agents and phone numbers change rapidly, and it is important to make sure that the essential entries are up to date. Be sure to note on the résumé the part that the actor reads for.

Sometimes the staff will want to look over the actor's résumé (or your comparable notes) before the actor is ushered in to read. This allows them to review the actor's background and judge his or her experience level before meeting him or her. In some other theater situations the actor may be judged solely on appearance and reading, and résumés or preliminary notes are intentionally ignored.

After the show has been cast, don't throw away the résumés or notes. If the résumé picture is an 8 x 10″ glossy print, it may be useful to the company publicity person as part of a publicity release or for posting in the lobby. Information on the résumé might be useful to you, the publicity person, or others. Keep the résumés of those not cast also. You might have to replace a cast member suddenly. When casting your next show, you just might remember someone right for a role by flipping through your collection of résumés.

If you save résumés for future productions, you will want to make some simple evaluation of the actor's ability and code the résumé. Your code might be: (1) excellent, exciting actor, (2) capable actor, (3) barely competent, (4) no talent; (A) well suited to the part, (B) possible for the part, (C) not suited for the part.

The value of such a code is that in invitational readings for future productions you would not call the 4's to read, and would start with the 1's. The letters, along with the names of the roles they read for, might remind you of the actors' physical types.

Controlling Scripts

During the casting call you are responsible for controlling scripts. If you have not already numbered your scripts, now would be a good time to do so. Jot down the names of the readers and the script numbers as you issue them. As the actors depart the interview area, be sure to reclaim the scripts and cross off their names.

PAM CLINE
555-3756

Height: 5'7"	Hair: Brown	Eyes: Blue
Weight: 125		Range: 15-35

SCHOOL PLAYS

"Taming of the Shrew"—
Bit Part

"Take Her She's Mine"—
Liz Michealson

"The Crucible"—
Student Director

"Valley of the Dolls"—
Neeley O'Hara

"Androcles and the Lion"—
Makeup

"Celebration"—
Crew

COMMUNITY THEATRE

"The Springs"—
Costume Designer
(original musical)

"Call Me Madam"—
Governess

"Lovers and Other Strangers"—
Joan

"Joe Egg"—
Pam

"You're a Good Man Charlie
Brown"—
Lucy

"Play it Again, Sam"—
Linda

"House of Blue Leaves"—
Corrina

"Except for Susie Finkle"—
Mike

NIGHTCLUBS

Toured nine months / Los Angeles area / variety act (singing,
dancing & comedy)

Figure 6-6   A Sample Résumé

Actors will beg to take home scripts in order to prepare for callbacks. You must frequently advise these actors that scripts are needed for auditions. You should be prepared to point out where scripts are available.

Obtaining Information

During auditions, at the first reading, and every time a newcomer joins your cast, crew, or staff, you will want to obtain information that you and other members of your staff can use. It is convenient to gather this

Photos by Edd Linskey

Figure 6-7 Composite of Photos to Accompany a Résumé

information on cards (3 × 5″ or 4 × 6″) or on standard-sized preprinted information sheets.

The information/audition card may be preprinted (see Figure 6-8), or you may post an explanation of the information you want and the format you want it in, and distribute blank cards (see Figure 6-9).

The former method is preferable, as you are more likely to get serviceable results. Whichever approach you use, it is best to check each card as it is completed to insure that it is legible and that both sides have been completed.

The following entries deserve special attention:

PLAYLAND THEATRE

AUDITION FORM   DATE_____ #_____

ADDRESS:_____AGE:_____SEX:_____

NAME:_____PHONE:_____

     ACTOR ☐   SINGER ☐   DANCER ☐

         COLOR   VOICE   VOICE

HT.:_____WT.:_____HAIR:_____EYES:_____TYPE:_____RANGE:_____

THEATRICAL UNION MEMBERSHIP:_____

THEATRICAL TRAINING & EXPERIENCE:_____

_____

_____

NAME & PHONE OF AGENT:_____

ARE YOU PREPARED TO SING IN THE ENSEMBLE?_____

SOCIAL SECURITY NO._____ _____

LAST NAME   FIRST   MIDDLE (Print)

Address   City/Zip

Phone Numbers (Home, work, service, other)

Equity, SAG, AFTRA, AGVA, SEG, Other

Circle Union Membership

Agency, Agent   (His phone)

Height, Weight, Color Eyes, Color Hair

RECENT CREDITS:

STUDIES:

CURRENT COMMITMENTS:

Figure 6-8 Printed Company Audition Form Cards

Age Range:

Some actors do not feel it necessary that you know their ages. If you ask for the range that they feel they can portray on stage, they do not feel pinned down. (You are welcome to your own opinion, but discreetly keep it to yourself.)

Rather than asking for the age range, you might offer the following multiple choice: (1) child, (2) ingenue, (3) mature. This offends no one (except the "aging ingenue").

Union Affiliation:

An actor who is a member of any of the performers' unions (AEA, SAG, AFTRA, or AGVA—discussed in Chapter Eighteen) may be prohibited by the union from performing in any non-union production. In

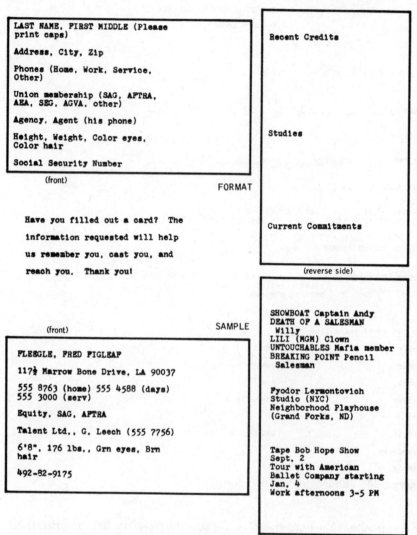

Figure 6-9 Posted Model-Examples for Audition Information Cards

auditioning for showcase productions and no-budget, non-union productions, actors have been known not to state their union affiliation on their audition cards in order to work. It is the producer's responsibility to check or face union sanctions.

When a preprinted audition form is used, an area may be set aside ("Do not write below this line.") for results of questions that the director or casting director will want to ask during interviews (see Figures 6-10 and 6-11).

The information cards or forms should be clipped to the actor's photo

```
                        THE ST. GENESIUS PLAYERS
                        THE ODD COUPLE


C A S T I N G


NAME _____ PHONE _____


ADDRESS_____


HEIGHT_____WEIGHT_____EYES_____HAIR_____


AGE RANGE_____


UNION:   AEA   SAG   SEG   AFTRA   AGVA   Other:_____
         (circle any to which you have ever belonged)


AGENCY, AGENT, PHONE (if any):_____


ACTING EXPERIENCE:  Use reverse side of this form to list
                    recent credits if you are not sub-
                    mitting a resume.


Do_not_write_below_line._ _ _ _ _ _ _ _ _ _ _ _ _

  Felix                      smokes

  Oscar                      poker

  Speed                      goal

  Murray                     schedule

  Roy                        SM

  Vinnie                     St. G?

  Gwendolyn

  Cecily
```

Figure 6-10   Full-length Audition Form

or composite. In school theaters, be sure to have the actors write their schedules of classes on their audition forms.

Controlling Forms

The first cast meeting after casting calls and callbacks is frequently a readthrough of the script. You should take advantage of a time when all the cast are present by getting the paperwork done. Take a few minutes of cast time to review the cast rules and to take care of the required forms. If you fail to get it all done at once, you will have to run after individual cast members to distribute and collect forms, and this can be time-consuming.

Plan this paperwork session ahead of time by grouping forms for

WORKSHOP APPLICATION

TALENT

NAME:_____

ADDRESS:_____

TELEPHONE NO:_____

UNION AFFILIATION:_____

    A.E.A._____   AGVA_____

    SAG_____   C.E._____

    AFTRA_____   OTHER_____

ACTOR_____
DIRECTOR_____
PLAYWRIGHT_____
ST. MANAGER_____
DESIGNER_____
TECHNICIAN_____
SINGER_____
DANCER_____
CHOREOGRAPHER_____
PRODUCER_____
MUSICIAN_____
OTHER_____

PROFESSIONAL BACKGROUND: (LIST ANY ADDITIONAL CREDITS ON REVERSE SIDE)
(RESUME & PICTURE, IF AVAILABLE)

TRAINING: Where and with whom have you studied?

CHECK SESSIONS YOU ARE INTERESTED IN ATTENDING:

_____ LECTURE SESSIONS

_____ WORKSHOP SCENES: Assignments. observations, critiques

_____ DIRECTING CLASS

_____ PRODUCTION: Panels, Budgeting, Stage Manager, Scenic Designer, Lighting, Etc.

_____ (Please do not write below this line) _____

Figure 6-11 Model of Workshop Application Form

each actor into a packet. Make sure that you have plenty of pens and pencils on hand. Each packet might include:

Cast keeps:
1. Rehearsal schedule,
2. Company rules,
3. Cast list (see Figure 6-15),
4. Guides to hotels, restaurants, points of interest (if cast is from out of town).

You need returned:
5. Biographical data form (see Figure 6-13) (check with your publicity person),

6. Costume size form (see Figure 6-14) (check with your costume designer),
7. Blue Cross form (if Equity company—see Figure 6-12),
8. Welfare Coverage form (if Equity company),
9. W-4 form (if paid company),
10. Life Insurance form (if Equity company).

If you have time, print the actor's name on each form before you distribute them. Then make sure that you get back the forms you need. The actors usually want to take them home. They may insist that they have the information written down at home and they can copy it if you will just allow them to take the forms home. Don't. You may never see the forms again. Insist that they fill out as much as they can, that you must have all forms back before they get up from the table. Have your tailor's tape handy for those who don't remember their costume sizes. Tell them that you will call them at home for the information they can't remember.

"I have my biography at home."

"My agent fills these in."

"I'm covered by my wife's insurance."

"I always forget how many of my husband's children by his first wife I'm supposed to claim."

Actors, like most other people, don't like to fill out forms. You must plead, cajole, and remain pleasant.

Check each return form on the spot to make sure that it is complete and legible.

Preparing a Cast List

The ability to reach any actor immediately is a function of prime importance to you. The cast list is an invaluable tool in that function. The list should include the character, full name of the actor who plays the character exactly as that actor wishes to have the name appear in the program, address, home phone, work or business phone, service number, agent's name and agent's phone number (see Figure 6-15).

Check for accuracy with each cast member before duplicating.

In rare cases actors will want to have their home phone and address withheld from all but you. Check this, too, before duplicating and distributing.

You never seem to have enough cast lists. Each cast member wants one so that she or he can contact other cast members (and send Christmas cards). The costume designer needs one. The publicist needs one. The payroll clerk needs one. The union insists on one. The program editor needs one. And as soon as you have given out your last copy, you find that there is still another person who needs one—the assistant director,

Figure 6-12 Forms That Professional Cast and Crew Must Complete

the assistant stage manager, the doorman, the receptionist, the box office, or the sign painter.

You can't go too far in obtaining extra phone numbers at which you can reach an actor. Ask for any other numbers at which he or she can be reached when not at home or at the theater. Note these numbers on your copy against the emergency situation when you will have to reach that actor in a hurry.

You will find a few good uses for a well-designed, complete cast

BIOGRAPHICAL DATA

Information requested below will be used for program
notes and publicity releases. Use reverse side to
complete comments if space below is not sufficient.
Thank you.

NAME _____ ROLE _____

Education:

Military service:

Theatrical training:

First stage appearance:

Credits:

Most recent stage:

Most recent film:

Most recent TV:

Current commitments (stage, film, TV):

Family:

Hobbies:

Highlight to date of your career:

Career ambition:

When did you come to Los Angeles? What brought you?

If you wish to add any unusual personal facts or viewpoints
which might aid in publicity, please use reverse side.

Figure 6-13   Model of Biographical Data Form

list. One should be posted near your home telephone. Another should
be indexed into your prompt script for handy reference during rehearsals. You can use still another copy, with a grid overlay (see Figure 6–
16), as a checklist. Every time you have a distribution to make, you can
check off each cast member to insure that everyone was told about a

COSTUMES

The costume department needs to know your measurements.
Please mark them on this sheet and return it to the
stage manager. Thank you.

NAME _____ ROLE _____

HEIGHT_____ft._____inches   WEIGHT _____lbs.

men only   women only

jacket size_____   bust _____

shirt _____   waist_____
          (neck) (sleeve)
                                   waist to floor _____
waist _____
                                   hips _____
inseam _____

shoes _____

sox _____

hat _____

Figure 6-14   Model Costume Size Form

pickup rehearsal, a cast picnic, or an invitation to see a matinee of another show.

Be sure to store a copy of each cast list for your personal files. This is the only list that has both home phone and home address, information you won't readily have available if you save only a program.

In a musical stock situation with only a one-week rehearsal period, you may not know all of the casting until the second day of rehearsals, which is only a few days before the printer needs that information in order to have programs for opening night. In such a case, it is desirable to run off lists with just the character name so that you may fill in cast members' names on the spot as casting is finalized, and hasten the information to the needy (see Figure 6-17).

You will also need a complete list of the staff and crew, with their addresses and telephone numbers. A grid overlay on such a list makes

THE TORCH-BEARERS   CAST

		HOME	WORK	SERVICE
Mr. Fred. Ritter	Albert Alvarez 1058 Bramercy Dr.	753 3691 (Jerry Rosen Agcy	870 5414 - 274 5861)	752 7975
Mr. Huxley Hossefrosse	Ben Blahzay 3916 Melrose	232 5756 (William Barnes	389 7726 - 273 0205)	none
Mr. Spindler	Charles Corn 12113 Redondo	268 6612 (Ted Cooper	231 1961 - 654 3050)	399 7171
Mr. Ralph Twiller	Dave Dumpling 161 S. Berendo	758 0058 (no agent)	292 5352	752 7975
Teddy Spearing	Earl Eastman 355 Douglas	665 1039 (GAC	none - 273 2400)	none
Mr. Stage Manager	Frank Farley 3607 W. 3rd	732 9444 (Coralie Jr.	778 3557 - 663 1268)	none
Mrs. Paula Ritter	Gina Glass 232 S. Serrano	567 6743 (Kurt Frings	652 7934 - 274 8881)	334 0101
Mrs. J. Duro Pampinelli	Helen Harvey 1510 S. Vermont	665 1605 (no agent)	none	none
Mrs. Nelly Fell	Ida Isely 2136 McPherson	221 2074 (Kumin-Olenick	295 1781 - 274 7281)	752 7975
Miss Flor. McCrickett	Judy Jennings 5716 Aldama Rd.	936 2325 (no agent)	627 4554	none
Mrs. Clara Sheppard	Karen Kirsten 3130 W. 11th	870 5079 (Kendall Agcy	none - 274 8107)	334 0101
Jenny	Louise Lehrer 139 E. 27th	877 2232 (Mishkin	754 3024 - 274 5261)	292 1333

Figure 6-15 Cast List for Duplication and Distribution

a handy coordination form to insure that you get all schedule changes and other necessary information to every member of the staff and crew.

Conducting the Deputy Election

At the first meeting of an Equity company, or the first rehearsal following casting at which the entire cast is present, you should conduct the election of the deputy. The deputy is that cast member who will represent her or his fellow union cast members in all union business.

You should not serve as deputy.

The union formally mails the official election form to you when your name is supplied to the union. If you do not receive the form prior to your first rehearsal, call the nearest Equity office (see Figure 6-18).

THE TORCH-BEARERS   CAST LIST/chEck List

		HOME	WORK	SERVICE
Mr. Fred. Ritter	Albert Alvarez 1058 Bramercy Dr.	753 3691 (J. Rosen Agcy	870 5414 - 274 5861)	752 7975
Mr. Huxley Hossefrosse	Ben Blahzay 3916 Melrose	232 5756 (Wm. Barnes	389 7726 - 273 0205)	none
Mr. Spindler	Charles Corn 12113 Redondo	268 6612 (Ted Cooper	231 1961 - 654 3050)	399 7171
Mr. Ralph Twiller	Dave Dumpling 161 S. Berendo	758 0058 (no agent)	292 5352	752 7975
Teddy Spearing	Earl Eastman 355 Douglas	665 1052 (GAC - 273 2400)	none	none
Mr. Stage Manager	Frank Farley 3607 W. 3rd	732 9444 (Coralie Jr.	778 3557 - 663 1268)	none
Mrs. Paula Ritter	Gina Glass 232 S. Serrano	567 6743 (Kurt Frings	652 7934 - 274 8881)	334 0101
Mrs. J. Duro Pampinelli	Helen Harvey 1510 S. Vermont	665 1605 (no agent)	none	none
Mrs. Nelly Fell	Ida Isely 2136 McPherson	221 2074 (Kumin-Oleniok	295 1781 - 274 7281)	752 7975
Miss Flor. McCrickett	Judy Jennings 5716 Aldama Rd.	936 2325 (no agent)	627 4554	none
Mrs. Clara Sheppard	Karen Kirsten 3130 W. 11th	870 5079 (Kendall Agcy	none - 274 8107)	334 0101
Jenny	Louise Lehrer 139 E. 27th	877 2232 (Mishkin	754 3024 - 274 5261)	292 1333

Contract / 8 x 10s / W-2 / bluex-GHI / AVAIL. TUES / Program Notes / Picnic / Pick up John

Figure 6-16 Duplicated Cast List with Overlay Grid for a Checklist

Take the time to read the official statement of election policy slowly and deliberately.

Secret ballots are desirable in large casts. This process slows the election enough to give voters time to think. In small casts members usually reach accord in an open discussion of who might best serve. Formality is not as important as thoughtfulness. Causing cast members to reflect, rather than simply "get it over with," is a matter of tactful persuasion.

Time to conduct this deputy election, and subsequent union meetings, should the need arise, out of paid rehearsal time, is guaranteed to union actors in their contract.

SHOW BOAT

OLD LADY ON LEVEE	_____
QUENNIE	*Bertha Powell*
PARTHY ANNE HAWKS	_____
CAPTAIN ANDY	*Marvin Miller*
ELLIE	_____
FRANK	*Dean Barlow*
JULIE	*Beverly Alvarez*
GAYLORD RAVENAL	*Alan Gilbert*
MAGNOLIA	*Kate Miller*
JOE	_____
WINDY	_____
STEVE	_____
PETE	_____
IKE VALLON	*Lou Boudreau*
BACKWOODSMAN	_____
BARKER	_____
FATIMA	_____
DAHOMEY QUEEN	_____
LANDLADY	_____
ETHEL	_____
MOTHER SUPERIOR	_____
KIM	_____
JAKE	_____
JIM	_____
MAN WITH GUITAR	_____
DOORMAN	_____
MISS SO-AND-SO	_____
MISS THINGAMABOB	_____
HEADWAITER	_____
ANNOUNCER	_____

Figure 6-17 Production Cast List with Characters in Appearance Order

First Cast Meeting or Readthrough

We have all seen trite first reading scenes in the movies in which the cast sits around a barren, coffee-stained table under a bleak work light. Why must it be this way?

DEPUTY ELECTION SHEET

The Stage Manager shall conduct the election and there shall be no person present at these proceedings who is not employed under an Equity contract (for this production). A Deputy may be elected by voice vote or, if more than one member is nominated, by secret ballot.

We, the undersigned Equity members, engaged under a standard form of Equity contract and constituting a majority of the cast of the (cross out inapplicable classification)

Principals
Ensemble Singers
Ensemble Dancers

of the_____ company

located at_____

under the management of _____

first day of rehearsal being_____ and opening on _____

do hereby elect_____ as Deputy

on this date_____19 _____

Figure 6-18 Election Form for Actor's Equity Deputy

I know one stage manager who brings from home a freshly pressed table cloth and a bouquet of flowers to place on the first reading table. It's a nice touch and it starts the cast off with the warm thought that someone went out of the way to make things a little better.

7

Budgeting

Keeping a record of your expenses is the very least that is expected of you in the area of budgeting. If you pay any money out of your pocket to further a production, whether it be a dime for a phone call to a late actor or the C.O.D. charge for a prop delivered to the theater, make a record of it, and, if possible, get a written receipt.

You may want to use an expenditures form (see Figure 7-1) and attach your receipts to it. Keep the form in your prompt script so that it is with you when you need it. Periodically you will turn in the receipts for reimbursement.

In some instances it is more convenient to set up a petty cash fund, from twenty-five to one hundred dollars, depending on needs. When it has been spent, turn over the receipts to the business manager or the box office treasurer, who can advance another twenty-five to one hundred dollars, or whatever sum has been arranged and budgeted.

In some companies a purchase order must be obtained from the business manager before anything can be bought.

In other cases it may be necessary for you as manager to control funds for the technical director, the costume designer, the property master (see Chapter Ten), and other backstage personnel. To make sure that each does not spend beyond the total budgeted for the production, you might need to use a purchase order system: any staff member must ask for a purchase order *before* buying. You must then check the budget to see if this particular expenditure is within reason, and then approve or disapprove by giving or by denying a purchase order.

A typical budget for a one-week musical stock production might be:

Lumber	$65.
Paint	$30.
Hardware	$20.
Fabrics	$15.
Rigging	$10.
Electrics	$10.
Tools	$ 5.
Props	
Running	$15. (expendable)
Purchase	$15. (permanent)
Car (gas, oil)	$15.
Truck (rental)	$20.

(See Figure 7-2).

EXPENDITURES

_____ production of "_____" _____
dates

Supplier	Item(s)	Purchased by	Date	Cost
1				
2				
3				
4				
5				
6				
7				
8				
9				
10				
11				
12				
13				

Page _____ of _____   Prepared by _____

LAWRENCE STERN
Production Stage Manager
555-3719

Figure 7-1 An Expenditures Record to Keep in the Prompt Script

NAME OF PRODUCTION *Camelot*

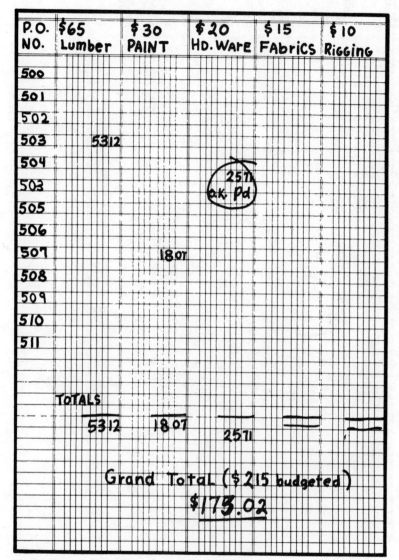

P.O. NO.	$65 Lumber	$30 PAINT	$20 HD. WAre	$15 FAbriCS	$10 RiGGinG
500					
501					
502					
503	5312				
504					
503			2571 o.k. Pd		
505					
506					
507		1807			
508					
509					
510					
511					
TOTALS	5312	1807	2571		

Grand Total ($215 budgeted)
$173.02

Figure 7-2 A Typical Production Budget Sheet

Example:

The technical director calls you from the lumber yard to say that the materials required to carry out the scene designer's plans will cost $98. Should you issue a purchase order?

Review the budget for this show and other shows this season.

Figure 7-2   *(Continued)*

There's $65 allotted to lumber. But, being familiar with the scene design and the show, you also know that there will be no flying of scenery or actors, or effects that require rigging. So you can add the rigging allocation of $10. You should also be aware of the budget situation for the season: tools have already cost $7.50 over the budget because of a lost sabre saw; the last two shows were under budget by $10 and $15, respectively, in lumber, and three of the four coming shows have been staged before in past seasons; therefore, since most of the scenery is stored, they should come in under budget. Sifting these factors, and perhaps some others, while the tech director waits on the phone, you might go ahead and give the purchase order number.

Or you might be under strict orders to clear all over-budget items with the business manager or other higher budget authority. In this case, you might have to ask the scene designer to streamline the design and bring it into line with the budget.

8

Rehearsal Procedures

Working with the Director during Rehearsal

As the closest assistant to the director, one of your most important functions will be to assist in getting the most productive results out of the time allotted to each rehearsal. To do this well it will be important to maintain a clear understanding of the director's function and a working relationship that will help his or her aims to be carried out smoothly.

The director is responsible for interpreting the playwright's work through the cast with the help of the staff. It is the director's artistic concept of the play that the cast, staff, and crew work to obtain.

When casting has been completed and rehearsals are under way, the director goes about her or his work in phases.

In the first phase the director insures that each cast member understands the character to be portrayed. This is accomplished at initial readings and in private discussions between the director and the actor. The director continues to influence characterization as reflected in line interpretations and business throughout the rehearsal period.

In the second phase, the director blocks—tells the actors where and how to move on stage and how to handle props.

Next, the director works on pace—the timing of lines and business, of scenes and acts. He or she imparts pace to the play the way an orchestra conductor imparts tempo to a symphony, one scene *presto*, another *moderato*.

In the last phase, the director works on polishing the interaction of characters with sets, with props, and most important, with one another.

The final quality of the performance is the product of all four phases of the director's work.

(In amateur theater, work sometimes does not go beyond the first two phases by opening night. Work on characterization consists of the actors learning their lines, and blocking means that they don't trip over one another. In professional theater, when a director is unable to progress beyond the first two phases, we call him or her a "traffic cop.")

The stage manager's functions in support of the director are twofold. First, she or he helps to expedite the rehearsals so that the director and cast will have as much time as possible to work on pace and interaction. Setting rehearsal furniture, taking blocking notation, and warning actors for their entrances during rehearsals are examples of the duties implied by this function.

Second, the stage manager accepts the responsibility for relieving the director of all concern for the mechanics of production so that the director may concentrate on bringing about an artistic interpretation of the script. Calling all sound and light cues, scheduling crew calls, and informing the director of progress on the sets are examples of the duties implied here.

The stage manager does not have any voice in the artistic interpretation of the script and must not intrude into this area. When prompting, for instance, he or she must not offer an interpretation of the lines to the actors.

What happens then, if the stage manager notices during a rehearsal that one actor is addressing a line to a second actor that the playwright obviously intended for a third actor? The mistake is repeated at the next rehearsal. Still the actors and director miss the obvious.

The stage manager should make a note in the prompt script and call the error to the attention of the director after the rehearsal and out of earshot of the cast. Let the director take remedial action.

Sometimes the stage manager observes very basic mistakes in direction. For example, focus is drawn away from an actress's important lines by an actor moving upstage of her during her speech. The stage manager observes that the director is oblivious or condones this at rehearsal after rehearsal. What should the stage manager do?

The stage manager calls such items to the director's attention, privately and tactfully.

Now let's take it to extremes. The stage manager notices during rehearsals that the director is demanding a light, comedy tone from an actress in a speech that simply won't work that way. It throws her fellow cast members off and it ruins the whole impact of the scene. What does the stage manager do?

The stage manager should exercise very careful judgment in deciding whether or not to discuss the matter with the director confidentially. I advise great caution until you get to know and understand the director. Certainly the stage manager should be extremely proficient in his or her own area before offering a director advice in another.

Although the stage manager does not participate in the creative interpretation of the script, he or she does make a conscientious effort

Figure 8-1   Preset Diagram of Set and Props

to identify and understand the director's interpretation so that he or she may retain it, if called upon to do so, in keeping the show in hand during a long run (Chapter Sixteen) or blocking replacements and rehearsing understudies (see the end of Chapter Sixteen). Again, in these last mentioned duties, it is the director's intent that the stage manager strives to retain; the stage manager does not impose his or her own artistic interpretation.

Preset Diagrams

As soon as the scene designer decides where the sets and set pieces are to be located, you should make a diagram that will allow you to place those sets (or indications of sets) and set pieces (or rehearsal substitutes) exactly where they should be (see Figure 8-1).

As frequently as placement changes in the course of rehearsals, you must update your diagrams.

When it is decided which props will be *discovered* (found on the set at the rise of the curtain), you should add these props to your diagram with exacting specifications on just how the props are to be set (i.e., the label on a bottle should face downstage, the envelope is to be placed under the telephone with the address up and the flap open and pointing downstage).

The purpose of the preset diagram is to allow you to make a visual inspection prior to every rehearsal and performance. You must insure that every part of the set, all set pieces, and all props are in exactly the position that the cast expects to find them. This ritual is one of your most sacred duties.

The preset diagram differs from a diagram of the stage (Chapter Five) in that it includes indications of sets and props, and it need not be drawn to scale. The preset diagram may be the same as a scene shift diagram (Chapter Twelve), but the shift diagrams are placed in the crew area to help brief the crew, whereas preset diagrams are placed in your prompt script.

Examples:

A. The property mistress is late. You know where everything goes from your diagram. You set the props in her absence and rehearsal is not delayed.

B. The crew, in setting for Act II, forgets to move a table on stage.

During the intermission you check your diagram for Act II, realize that the table is not in place, and remind the crew.

C. An actor omits the business of closing the drapes on the set in Act II.

Checking your diagram for Act III you realize that the drapes are supposed to be discovered closed. You make the adjustment.

Actors become very dependent psychologically upon the exact placement of set pieces and props. Their timing for business is dependent on this placement. Adjusting to misplacement puts a strain on them, and sometimes it throws them off completely.

Your preset diagram should extend to the wings and include all stacked set pieces and props that are offstage. You must check their presence just as carefully as the units on stage.

Example:

A ladder and hammer, used as a set piece and prop in Scene 2, are borrowed for practical use in the shop and not returned. The items are not preset for Scene 1. If the crew waits until their cue for the Scene 1–2 fast change to discover that the props are missing, the change will be delayed. Your inspection of the offstage sets and props avoids this type of incident.

Rehearsals away from Your Stage

When stage time is not available for rehearsals and scenes must be rehearsed in other areas, preset diagrams, drawn to scale, allow you to lay out the exact dimensions of the scene using measuring tape and masking tape and/or spare rehearsal furniture to indicate flats and doors. Physical barricades used to indicate flats are better than tape. Actors tend to move closer to the taped lines or even step over them. They later feel cramped when they get onto the actual set. Your care in setting up the makeshift rehearsal area saves the time and energy of the cast in reblocking on the actual set.

Your Rehearsal Call

Usually you should arrive in the rehearsal area thirty to forty minutes prior to the rehearsal call, depending on how much work must be done to ready the area.

Besides arranging sets and props according to your present diagram, you should check on working conditions. Sweep the stage and dust the rehearsal furniture, if necessary, and make whatever improvements you can in ventilation, temperature, and lighting.

You should also prepare a work area for yourself and the director. Usually you will place a desk with two chairs in front of the apron. (Some directors prefer to use a music stand to hold their script as they remain standing during rehearsals.) Is there adequate room for your prompt script, the director's script, scratch paper, pencils, and refreshments? Insure that there is satisfactory lighting so that you may follow your scripts comfortably.

Now, is everything ready to start rehearsal at the minute it is called? Or will the cast have to stand around fifteen minutes waiting and/or adjusting things and not really rehearsing? Fifteen minutes of pre-rehearsal work by you can save two or three hours of cast time at every rehearsal. These hours saved and devoted to the quality of the final production are one of your very valuable contributions to the production process.

You should try to anticipate the entire course of the rehearsal and have all working materials at hand so that you may be stationary or at the director's side throughout. As the director's closest assistant, you must be able to devote your full attention to the rehearsal because it is your busiest and most demanding work period. You have many duties and a few run concurrently:

A. Calling all sound and light cues and special effects, pinpointing cues,
B. Taking blocking notation,
C. Prompting,
D. Warning,
E. Maintaining order,
F. Spiking set pieces,
G. Timing.

Calling and Pinpointing Cues

From the very first rehearsal you should call every light, sound, and special-effect cue. You should do it with such regularity and accuracy that no cast member ever doubts for a second that you will miss a cue during the production.

No matter how many times the director reruns the same scene, you always call the cues.

At first you go by the script. You ring the phone at the place indicated by the script and the place where you inserted your light pencil rough cue (discussed in Chapter Three). But during rehearsals you discuss the exact pinpointing of the cue with the director. Perhaps the director wants the phone to ring two lines prior, and the actors to allow it to ring twice in order to heighten suspense as to which of the actors will answer the phone. Or the director decides that she or he doesn't want the first phone ring to come at the end of the actor's line, but three words from the end so that the actor may cross to the phone on the last words of his line. Now the cue is specific. You should caret the exact point in your script. Later, just prior to the technical rehearsal, or during it, you will mark the exact cue with bold marking pen.

I use those fluorescent self-stick dots in my prompt script as I work in a very dim corner during performances. They show up nicely in my blue light.

Patty Kilpatric
Stage Manager
Charles Town, West Virginia

It is handy for you to have a bell/buzzer device in your kit (see Chapter Five) to provide some basic rehearsal sound effects. If you don't, simply call out, "Phone," "Doorbell," "Auto horn," or whatever sound is called for.

Similarly you should call all lighting effects to which the actors must react. You call "Curtain," and/or "Lights," at the beginning and end of every act.

You will also call the beginning, and sometimes the end, of all special effects: "Fog rolls in," "Vase rises from bookcase," "Rain begins," "Rain ends."

You should call all cues *resolutely*, letting the cast know that you know your business and are self-assured.

For a large stage:

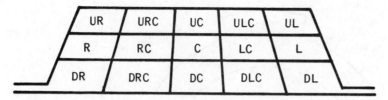

C - Center of the stage

D - Down (toward the audience)

U - Up (away from the audience)

R - Right (actor's right facing the audience)

L - Left (actor's left facing the audience)

For a small stage:

Figure 8-2 Divisions of Proscenium Stage for Blocking Notation

Taking Blocking Notation

Recording the movement of the actors helps to expedite rehearsals. With a written record of where they move on their lines, you are able to remind them when they forget. You will also use this notation to block in replacements and conduct understudy rehearsals (see Chapter Sixteen).

Normally you simply observe the initial blocking that the director gives the actors. You do not start to take blocking notations until the blocking starts to jell.

There are several systems for making such notation.

Method I

The stage is divided as shown in Figure 8-2. Blocking notations using this method might read:

XDR—The actor crosses to the down right area of the stage.
XLC—The actor crosses to the left center area of the stage.

Figure 8-3   Divisions of Round Stage for Blocking Notation

Method II (for theater in the round)

The stage is divided as shown in Figure 8-3. The stage is thought of as a clock, with the orchestra pit at 12 o'clock, and then divided into four concentric circles numbered from the audience to the center of the stage. Blocking notations might read as follows:

> X3.2—The actor crosses to the second ring at 3 o'clock.
> X11.1—The actor crosses to the first ring at 11 o'clock.

Method III

All notations are made, regardless of the shape of the stage, with reference to the destination of the actor and the number of steps she or he takes in the direction of that destination. Blocking notations might read:

> X door 2—The actor takes two steps toward the door.
> X Pat 5—The actor crosses five steps toward Pat, another character.

With this type of notation it is not possible to understand from reading a single entry where on stage the actor is located. This disadvantage should be countered by using extensive "French-scene" diagrams described below.

Method IV (Combinations)

Prior methods are combined. Blocking notations might read:

X DR door—The actor crosses to the down right door.
X2 DR door—The actor takes two steps toward the down right door.
    X2DR—The actor takes two steps toward the down right area.
  X3.2 door—The actor crosses to the door in the 3.2 area.
X2 3.2 door—The actor takes two steps toward the 3.2 door.

The best method is the method that works best for you.

Most often the actors move on their lines, that is, they cross while delivering a line of dialogue. They frequently start to move at the beginning of the line and stop moving with the last word of it. So when you make a blocking notation adjacent to an actor's line, it automatically indicates that the actor is moving on the line.

If an actor is blocked to move on another actor's line—not usually the case—this must be indicated. For these instances, and for the purpose of "French-scene" diagrams, it is convenient to have a symbol for each actor:

Constance—C
Irene—I
George—G

Now, if George moves on Irene's line:

Irene: One or Two? *G XDR* table

Or if two or more actors move at the same time:

Constance: I won't insist. *XDL; I XDR; G XULC*

(On Constance's line she crosses down left, Irene crosses down right, and George crosses up left center.)

What if the actor moves before or after his or her line but not on another actor's line?
Use carets:

Constance:∧I won't insist. *XDL*

This indicates that Constance starts her cross prior to her line and finishes it with the end of her line.

> *Constance:*∧∧I won't insist. *XDL*

These carets indicate that Constance begins and ends her cross prior to her line, but not on another actor's line.

> *Constance*: I won't∧insist.∧*XDL*

She starts her cross with the word indicated and completes the cross after the line.

> *Constance*: I won't insist.∧∧*XDL*.

She begins and ends her cross after her line.

Blocking notation is not an exact science. Some stage managers find that they can remember where and when an actor moves without precise notation. Others rely very heavily on notation and longhand notes (see Figure 8-4).

After you have observed the first few rough blocking rehearsals, you will start to make your notations, realizing that the blocking is not yet set (permanent). It is best to take notation in light pencil. If you do not care to erase, you may make changes in columns at the side of the original blocking:

> *Constance*: I won't insist. *XDL / XULC / XRC*

Using columns may be advantageous. When a director wants to go back to an earlier blocking, you will be able to tell the actors how they used to move.

After a few rehearsals when the same blocking is repeated, it is safe to assume that the blocking is set. A director may still change all or part of the blocking after this point, but it is set insofar as the director expects the actors to repeat their movement unless he or she changes it. The time when this happens varies with the director's technique. Some directors rough block at home, using diagrams of the stage and tokens for actors. They bring in their own notation of projected blocking and start early rehearsals with very firm blocking. Other directors allow cast members to drift at will as they recite their lines, and then try to arrange the drifting, sometimes called organic blocking.

When you feel that the blocking is set, you should start to prompt on blocking.

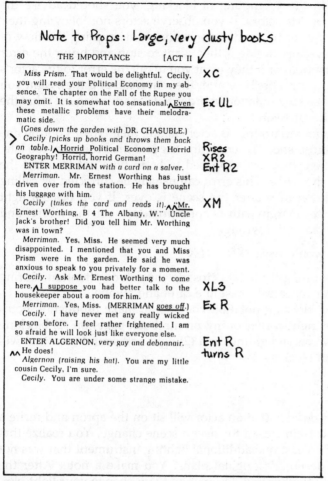

"Note to Props: Large, very dusty books"

80 THE IMPORTANCE [ACT II ✓

Miss Prism. That would be delightful. Cecily, you will read your Political Economy in my absence. The chapter on the Fall of the Rupee you may omit. It is somewhat too sensational. Even these metallic problems have their melodramatic side.

(Goes down the garden with DR. CHASUBLE.)

Cecily (picks up books and throws them back on table.) Horrid Political Economy! Horrid Geography! Horrid, horrid German!

ENTER MERRIMAN *with a card on a salver.*

Merriman. Mr. Ernest Worthing has just driven over from the station. He has brought his luggage with him.

Cecily (takes the card and reads it). "Mr. Ernest Worthing, B 4 The Albany, W." Uncle Jack's brother! Did you tell him Mr. Worthing was in town?

Merriman. Yes, Miss. He seemed very much disappointed. I mentioned that you and Miss Prism were in the garden. He said he was anxious to speak to you privately for a moment.

Cecily. Ask Mr. Ernest Worthing to come here. I suppose you had better talk to the housekeeper about a room for him.

Merriman. Yes, Miss. (MERRIMAN *goes off.*)

Cecily. I have never met any really wicked person before. I feel rather frightened. I am so afraid he will look just like everyone else.

ENTER ALGERNON, *very gay and debonnair.* He does!

Algernon (raising his hat). You are my little cousin Cecily, I'm sure.

Cecily. You are under some strange mistake.

Blocking notations (margin):
XC
Ex UL
Rises
XR2
Ent R2
XM
XL3
Ex R
Ent R
turns R

Figure 8-4 Blocking Notation as Entered on Prompt Script Page

Example A:

An actor says: "I know I was supposed to move on that line but I've forgotten where."

You: "Your cross is down left."

Example B:

A director says to an actor: "You're not supposed to be there when Sam enters."

You advise the director (not the actor): "He missed his cross down left three lines back on 'Hark, here comes the king'."

In general, in the prompting of blocking, you should advise the *director* rather than the actors. If you observe actors not following their blocking, you whisper to the director without interrupting the flow of the scene. Let directors decide if they want to stop and bring the error to the actor's attention, or if they want you to call the error to the actor's attention later, during a break or after the rehearsal, or if they want you to change your blocking notation in order to take advantage of what the actor has done instinctively.

A very common occurrence is actors taking their crosses on the line following their cross line. The cross line triggers their memory too late. But they get where they are supposed to be in time not to upset the overall effect of the scene. This error can usually be corrected by calling the actor's attention to it after the scene is over. If you place a light penciled caret in the margin with an appropriate symbol, this will remind you of what the actor did wrong.

Constance: I won't insist. *XDL <LX*

When you have brought the late cross to the actor's attention, during the break or after rehearsal, erase the caret and symbol.

While taking blocking notation you should make production notes (I use the upper right corner of my promptbook page) on (1) blocking that will require special lighting, and (2) light and sound cues that will be dependent on blocking.

Example A:

The director decides that an actor will sit on the apron and recite a poem with the curtain closed to cover a scene change. You realize that this will call for at least one additional lighting instrument that was not in the lighting designer's original plans. You make a note. After the rehearsal you tell the lighting designer and you change your light plot. You also place new cues in your prompt script.

Example B:

The director decides that the nurse will rise and cross to a table to examine a knife before she hears a bell that summons her offstage. Formerly the cue for the bell was the doctor's line to the nurse. You realize that the cue for the bell is now a visual one rather than an oral one, so you make this change in your prompt script immediately.

French-Scene Diagrams

Within a scene there may be many "French-scenes." Every time a character enters or exits, a new French-scene is begun (after the conventional

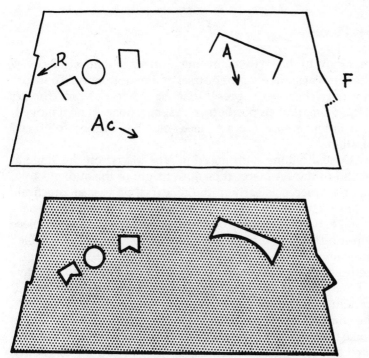

Figure 8-5   "French-Scene" Cardboard Template and Scene Diagram

scene designations in classical French drama). A French-scene is that part of a scene or act in which the number of characters is constant.

The director usually starts or resumes rehearsing from the beginning of a French-scene. You may find it quite helpful to make small diagrams of the position of the cast at the beginning of each French-scene (see Figure 8-5).

If the director says, "Let's take it from the top of page 83 where Fran enters," the cast members will probably not remember where they are supposed to be for Fran's entrance. If you review your blocking notation just prior to Fran's entrance, you may eventually be able to determine where they are, but it will take time. But if you have made a diagram, you can say immediately (from Figure 8-5), "Al is seated on the couch facing down left, Ralph is looking out the window, and Alice is standing down right center facing down left."

As there are frequently many French-scenes in every act, you may expedite your diagraming with a cardboard template of the set and set pieces (see Figure 8-5). At the top of every promptbook page on which a character enters or exits, you simply copy your scene diagram. Jotting in the positions of the cast then takes very little effort.

Spiking Set Pieces

It is very important to the actors' movement on stage that set pieces be in exactly the same place at every rehearsal and performance. To insure this, you not only check your preset diagrams, but also *spike* the set pieces, that is, you mark their position on the stage floor. Then if moved, accidentally or intentionally, the set pieces may be returned to exactly the same location.

Spiking is usually done with masking tape placed on the stage at the upstage end of the set piece, thus out of sight of the audience.

Spike your set pieces as early in the rehearsal process as practical.

When many scenes are to play in the same area, it becomes necessary to code the spike marks—to write on the masking tape which set piece plays there during which scene. Next to one tape marked "II–2 table" there might be another tape marked "III–7 chair."

Frequently shifts must be made so fast that stagehands do not have time to read the tapes. In these cases the tapes should be color-coded, painted a certain color for each scene.

Or if the changes are to be made in blackouts, it may be helpful to paint the spike marks with luminous paint. The stage lighting will usually "heat up" the luminous paint so that it will glow during blackouts. If you are using luminous paint in areas where it is not hit by stage lights, you can heat it up by shining a spot or sunlamp on it at close range for a few minutes prior to performance.

Prompting

Prompting procedure is determined by the director. You should ask the director privately, prior to rehearsals, how he or she wants the cast prompted. How close are the actors to be held to the lines in the script? Letter-perfect? Or may they paraphrase as long as they get the sense of the line? How are the actors to call for lines? When and how are you to review lines with actors? Ask the director to brief the cast at the outset of rehearsals on just what he or she expects in the prompting process.

The few words on the subject might go like this: "Our stage manager has been instructed to hold you very close to the script. If you deliver a line and our stage manager calls out the correct one, repeat the line as he gives it, without breaking character, and carry on. Do not argue about changing the line. See me before or after rehearsals about any possible line changes. Our stage manager will also approach you during breaks and after rehearsals to cite lines or cues that were missed. Please do not argue. Simply repeat out loud the line cited and then say, 'Thank you.' Call for lines by saying 'line,' and in no other way."

Some directors insist that the cast be held letter-perfect to the script, particularly if the playwright's reputation is great. They allow their casts greater latitude with the works of lesser-known playwrights. Some directors feel that they must update plays and encourage their cast members to experiment with and modernize the dialogue.

Some directors insist that the stage manager throw the exact line whenever an actor hesitates or paraphrases, as well as when an actor calls for a line. Other directors want lines thrown only when the actor calls for them or when the cast jumps out of sequence. But they want all errors in lines brought to the attention of the cast during breaks or after rehearsals.

Some directors want cast members to say "line" when asking for a line. Others want them to snap their fingers but otherwise to remain in character. Some directors do not want their actors to call for lines at all. Some set a date in the rehearsal schedule after which actors are not to call for lines. Many directors resent any other remarks that actors throw when calling for lines, such as, "Oh, I always forget that one."

Talk it over with your director. If she or he does not give specific instructions to the cast explaining the prompting interaction expected, start out in the way you feel is best, and apply her or his criticism of your prompting technique as you go along.

To prompt efficiently, read the script to yourself, mouthing the words as the actors recite them. That way you are right there with them. Actors appreciate getting their line immediately after they call for it. If they and the director have to wait while you search for the line, then you are delaying the rehearsal.

When you prompt, give the actor the line in a clear, resolute, but emotionless tone of voice. Do not interpret the actor's line for him or her.

Be sure to make line changes in your prompt script as they are decided upon. Prompt the new lines as if they were the old lines.

As you prompt, draw a caret in the margin to indicate every line that was delivered improperly. Use a code to indicate the type of error. Work in light pencil.

C — called for line
P — paraphrased
BB — bobbled
L — late (cite cue to actor)
PR — pronunciation
J — jumped cue
H — handle—added extra word not in script prior to line
S — sequence, jumped out of

Use any code that works for you.

At the next break or after rehearsal, go to each actor, point out the missed line, and ask the actor to read it aloud. It is not necessary to say

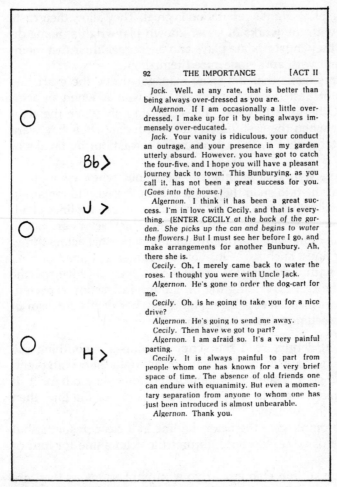

92   THE IMPORTANCE   [ACT II

Jack. Well, at any rate, that is better than being always over-dressed as you are.

Algernon. If I am occasionally a little over-dressed, I make up for it by being always immensely over-educated.

Jack. Your vanity is ridiculous, your conduct an outrage, and your presence in my garden utterly absurd. However, you have got to catch the four-five, and I hope you will have a pleasant journey back to town. This Bunburying, as you call it, has not been a great success for you. *(Goes into the house.)*

Algernon. I think it has been a great success. I'm in love with Cecily, and that is everything. *(ENTER CECILY at the back of the garden. She picks up the can and begins to water the flowers.)* But I must see her before I go, and make arrangements for another Bunbury. Ah, there she is.

Cecily. Oh, I merely came back to water the roses. I thought you were with Uncle Jack.

Algernon. He's gone to order the dog-cart for me.

Cecily. Oh, is he going to take you for a nice drive?

Algernon. He's going to send me away.

Cecily. Then have we got to part?

Algernon. I am afraid so. It's a very painful parting.

Cecily. It is always painful to part from people whom one has known for a very brief space of time. The absence of old friends one can endure with equanimity. But even a momentary separation from anyone to whom one has just been introduced is almost unbearable.

Algernon. Thank you.

Figure 8-6 Prompting Cites, Lightly Penciled on Inside Script Margin

why you marked the line unless you are asked. Then erase the caret and code (see Figure 8-6).

Most professional actors are grateful for this service. If you should meet with resentment ("That's exactly what I said." "I know I missed it. You don't have to tell me."), say, "Thank you," politely, and walk away. Try it again at the next rehearsal and see how the actor accepts your help more graciously. When the actors are convinced that you are trying to help them, they are appreciative.

If there is an intentional pause prior to, or during a line, you should mark your script with an inverted caret (V) at the pause point so that you are reminded not to prompt there (and don't panic on opening night).

Sometimes it is convenient to write out line cites during rehearsal so that you can hand each actor a list of lines that need to be reviewed. This allows you to dismiss the cast faster after rehearsal, rather than hold them while you flip through pages of the script. If the director habitually holds the cast after rehearsals to review notes with them, you might use that same time to cite lines, doing it as unobtrusively as possible, and not interfering with the director's notes.

Getting up on lines is basic to any production. You helped establish deadlines for line memorization in making up the master calendar and rehearsal schedule. Now, how can you help the actors meet those deadlines? Are you willing to run lines with them before or after rehearsals? Can you arrange extra pre-rehearsal sessions for cast members when they can help each other by running lines? Can you assign a gopher to run lines with an actor who is offstage?

Start prompting with gusto just as soon as cast members are willing to put down their scripts. Let the cast know that you mean to help them get up on their lines quickly and accurately. It is easier to start working hard than to start leniently and then apply pressure after the cast has gotten into sloppy habits.

If you can make every actor feel that you are earnestly trying to help rather than criticize, your prompting technique is good.

Prompting during a performance is a matter of the director's policy. Once a production has opened it is generally considered very unprofessional to prompt, and actors are expected to ad-lib their way out of any situation.

Warning

During rehearsals actors may wander out of the rehearsal area. If they leave, they must always check out with the stage manager to say where they are going. ("I'm going to get this sewn up in costumes." "We're running lines in the lobby.") They should also check in with the stage manager when they return (see Chapter Three, "Actors and Their Entrance Cues").

You must think ahead. Which scene will the director work on next? You must warn wandering actors to be ready to appear. Waiting for an actor to be summoned so that a rehearsal can continue wastes a lot of time. If you observe your entrance warns (see Chapter Three and Figure 3-9), you can avoid such delays.

If an actor is on the premises and rehearsal is delayed while waiting for that actor to appear, the fault is yours.

Sometimes an actor will be summoned only to find that the director wishes to rerun the scene prior to her or his entrance. It is better that a single actor be inconvenienced than that several be hung up by her or his absence. When you work at mounting a few plays with the same director, you will develop a sixth sense as to whether the director will press on or rerun.

If possible, don't leave your post to summon a wandering actor. Send a gopher or another actor.

During performances you are not responsible for warning actors for individual entrances, but you are responsible for warning the crew about impending shifts and the orchestra about musical cues, as necessary. (See Chapter Three, p. 32, for discussion of exceptions.)

Maintaining Order

A director should never have to ask for quiet working conditions that will allow him or her and the cast to concentrate on their work. You should be aware of any noise or other disruptions and try to remedy the situation.

Try personal contact. Approach the noisy offender and explain, eye-ball to eyeball, that rehearsals require silence from those who are not on stage, that it is a matter of courtesy.

Do not hesitate to shout, "Quiet, PLEASE!" if personal contact fails.

Some people have greater tolerance of noise levels than others. If you can read Christopher Fry during an air raid, but your director gets shell shock from seats squeaking, try to sympathize with his or her problem and hold the cast down to the level he or she can tolerate.

Giving Rehearsal, Publicity, and Costume Calls

The last official voice that every actor should hear as she or he leaves a rehearsal is yours, giving the next call, whether that call is for a rehearsal, publicity meeting with a TV interviewer, costume call at a supply house across town, or conference with the producer.

It should be standard procedure that every actor check out, after rehearsal or performance, with the stage manager. This might simply mean a cheerful "Goodnight," to which you might answer with an equally informal, "See you at ten tomorrow." That informal "ten tomorrow" is an order to appear at 10 o'clock sharp.

It is not enough to publish, post, and distribute rehearsal schedules. You must give the calls in person, face to face. You must then mentally or physically check off each cast member; if anyone left early and failed to check out with you, you must phone that individual to give the call.

If you are working with a large cast, divided into principals, chorus, and dancers, or other major groups, you may wish to use a special callboard.

The term *callboard* has come to mean a bulletin board where any information, including the next call, can be brought to the attention of

YOUR C A L LFOR

TUES. July 14
(DATE)

	TIME	PLACE
PRINCIPALS		
FrANK *	10:00	TenT
JUlIE *	10:30	MUSIC ROOM
RAVENAL	10:30	COStUME SHOP
All Others	10:30	Tent
SINGING ENSEMBLE		
BOYS	Off	
GIRLS	11:00	ChORUS ROOM
DANCING ENSEMBLE		
BOYS	11:00	COStUME Shop
GIRLS	11:00	ChoRUS ROOM
LOCAL CHORUS		
BOYS	5:30	COStUME SHOP
GIRLS	5:30	COStUME SHOP
*SPECIAL APPOINTMENTS		
FrANK	Publicity Lunch, 12:00	FlorentinE ROOM
JUliE	HAIRDRESSER 6:00	Claire's 140 W. 2ND

Figure 8-7 Special Callboard Format, for Next Upcoming Calls

the cast. *Special callboard* is used here to mean a board display with only the next call (see Figure 8-7). Rather than placing it on the general callboard, it is effective to place the special callboard by itself near the exit through which the cast must leave.

The special callboard form can be covered with plastic, glass, or even a plastic film wrap so that the blanks may be filled in with crayon and then erased with a rag.

When photo calls are scheduled in the rehearsal area, whether for publicity, cast souvenirs, or the theater scrapbook, it is often helpful to post a picture schedule (see Figure 8-8).

The publicity person usually decides who is to appear in the pictures. But to save time in posing the shots, you might want to pre-select emotional peak scenes from the script. During the call you can then

PICTURE CALL

Thursday night after performance pictures will be taken.
Please remain in costume and change for subsequent shots.

1. Entire cast (curtain call order) and crew.

2. III-2: "So I'll say goodnight..." - Arlene, Jonas, Terry

3. III-1: "...because I'm going to get married." - Arlene,
    Sandy, Rita, Larry

4. III-1: "My arms, my lips..." - Larry, Rita, Sandy

5. II-3 : "I'm going to be frank with you, Pa." - Jonas,
    Dave, JoAnne

6. II-3: "We going to be here that long?" - Dave, JoAnne,
    Terry

7. II-1: "I want to go to a hotel." - Jonas, Arlene

8. II-1: "He don't look like no Cary Grant to me." - Dee,
    Sandy, Norma, Jonas, Rita

9. I-3: "Then start going out on dates again." - Arlene,
    Jonas

10. I-2: "Stop trying to fix me up with all your friends."
    Shirley-May, Jonas, Terry

11. I-2: "Rosalind, do me a favor." - Terry, Vicky, Jonas,
    JoAnne

12. I-2: "Rosalind, you know my brother Jerry." - Vicky,
    Jonas, Terry

13. I-1: "I'm in trouble now, Ma." - Arlene, Rita

14. I-1: "Will you get dressed and go to school." - Arlene,
    Rita, Sandy

Figure 8-8 Picture Call Schedule

throw a line before the emotional peak and have the cast pick it up in
character. If someone will shout "Freeze" when they come to the peak
line, this process will usually result in an interesting tableau.

It is often necessary for the photographer to tighten the shot by
moving the actors closer to one another than they normally appear in
that sequence. But reposing and rerunning still saves time over the
unplanned approach of deciding in front of the camera just what poses
are appropriate.

If the picture call follows a run-through or dress rehearsal or performance, it is desirable to start with poses selected from the last scene
of the last act and work backwards so that cast members are saved an
unnecessary costume change.

Posting a picture call and picture schedule well in advance allows cast members to plan for the session in terms of shaving, hair style, makeup, costumes, and time.

Posting the Running Order

The running order is a list, in production sequence, of the scenes, giving the place of the scene, the cast members in the scene, the songs or dance numbers (if any) in that scene, and special cue lines (see Figure 8-9). You should post it on the first day of rehearsal or as soon thereafter as possible, and update it as necessary.

The function of the running order is to help remind cast members when they appear next.

Why is this necessary? Shouldn't every cast member know when he or she appears next?

Sometimes it is very confusing. In a one-week rehearsal for a musical stock show the chorus may have rehearsed their songs in a chorus room, their dances in a rehearsal hall, and many will not have gone through the show in production sequence until the "put together," possibly the day before dress rehearsal, and only two days before opening night. So, as the chorus members dash from the stage to the dressing room, they need to have some easily accessible reference to answer the questions, "What do I do next?" and "Which of my eight costumes do I change into?"

In the rewrite phase of a new musical the chorus might come in for half hour call to find that the running order has been drastically changed. The finale will be sung as the opening number, the show done as a flashback, and the principals will reprise the finale at the final curtain with the chorus humming the bridge from the wings. Then, the next night at half hour call, the chorus learns that the finale will be sung at the second act curtain and that they will reprise their Act I, Scene 2 hit song as the finale. Their actual performance sequence will vary from day to day. So in addition to briefings from the staff, they need a written running order that they can refer to in haste.

The running order should be BIG!, possibly two feet wide by three feet tall, and carefully lettered so that it is easily legible. It should be placed along the path from the stage to the dressing rooms so that cast members don't have to detour to read it. It should be well lighted. It should be in the same place from the time it is posted until closing night, so that cast members don't have to search for it.

If there is a blackout within a scene to denote time lapse, a "false blackout," this should be noted on the running order so that cast members will be forewarned not to enter on that blackout for the following scene. A song or line that occurs after the time lapse blackout should

TAKE   ME   ALONG

RUNNING ORDER

ACT   I

I-1   OUTSIDE MILLER HOME

    Townspeople
       "Fire Machine"

    Fire Chief, Nat, Essie, Art, Tommy, Mildred
       "Oh, Please"

    Lilly
       reprise: "Oh, Please"

I-2   MACOMBER HOUSE

    Richard, Muriel
       "I Would Die"

    Macomber

I-3 CARBARN

  Sid, Voices
     "Sid, Ol' Kid"

I-4   STREET   (Played In Aisle)

    Art, Sid

I-5   MILLER HOME

    Essie, Lilly, Tommy, Mildred, Nat, Richard, Macomber
       "Staying Young"

    Art, Sid
       "I Get Embarrassed"
       "We're Home"
       "Take Me Along"

I-6   PICNIC

    Sid, Carter, McDonald, Nat
    "For Sweet Charity"

Figure 8-9   Running Order on a Large Board, Easily Legible

be listed so that cast members will have an accurate cue for their entrance blackout.

All reprises should be carefully designated as reprises so that there is no confusion as to whether the song or the reprise is the cue. This is a particular problem when the song and the reprise occur within the same scene.

To make the entries on your running order immediately discernible, write your song titles in one color or style of script (e.g., letters underlined), the names of the scenes in a second color or style (e.g., large capitals), the cast members involved in a third (e.g., small capitals), and special notes about cue lines and blackouts in still another (e.g., cursive script). A work of art is not your goal, but any scheme that will help cast members to decipher the running order quickly is helpful.

You must call all revisions to the attention of the cast and discuss with them the problems incurred by changes.

Typed copies of the running order should be placed in the crew area and on the callboard. You are very definitely responsible for alerting all crew members (props, lights, scene changes, costumes, etc.) to changes. The crew is not expected to decipher and apply a revised running order without a briefing from you and your immediate close supervision.

When changes in the production sequence are made, the running order should not be done over, but revisions should be cited with bold marking pen so that cast members can pick out the changes without studying the whole running order.

Summer stock running orders rarely parallel the New York productions as reflected in published scripts, so the running order must be coordinated with the staff before it is posted.

Timing of Rehearsals and Performances

You should carefully time each scene, and sometimes critical parts of scenes. The purpose of timing during rehearsals is to help the director know what the total playing time is, and to let the box office and house manager know what time the show will be out and what time to expect intermissions. The purpose of timing during performances is to keep track of the pace of each scene and act.

Using a stopwatch is desirable, but an ordinary watch with a sweep second hand may be used.

Start to time scenes just as soon in rehearsal as the scenes are run without interruption. At the end of each rehearsal, advise the director of the running times. Tell him or her not only how long the scenes took, but how long it took last time they were run, and the shortest time in which they were run.

As soon as every scene in the play has been timed once, give the director some projection of the total running time.

During the run, time each scene at every performance. You will find that running time of each scene varies from performance to performance. Sometimes it's audience response; sometimes it's actors who are not picking up their lines or are adding pauses. Sometimes a bit of business will vary in time. There are many reasons for differences in the timing of scenes. If the director is "with the show" (attending performances regularly or even periodically), judgment as to why the times vary may

WEEKLY TIME CHART

PRODUCTION **The Bunny**   WEEK OF **Oct. 10, 53**

	Tues Dress	Wed Dress	Thur opening	Fri	Sat early	Sat late	Sun
Announced Curtain	8:00	8:00	8:30	8:30	8:00	10:30	8:30
Actual Curtain	8:06	8:14	8:41	8:35	8:04	10:31	8:36
I-1	8:14 / 8	8:22 / 8	8:48 / 7	8:43 / 8	8:12 / 8	10:40 / 9	8:45 / 9
Blackout	8:14 / :30	8:38 / :16	8:48 / :25	8:43 / :20	8:12 / :20	10:40 / :20	8:45 / :20
I-2	8:29 / 15	8:39 / 17	9:03 / 15	8:58 / 15	8:27 / 15	10:54 / 14	9:00 / 15
Blackout	8:30 / :35	8:39 / :30	9:04 / :30	8:59 / :30	8:28 / :30	10:55 / :30	9:01 / :30
I-3	8:47 / 17	8:55 / 16	9:19 / 15	9:14 / 15	8:44 / 16	11:10 / 15	9:16 / 15
Intermission	9:09 / 22	9:07 / 12	9:30 / 11	9:25 / 11	8:53 / 9	11:20 / 10	9:26 / :10
II-1	9:25 / 16	9:23 / 16	9:46 / 16	9:42 / 17	9:10 / 17	11:36 / 16	9:42 / 16
Blackout	9:26 / :48	9:24 / :45	9:47 / :40	9:43 / :35	9:11 / :35	11:37 / :35	9:43 / :30
II-2	9:37 / 11	9:34 / 10	9:56 / 9	9:52 / 9	9:20 / 9	11:46 / 9	9:52 / 9
Blackout	9:37 / :25	9:34 / :25	9:56 / :25	9:53 / :30	9:20 / :25	11:46 / :25	9:52 / :25
II-3	9:57 / 20	9:53 / 19	10:14 / 18	10:11 / 18	9:39 / 19	12:04 / 18	10:10 / 18
Total Running Time	1:27	1:26	1:20	1:22	1:24	1:21	1:22

Figure 8-10   Chart Record of Running Time

be left to her or him. If the director has left the show, or if the show is on the road, then it is your responsibility to evaluate the running times and take appropriate action (see Chapter Sixteen).

If you index a weekly time chart (see Figure 8-10) into your prompt script, you will be easily able to make the necessary comparisons and have the information readily available to your staff.

In most theater situations you will be responsible for the timing of blackouts and intermissions. You must direct the blackouts and the backstage aspects of the intermissions just as carefully as the director directs the scenes. Some of the factors in a blackout or intermission are changes of sets, striking and/or setting of props, change of position of actors, changes in costumes, patching of the lighting board, re-gelling of instruments, etc. (see Chapter Eleven).

During a blackout, audience attention wanders. Perhaps the first 10 seconds of a blackout are consumed in applause and/or mental reaction to what has just happened. After that, coughing, fidgeting, and conversations indicate that the audience is no longer involved with the scene that is past. The longer the audience is left in darkness, the harder it is for the actors in the following scene to regain the audience's attention, emotional focus, and/or intellectual concern.

So it is very important that you be able to organize the proceedings during blackouts to make them as short as possible. Some directors insist that no blackouts be longer than 20 seconds. During the technical rehearsal and subsequent dress rehearsals you must ask to run, rerun, and if necessary, choreograph blackouts until you and the director are satisfied that they are run in minimum time.

During the rehearsals you should also time certain of the sound effects and special effects to figure out the length for your plots.

Example:

You realize during a rehearsal that an alarm bell sound effect must last long enough to cover an actor's business of opening a safe, ransacking it, and escaping through a window, and it must also last long enough to cover the entrance of two other characters, their reaction, and the closing of the curtain. How long should a tape of that alarm bell effect be? During the rehearsals you carefully time the business and either make a production note in your script or add this timing to your sound plot. Then at the sound session you are prepared to say, "We will need at least three minutes of the alarm bell on tape."

Keeping a Rehearsal Log

The rehearsal log is a very brief diary of what happened or failed to happen at rehearsals. You should always be able to answer the question, "How did we come to this state of affairs?" with specifics. It is not always possible to remember the specifics unless you keep notes. It is convenient to tab your log into your prompt script.

Entries in the rehearsal log should include date, cast members who are late or absent, cast changes, the scene or scenes that were blocked or run, the number of times these scenes were run, delays and causes of delays in rehearsals, failure to run a scheduled scene, and any significant occurrence out of the ordinary—e.g., an accident, failure to meet a deadline, or mechanical failure of equipment (see Figure 8-11).

If you have the opportunity to help critique a production, your rehearsal log will be an invaluable asset (see Chapter Nineteen).

Submitting Rehearsal Reports

In some companies the producer or top management may require a daily written report from the stage manager. This report usually requires the

REHEARSAL LOG

Sunday, May 28 — Read through script (Mike, Will, Jackie out).

Monday, May 29 — Read through again, made a few revisions (Jackie still out).

Friday, June 2 — Blocked Act I to p. 17.

Saturday, June 3 — Started 15 minutes late. (Dick claimed shooting wound up late.) Blocked remainder of Act I.

Sunday, June 4 — Jackie, Dick only - script changes.

Monday, June 5 — Jackie, Dick only - blocked their scenes in Act II.

Tuesday, June 6 — Billy only. Worked him through all blocking as Eric's replacement.

Wednesday, June 7 — Ran Act I twice. Sound session after rehearsal. (Steve was late but no delay in rehearsal.)

Thursday, June 8 — Blocked Act II (except Jackie, Dick scenes.)

Friday, June 9 — Attempted to integrate sound but amplifier went out. Ran Act II twice.

Saturday, June 10 — First runthrough, integrated sound cues.

Sunday, June 11 — Polished Act I, ran five times.

Tuesday, June 13 — Ran Act II twice. Dick, Pandora out so rehearsal suffered;did not run Dick-Jackie scenes (Dick was shooting, Pandora's husband in auto accident.)

Figure 8-11 Rehearsal Log with Typical Entries

same information that you would want to keep in your log, but in a more formal format (see Figure 8-12). If you were to keep a copy of this report, you would not have to keep a log, as the same purpose would be served.

Note that in the rehearsal report, under the heading "Engaged/

COMPANY *J. Gill*

STAGE MANAGER's REHEARSAL REPORT FORM

PLACE: *Loft*   DATE: *Aug. 13, '69*

CALL: 7:30 SCENES: I-4 II-2	Rehearsal started: 7:30 Lunch/Dinner break: — Rehearsal resumed: — Rehearsal ended: 10:00 Rehearsal time: 2:30 Overtime (if any): —
	Expenses: —
Engaged/Dismissed: —	Injuries: Dinah Left Early — *see report*
Absent/Excused: AL — still out sick	Late: —

Remarks: Good work done on both scenes despite AL's absence. — Dinah did well before she left.

Laurence Stern
Stage Manager

Figure 8-12   Rehearsal Report Form

Dismissed," you are expected to indicate those cast members who joined or left the company. The payroll department and Equity must be notified in these cases.

In some companies the stage manager is also required to submit a report to Equity (see Figure 8-13).

Accident Prevention and Reports

You must always be alert to situations that might cause accidents: set construction materials left on stage or backstage, materials left perched precariously on ladders and on flats, nails and boards protruding upstage of flats which might tear actors' costumes or skin, wires not secured on which to trip, sharp edges on corners in dark areas backstage, etc. The list is endless.

Check flying cables, whether or not you have immediate plans to

STAGE MANAGER'S WEEKLY REPORT

Location: _____ Week Ending: _____

Name of Theatre: _____

Violations by Actor

1. List the name of the Actor.

2. Type of violation (lateness for half-hour, altering direction, etc.

3. Indicate in column 1 if sufficient explanation given so that violation should be considered excused (E for excused, U for unexcused)

4. Has the Actor been spoken to about this type of violation before? Indicate in column 2 (R for repeated, 1 for the first time, 2 for second time, etc.)

NAME	VIOLATION	COLUMN 1 2

Violations by Manager

1. List only violations by Manager which he has not corrected after being informed by you, the Deputy or Equity.

Signed:_____
Stage Manager

7/29/68 Rev. 4/72   USE REVERSE SIDE FOR REMARKS   PO-5

Figure 8-13   Report Form to Actor's Equity

use them, to be sure they will hold under strain. Twist the cables open to check the condition of the inside. If rotten, replace.

It takes constant vigilance to prevent carelessness and inconsideration from turning into serious accidents.

You should encourage all members of the staff, cast, and crew to report unsafe conditions to you, and you should take immediate steps to correct them.

Most large or long-established theaters are covered by accident insurance as a form of protection against suit by actors or patrons for accidents that occur on the theater premises. Most insurance companies want to have the same information about any accident that occurs (see Figure 8-14).

If your theater does have such insurance, make sure that you have accident report forms on hand.

In the event of an accident, whether or not your theater has insur-

E M P L O Y E R	1 FIRM NAME	1A. POLICY NUMBER
	2 MAILING ADDRESS (Please include city, Zip)	2A. PHONE NUMBER
	3 LOCATION IF DIFFERENT FROM MAIL ADDRESS	
	4 NATURE OF BUSINESS e.g. painting contractor, wholesale grocer, sawmill, hotel, etc.	5. State Unemployment Insurance Acct. No

E M P L O Y E E	6 NAME	7. DATE OF BIRTH / / Month Day Year
	8 HOME ADDRESS (number and street, city, Zip)	8A. PHONE NUMBER
	9 SEX ☐ Male ☐ Female	10. OCCUPATION (Regular job title, not specific activity at time of injury)	11. SOCIAL SECURITY NUMBER

12 DEPARTMENT IN WHICH REGULARLY EMPLOYED | 12A. DATE OF HIRE / / Month Day Year

13 HOURS USUALLY WORKED

EMPLOYEE WORKS _____ HOURS PER DAY FOR _____ DAYS PER WEEK | 13A. WEEKLY HOURS | 13B. Under what class code of your policy were wages assigned?

14 GROSS WAGES/SALARY

EMPLOYEE EARNS $ _____ PER ☐ HOUR ☐ DAY ☐ WEEK ☐ EVERY TWO WEEKS ☐ MONTH ☐ OTHER _____

I N J U R Y O R I L L N E S S	15 WHERE DID ACCIDENT OR EXPOSURE OCCUR? (number, and street, city)	15A. COUNTY	15B ON EMPLOYER'S PREMISES? ☐ YES ☐ NO

16 WHAT WAS EMPLOYEE DOING WHEN INJURED? (Please be specific. Identify tools, equipment or material the employee was using.)

17 HOW DID THE ACCIDENT OR EXPOSURE OCCUR? (Please describe fully the events that resulted in injury or occupational disease. Tell what happened and how it happened. Please use separate sheet if necessary.)

18 OBJECT OR SUBSTANCE THAT DIRECTLY INJURED EMPLOYEE e.g. the machine employee struck against or which struck him; the vapor or poison inhaled or swallowed the chemical that irritated his skin; in cases of strains, the thing he was lifting, pulling, etc.

19A DESCRIBE THE INJURY OR ILLNESS e.g. cut, strain, fracture, skin rash, etc	19B PART OF BODY AFFECTED e.g., back, left wrist, right eye, etc.

20 NAME AND ADDRESS OF PHYSICIAN

21 IF HOSPITALIZED, NAME AND ADDRESS OF HOSPITAL

22 DATE OF INJURY OR ILLNESS / / Month Day Year	23 TIME OF DAY _____ a.m. _____ p.m.	24 Did employee lose at least one full day's work after the injury? ☐ Yes, date last worked _____ ☐ No
25 HAS EMPLOYEE RETURNED TO WORK? ☐ Yes, date returned _____ ☐ No, still off work		26 DID EMPLOYEE DIE? ☐ Yes, date _____ ☐ No

Completed by (type or print)	Signature	Title	Date

Form 5020 (Rev 4)
January 1983

FILING OF THIS REPORT IS NOT AN ADMISSION OF LIABILITY

Figure 8-14 Accident Report Form

ance, obtain all of the information required in the illustration and write a brief narrative of what happened. Ask the individual involved to write his or her own brief narrative, and have him or her sign it.

No matter how many copies of the accident form are required by the insurance company, make one additional copy for your files.

Wednesday

1. Touch up staples reflecting lights

2. weight bottom of flaps swinging in draft.

3. Call Norman on plans for ramp

4. Get sack of wheat paste.

5. tell Nick he won't be needed Friday night

6. Call photographer for schedule

<u>remind Chuck:</u>
    1. mortar & pestle
    2. Bring in III revisions
    3. Call Ray 7:00 PM

Figure 8-15 Manager's Daily Do-List and Reminder Checklist

Keeping a Do-List

A *do-list* (talk of redundant definitions!) is a self-kept list of things that you need to do. It is usually kept on your clipboard, but might just as practically be attached to the inside front cover of your prompt script. Anyone who has ever made out a shopping list can write one, and anyone who has ever made out a shopping list will appreciate the necessity for one (see Figure 8-15).

Your do-list should always be with you. Whenever staff, crew, or cast tell you anything that requires an action on your part, you should make a note of it. Any change of schedule should be noted so that you can figure out the consequences and deal with them. You will also want to note information that must be relayed to other staff members. Do not trust to memory. There are simply too many things to be done.

Writing something on your list implies that you will take care of it or see that it is taken care of. It is reassuring to a director to see you make a note when he or she asks for something.

Take time at the end of each day to review your list and to assess what must be done first tomorrow and what may be delegated to others.

Keep a special area for notes for the director. In doing so you will be functioning not only as the director's assistant but as the director's secretary. When the director promises to do something—bring in a prop, contact a scene designer with whom he or she has worked in the past, write a letter of introduction for a cast member who will be going to New York—jot down a note for him or her. After rehearsal, present your notes with tact. Obviously, if the director does not appreciate this, discontinue. You'll find most directors grateful.

Your book helped me to survive my first summer stock experience, but unfortunately you did not touch one area which is fast becoming the difference between the "men and boys" in stage management: coffee. I found that the making of a good pot of java brings the same respect as calling cues on time. It's a way of getting ahead in this business. The choices are difficult: Coffee-mate vs. Cremora; Sweet 'N Low or Sweet 10 or Equal or Sugar Twin or Necta Sweet. Remember, most coffee machines must be cleaned once a week. A solution of vinegar and water works wonders.

Gary L. Schaffer
Assistant Stage Manager
Pittsburgh Ballet Company

It's a good idea to have some tea and herb tea on hand as well.

Avoiding Rehearsal Problems

I'll take a few paragraphs here to throw in a little philosophy—the Gospel according to Stern—very little and not too deep:

My "Discipline of the Theater" theory is an oversimplification and may be stated very briefly: The play exists *only* on stage when the curtain is up. Prior to performance, the play exists *only* in the mind of the director, and *everyone* works to realize his or her concept.

In reality, this theory never quite works. Still, I feel that it is the premise on which everyone should work, and it is a premise that serves stage managers well in deciding what their words and deeds should be.

Play production is a process of compromise. From the first casting audition, the director may find that an actor brings forth an aspect of characterization that is superior to her or his original concept. Or, she or he may find that no actor really lives up to that concept, so the best available actor is cast. Either way, the original concept is changed. Compromise.

During rehearsals the director attempts to bring forth from the cast his or her concept. Actors experiment in early rehearsals and present the director with their concepts. Further compromise.

The scene designer talks to the director to understand the director's concept of the play and then supports the director by designing a set that will put the director's concept on the stage. It is the same with the costume designer, the lighting designer, sound designer, and all of the other creative people concerned with the production. In reality there are further compromises as the designers try to turn the director's inspired or approved concepts into reality.

The stage manager is concerned with this process because the inevitable compromises are sometimes preceded by confrontations that disrupt rehearsals or pre-production work and/or demoralize cast members.

Sometimes problems arise between the producer and the director. In theory the producer is responsible for obtaining the materials and personnel to make the play happen. He or she generally hires or selects the director. Thereafter, the producer is supposed to work to realize the director's concept along with everyone else. But the producer hires the director and can usually fire the director. In commercial theater the producer is concerned with possible loss of great amounts of money if the director's concept does not pay off. In theory, the producer should discuss and evaluate the director's concept before hiring her or him; once the producer has hired, he or she should go with the director.

In practice, however, the producer feels that his or her powers should allow him or her to influence the director, not only as to general concepts, but also with respect to specifics. So there are many incidents of producers directing over the director's shoulder—pulling strings in casting, changing designs that the director and designers have agreed upon, demanding that changes in the director's realm be made up to the very last minute.

Even if the producers do not subscribe to my oversimplified theory, they should honor some ethics of supervision:

1. The authority of any supervisor should not be diminished before his or her subordinates.
2. A person can only follow the dictates of one supervisor.

Translated into theater practice this means that a director and producer should never discuss their differences of opinion in front of cast members, staff, or crew. Once their differences have been ironed out, all resulting changes should be announced by the director. They should not be prefaced with any disclaimers, such as, "I don't feel this way, but due to circumstances beyond my control. . . . " If the director can't say firmly, "I have decided that . . . ," then she or he should firmly announce, "I have quit and it's up to the producer to provide another director."

As stage manager, if you should observe that producer-director conflicts during rehearsals are demoralizing cast members or disrupting rehearsals or work calls, you should call the director and producer aside and tactfully request that their disputes be resolved in private. It's psychologically hard to back down in public, but significantly easier to listen to reason and change one's mind in private.

Theater is not a democratic process in which the producer and director debate and then resolve their differences by a vote of the cast.

It is always preferable to anticipate such problems and to discuss problem-solving procedures at early staff meetings before they erupt into rehearsal delays.

Playwright at Work

What happens when the playwright is present? The play still exists in only one place prior to the curtain's rise—in the director's mind. I know this sounds improbable, and I've never met a playwright who could accept it. But once the playwright commits her or his work to paper and the producer turns it over to the director, the play is a concept in the director's mind.

Of course, some changes can and should be made as the playwright and director see the play come to life. But the playwright should go through the director privately to work on changes and should not communicate directly with the cast. The director should also suggest changes to the playwright privately.

I have seen playwrights angrily interrupt rehearsals because an actor paraphrased a line. I have seen casts thoroughly demoralized by director-playwright conflicts during rehearsals. If you are going into any production in which the playwright will be allowed in the rehearsal area, please discuss in advance with the director, playwright, and producer what procedures will be used to resolve disputes, and particularly *where* disputes will be handled—in private and outside the rehearsal area, I hope.

I have the greatest respect for playwrights. None of us could work without their words and ideas. But I believe that if they cannot accept the principles above, they should write novels or greeting cards, or direct their own plays.

[Another rule that I would like to see accepted by playwrights, I have the decency to put in brackets because I know that this is a book on stage management and not on playwriting or directing: Every director should have the right to cut 5 percent of a playwright's lines without negotiation. There isn't a play by Shakespeare, Eugene O'Neill, Arthur Miller, Tennessee Williams, or Neil Simon that could not survive a 5 percent cut easily. It's hard for playwrights to see this.

[I find that inexperienced playwrights become emotionally involved—love!—with their every word, article, and comma. Directors bring a different perspective to a script. Experienced directors know instinctively when action is bogging down in verbiage, when a scene is not playing. They don't need to wait for audience reaction to know.

[When it comes to discussions or arguments between playwright and director, the playwright can always rationalize every syllable that he or she has committed to paper. "It reveals character." "It'll get a laugh." "It advances the plot." "It foreshadows." The playwright knows all the good writing craft reasons why every word is immortal. The director knows only that those immortal words don't play.

[If the playwright doesn't trust the director enough with his or her baby to allow the director to change the diapers, he or she ought to find another director.

[But this is not a book on directing or playwriting, and stage managers do not make rules for the relationship between directors and playwrights; they only make things run smoothly by getting an understanding of what the rules are, and insuring that everyone knows them.

[Sometimes actors approach a playwright to ask if they are giving the playwright the interpretation of the role he or she wants. Actually the actors are looking for reassurance or seeking praise. The playwright launches into a discussion of characterization, completely confusing the actor, not only by giving specifics that conflict with the director's but also by talking an entirely different language. Playwrights should have a stock of supportive generalizations to offer insecure actors: "I really appreciate all the hard work you are putting into this production." "I really admire the way you take direction." "I'm very well pleased with the way the director is interpreting my work and the way the cast is supporting her interpretation."

[The best time for the playwright to clarify his or her intent is when he or she is writing the play. If it isn't in the script, he or she shouldn't expect his or her presence at rehearsals to put it on the stage. If he or she must have contact with the cast, he or she may give extensive notes at an early reading. But when the director and cast are in blocking, pacing, and polishing rehearsals, all further changes and clarifications should be discussed between the playwright and the director privately and then any agreed-upon changes should issue from the director.]

A "no more changes" deadline should be established at an early staff meeting. Additionally, playwrights should understand that the later changes are made in rehearsals, the less chance there is for a polished performance.

Stage managers who are new to their work or are working with a new company should raise the issue of change procedures at the very first production meeting to arrive at an understanding among director, producer, and playwright. Tell them that you or your fellow stage managers have had bad experiences in the past and that you want to prevent future problems by getting procedures spelled out in advance. If the playwright, producer, and director can't agree, or if you can't live by their agreement, find another job.

9

Keeping the Cast on Time

You are (of course) personally so punctual that it is hard for you to understand those who are late. Your mental clock is ten minutes ahead of real time. You always feel that if you are not ten minutes early for an appointment, you're late. You know that you are being paid to think ahead. You plan ahead with master calendars and schedules. You work ahead of others, arriving at the theater before the staff and cast to open up and prepare for rehearsals and performances. You are never late. With that kind of orientation, and with punctuality so deeply infused into the fiber of your being, you find it difficult to comprehend how an actor can possibly show up twenty-two minutes late for a rehearsal. Yet it happens.

When an actor does arrive late, the rehearsal should not come to a halt while that actor is questioned. You should tell the late actor what page of the script you are on, or the scene if you are off book, and ask the late actor to take her or his place. The late actor should be advised not to apologize, but simply to get to work. If the late actor is not in the scene, you should tell her or him which scene will be worked on next, and ask the late actor to go over lines until she or he is needed.

Under no circumstances should you allow other cast members to sit around to wait for a late actor. Urge your director to do the scene that was scheduled. Either throw the missing actor's lines or have another cast member or understudy read the part. Make use of the time as best you can. Perhaps the director will allow you to check your visual display of characters and select a sequence that can be rehearsed without the missing actor. If there is only one actor present on time, regardless of the minimum number needed to do a scene, start working with that one actor. It is important to the play, to the on-time actors, and to the late actors that work be in progress from the minute that the rehearsal was called!

At the end of the rehearsal period, you should discuss tardiness with the late actor, privately. First, especially in a professional situation, you should turn to your log in the presence of the actor and write the number of minutes that he or she was late. Ask the reason that he or she was late, and write it also. Then ask him or her to sign the log. In any case, confront him or her politely with the facts and ask if the rehearsal schedule was clear and if he or she understood what time he or she was expected. Ask him or her if there is anything you can do to help overcome the cause of the tardiness. Ask him or her if he or she needs to be called prior to the next rehearsal. If necessary, review the importance of rehearsal time, the fact that twenty-two minutes of tardiness represents over two hours of lost rehearsal time in terms of complete cast interaction, that not only the tardy actor but all of the other actors in the scene suffer, and ultimately the quality of the play suffers. Stress the positive factors, that early arrival at rehearsals allows the actor to review lines and to run lines with other actors, that the director is going for the kind of polished performance that needs every possible minute of rehearsal time, and that since this is also the tardy actor's goal, you know that you can count on future cooperation. In short, make it absolutely clear that you care, that it is important to you that actors be on time.

In professional theaters steps may be taken against habitually tardy actors through their union, but in both union and non-union situations you should try to educate and stress the positive rather than threaten and punish.

Directors should not have to discuss tardiness with actors. They should be able to rely on you in this matter.

Sign-In Sheets

As early as dress rehearsals, sign-in sheets should be posted. Cast members should be reminded to initial in, until they get into the habit (see Figure 9-1). Initialing prevents actors from placing a check mark in the wrong block. If they initial the wrong block, the error can be traced. Alternate lines of the sign-in sheet may be set up in different colors or in different indention patterns; this makes it easier to find the correct space to initial.

The sign-in sheet saves you work. It allows you to see if the cast is there by looking in only one place. If anyone has not initialed in by half hour call, you must check the dressing rooms. Then you must phone those who are late.

Placement of the sign-in sheet on the callboard insures that cast

Please ~~Initial~~ In !

ALBATROSS

SIGN IN

	TUE	WED	THUR	FRI	SAT	SUN
Frank Aletter						
Jenny Gillespie						
Pauline Meyers						
Lee Meriwether						
James R. Sweeney						
James B. Sikking						
Marge Redmond						
Paul Bryar						
Kathleen Freeman						
Dick Ramos						
Ellen Webb						

Figure 9-1 Sign-In Sheet for Cast Members

members will be close enough to the callboard to read any urgent new information that has been posted.

If you have a cast of two, you may elect not to post a sign-in sheet. If you have a cast of one hundred, you may elect to turn the sign-in sheet over to a gate man or stage door guard and have that individual check in the cast. You would still check with that individual for tardiness.

Calling any actor who has failed to sign in by half hour call (see below, "The Calls") is an important responsibility. Nothing should get in the way of your carrying out that duty.

Examples:

During a three-month run the home of a habitually late actor was frequently called. His wife always answered the phone and told the stage manager that the actor had left for the theater. When the actor arrived, the stage manager explained that he had called his home. The actor complained that the stage manager was needlessly alarming his wife, who would worry about traffic accidents until he called her to reassure her that he'd arrived safely. The stage manager's complaint that he was late and the actor's complaint that the stage manager was needlessly worrying his wife were frequently voiced—until the evening that the stage manager called and woke him up!

On opening night of a musical five principals and the director were late for half hour call. None responded to the stage manager's phone calls. The stage manager assumed that they were on their way. At fifteen minute call they were still not there. The stage manager alerted the house manager and the producer. Then a chorus member remembered that one of the principals had mentioned that they were going out to dinner before the show. The restaurant was called. They had been there and left—thirty-five minutes ago. At five minute call they had still not arrived. Now the producer and the house manager were pacing the lobby. An audience of 1,400 waited, completely unaware that they were missing quite a drama. At curtain time there were still no principals and no word from them. The producer's guidance was, "Stay calm," but he was clearly upset. How could such a thing happen? Why hadn't they called? The stage manager was numb.

At seven minutes past curtain the principals and director arrived. Blocked road, train accident, waited to clear road, hemmed in by other cars, no way out, no phone or house visible to horizon.

At thirteen minutes past curtain time the overture began.

And that was the night that one of the bit players who lived next door to the theater overslept and missed his one line. The stage manager had failed to call him.

In a situation of complete pandemonium, don't fail to carry out your basic duties!

During the run of any production, if an actor is late for half hour call, she or he should be reminded that the half hour prior to performance is meant to be used by the actor to get into costume, makeup, and character, and to relax in order to store up energy for the performance.

Actors sometimes argue the necessity of being at the theater one half hour prior to curtain. They claim that they can get into costume, makeup, and character in seven and one half minutes, they can relax at home, and they have plenty of energy. Then too, they don't like to wait backstage because it's musty, crowded, etc.

Regardless of such arguments you should continue to expect punctuality. Call every time the actor is late and use whatever methods you can to convince the actor to be at the theater for half hour call.

Should an actor who drives for forty-five minutes to get to the theater still have the same call as other cast members? Should you call that actor's home forty-five minutes prior to curtain to assure yourself that the actor is on the way? What if that same actor does not appear until fifteen minutes into the first act?

Should another actor who does not appear until the third act be granted a late call? Should an actress who puts on her makeup and costume at home to avoid using the overcrowded dressing room be allowed to sign in after half hour call?

These are but a few of the practical questions that will come up. To answer them you must ask yourself: Can I help insure that this actor will get to the theater on time? Can I insure that the cast will not be rushed in putting on makeup, getting into costume and into character? Can I assure myself that I will have adequate time to call actors and still carry out my other pre-curtain duties?

If an actor is ever granted a late call, the call should coincide with a period of time that you have free to check on his or her arrival.

The Calls

Calls—announcements of the time to the curtain—are given in order to alert cast members to how much time they have before the play begins. The traditional calls are:

Half hour, please.
Fifteen minutes, please.
Five minutes, please.
Places, please.

The first three calls are given thirty, fifteen, and five minutes prior to the announced curtain time. The "places" call is given after the house manager has turned the house over to you and when you are ready to run the show.

Notice that "please" is a part of the call. Don't omit it.

It is traditional that all cast members acknowledge your calls with a cheery "Thank you." If cast members are unaware of this custom, you might bring it to their attention.

In some cases the curtain will be delayed—last-minute rush at the box office, bad weather, traffic and parking problems, late arrival of theater parties, etc. The house manager might ask you to hold the curtain for five, ten, or fifteen minutes. You should relay these holds to the cast with an additional call of "Five minute hold, please." If possible you should explain to the cast the reason for the delay.

At intermissions the calls are "Five minutes, please," and "Places, please."

Do not rely on a one-way speaker system from your work area to the dressing rooms to give the calls. You not only run the risk of mechanical failure, but you lose that bit of contact with the cast.

A two-way communications system is only slightly better because mechanical failure is immediately noticeable and cast members have a chance to respond. But a face-to-face exchange is much better.

Only if it is absolutely impossible for you to give the calls should you assign this duty to an assistant or call boy. But this is not a task that should be delegated. This is one of your more important duties.

If you cannot greet and chat with each cast member as that cast member arrives at the theater, you have all too little contact. The call itself is not sufficient. There has to be a little dialogue between you and cast members. The subtext is, "Are you all right? Can you give a good performance tonight? Are you overtired? Did you get too sunburned? Did you have too much to drink? Do you have a stomachache?"

There is very little that you can do to relieve the pains and suffering of the acting condition. But some hot coffee, a few aspirins, and some kind words can go a long way in boosting cast morale to performance level. If you are effective, you can make just a few words and a friendly, sympathetic smile serve as a mental rubdown.

Under normal conditions you are not expected to give calls or warns for individual actor entrances once the act has begun. Actors are expected to listen for their cues in the wings, or if available, on dressing room monitors.

There are exceptions.

Example:

A big name personality who had played the same role in hundreds of theaters in the round across the country had become so indifferent to the script and local variations in blocking, that he had to be led out of his dressing room by the hand, pointed down the correct aisle, and pushed on cue. He also had to be retrieved as he exited, whenever and wherever he chose, and led back to his dressing room, as he could never remember where the dressing room was. The stage manager assigned the big name a "seeing-eye gopher."

If you are a new stage manager, do not worry about gaining the respect of the actors. Just assume that you already have it. You do have it by virtue of your title and you will earn it by virtue of your work. Respect is reciprocal. The more you give, the more you can count on getting back. As soon as the actors realize that you respect them, you will also gain their utmost cooperation.

10

Department Management and Property Management

The Manager as Supervisor

Stage managers are called upon to work with, coordinate the efforts of, and/or supervise many theater workers—the builders on the "premises of illusion": set designers, lighting designers, technical directors, master carpenters, lighting technicians, crew members, costume designers, property masters, and others.

To do this, (1) stage managers must first be knowledgeable about their work. They must understand the technical aspects of making theater. This they gain through observation and study.

Next, (2) they must understand their personal relationship to co-workers. As stage managers move from theater to theater, from educational to community to professional levels, they find the titles and relationships of the builders changing frequently. At one theater the set designer is the technical director. At another, there is no technical director, and the stage manager and set designer work together in supervising the construction and painting of sets. At still another there are both a resident scene designer and resident technical director, and the latter supervises both the stage manager and the master carpenter.

Despite the wide range of job titles and descriptions and the deviations in the chain of command, stage managers quickly find out who does what and who reports to whom by observation and through conversations with the staff (see Chapter Five).

Once she or he determines which of the staff are directly responsible to her or him, (3) she or he exerts control over their work. She or he acts as the foreman for the producer or management, coordinating their work through the master calendar and the schedules she or he distributes. She or he personally oversees their work as necessary.

Getting along with subordinates and managing their work is an art form in itself. Stage management is certainly a proving ground for this art. Here are a few simple recommendations for supervising subordinates:

a. Take time to give your instructions with great clarity, making sure that you are understood, or that the director's or producer's intention, which you are passing on, is understood.

b. Give instructions in bite-size portions. Don't give a gopher twenty things to do. Give one, and when it's finished, then give the next.

c. Don't give an individual more work than you feel confident he or she can accomplish. If you expect that he or she will need more labor or more time than immediately available, explain that you only expect him or her to make a start on the work.

d. Deliver instruction with calmness and self-confidence.

e. Follow up on the work you assign, checking on problems and reviving interest in projects as necessary by showing your interest and appreciation. Re-emphasize goals when the enthusiasm of your subordinates is flagging.

f. Whenever you assign work, remember that the responsibility for its completion remains with you.

Additional comments on getting along with others and supervising department heads may be found in Chapter Two.

Supervision of Department Heads

In the course of your work you are likely to be supervising the property manager, but you may also be asked to supervise a few other department heads—sometimes the costumer and sometimes the technical director.

If so, during the rehearsal period you will want to see that the department heads (a) are working, (b) are on schedule, and (c) have not run into any "insurmountable" problems.

a. Department heads and their assistants don't usually punch clocks. But if they are not there to do the work, the production will not be able to open on time. You informally make the rounds to see if the staff is at work. It may occasionally mean rousing a late sleeper or providing transportation for someone with an unreliable auto. When you make the rounds, you chat about progress on the current production.

b. Falling behind on the schedule sometimes means that a department will need more staff. Can you send over an assistant, some apprentices, or your gopher to help the shop wire on the ornamental grapes that light up? Or will you have to approach the business manager because the costumer insists on another union costume technician at union wages in order to accomplish the costume work on time?

c. Problem solving is frequently the same as listening well. If every department head feels able to express her- or himself to you, she or he will air "insurmountable" problems. In doing so, she or he will usually come up with the solution. If you should observe that the department heads themselves are largely the cause of their own problems, you keep this to yourself and praise their solutions.

By asking questions (What if . . . ? What would happen if . . . ?) rather than imposing solutions (You should . . .) or placing blame (You should have . . .), you tactfully get department heads to feel that they are in command of the situation, and the commander usually works harder than the guy who is merely following orders.

In supervision, tact can usually get it done.

Property Management and You

Regardless of theater level, the function of the property person remains the same—to get the props. Your usual function is to supervise. To do this you should know all aspects of property management.

In union theaters, the property person is paid for services. In community, educational, showcase, and children's theater, the property person is usually an unpaid volunteer. Some people do not consider working on props particularly exciting or glamorous. It calls for someone who is methodical and persistent.

Finding and motivating a competent property person is a problem that plagues many theaters. Sometimes when a property person cannot be found, you find yourself either working as property person or retaining overall responsibility for props and dividing the prop work among the staff and cast.

Whether supervising or doing it yourself, you should appreciate the importance of having props available for rehearsals.

As soon as the actors set down their scripts, having memorized their lines, they should be able to pick up their props. Using props early in the rehearsal period allows the cast and director to experiment and to develop suitable business. This is highly desirable as it may add immeasurably to the quality of the production.

Conversely, not having props on time leads to serious problems.

Examples:

Scenes may have to be reblocked because an actor did not allow enough room for his imagined sword.

The leading lady sneezes through opening night because of the bouquet. The wadded-up newspaper used as a rehearsal prop did not affect her allergies.

Property Person's Checklist

To help determine the extent of the property person's responsibilities, you might review the following:

Before Rehearsals

Before rehearsals will the property person

1. Be responsible for hand properties?
2. Be responsible for set pieces? Which ones?
3. Be responsible for obtaining transportation to pick up and return all props?
4. Coordinate with the director, scene designer, and producer to assure appropriate props?
5. Insure that set pieces arrive on time for the take-in?
6. Obtain hand props as soon as possible in order to give actors maximum rehearsal time to work with them?
7. Provide temporary rehearsal props for unusual or costly props that cannot be obtained until later in the rehearsal period?
8. Give a written receipt to lenders of props and set pieces? Note on both the original and carbon copy the condition of the prop and the intended date of return?
9. Coordinate with the producer, through the stage manager, prior to rental of expensive props?
10. Be able to give———hours per week for———weeks to this work?
11. Need assistance (an assistant property master)?
12. Report to the stage manager any difficulties that he or she encounters in sufficient time to avert a last-minute rush?

During Rehearsals

During rehearsals will the property person

1. Attend rehearsals to make notes of additional props, where and how props are used, which actors use them, and from which entrance they come on stage?
2. Bring in large boxes and label them by act or scene as necessary in order to store the props?

3. Set props for each scene fifteen minutes before rehearsal is scheduled?
4. Lock up or otherwise secure all props after rehearsals?
5. Draw maps of prop tables and post them on or above the prop tables offstage to insure quick, accurate checks of all props prior to rehearsals and performances?
6. Make maps of locations of props in each scene so that he or she can change or supervise changes of props between scenes?
7. Draw diagrams on stage surfaces (tables, bars, mantels, etc.) to indicate exact placement of props?

Prior to Performance

Prior to the performance will the property person

1. Check presence and condition of all props, and report to the stage manager? (usually forty-five minutes prior to performance)
2. Replace expendable items (water in pitcher, tea in booze bottles, telegram that gets crumpled, etc.) prior to each performance?

Simply put eight drops of yellow food color, three drops of red, and one drop of green into whatever bottle one is using, add water and you have perfect whiskey. (This process eliminates the bubbles that you get when using instant tea.)

William J. Buckley, III
Stage Manager
Woodstock Playhouse, Woodstock NY

Be sure to clean the bottle thoroughly first!!!!!!

During Performance

During the performance will the property person

1. Change properties on the stage between acts as needed?

After Performance

After the performance will the property person

1. Check for return of all props to the property tables?

BORROWED ITEMS

_____ production of "_____" _____

dates

Item(s) Borrowed	Date Received	Borrowed From*	Date (to be) Returned
1			
2			
3			
4			
5			
6			
7			
8			
9			
10			
11			
12			
13			

*include company name, address, phone no., extension, and personal contact!

page____of _____   Prepared by _____

LAWRENCE STERN
Production Stage Manager
555-3719

Figure 10-1 Property Master's Control Form and Record of Borrowed Items

2. Store props between performances, providing secure storage for expensive props?

After Production

After the production will the property person

1. Clean or repair borrowed items to insure goodwill for future borrowing?
2. Obtain receipts for return of items borrowed, give notes of thanks, and thank contributors personally?
3. Be financially responsible for all lost props?
4. Keep a list of sources, and the types of props that can be borrowed from each, as an aid to future productions?

ACKNOWLEDGMENT OF BORROWED ITEMS (RETURNED)

The following items, loaned to the_____production

of "_____" were returned on _____
                                            date
by _____in satisfactory condition:

1.

2.

3.

4.

5.

6.

7.

8.

9.

10.

11.

12.

13.

14.

15.

      Received by:
        name_____

       position_____
LAWRENCE STERN
Production Stage Manager
555-3719   company_____

Figure 10-2 Acknowledgment Form for Borrowed
Items

5. Write a critique of his or her experience, emphasizing problem
   areas, in order to help the next property master?

Although it is desirable, it is not necessary that the property person
do everything reflected in the questions above. Rather than review the
above list with the property person, you might want to give her or him
just a few items at a time, or as much responsibility as you feel she or
he can accept at one time. A new property person might accept more
and more responsibility gradually but might balk if presented with the
whole range.

It is necessary, however, that you and the property person come to
a clear understanding of her or his exact duties.

Property Forms

The two forms, "Borrowed Items," and "Acknowledgment of Borrowed
Items (Returned)," may be used by the property person to control props

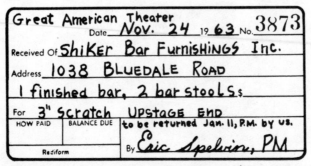

Figure 10-3 Receipt Form Acknowledgment for a Borrowed Item. Note: Original is kept by the property master and duplicate is issued to the lender. Both copies should specify the date of return and the condition of the prop.

(see Figures 10-1 and 10-2). When she or he picks up a prop, the property master fills out the "Acknowledgment" form and gives it to the lender. She or he then notes on the "Borrowed Items" form the program credit line that is expected and other information. When she or he returns the prop, she or he picks up the "Acknowledgment" form.

Receipt forms, found in most stationery stores, may be used in place of the forms above (see Figure 10–3). One receipt and a carbon are made out for each borrowed prop. The carbon is issued to the lender and retrieved when the prop is returned. The original is kept by the property master.

In some cases it is easier to use the prop plot (Figure 3-8) as a control form. If many copies of the prop plot can be duplicated, then they may be posted on prop storage boxes, placed on prop tables, and even given to cast and staff as reminders of the props they have pledged to bring in.

The cost of all props which must be purchased by the theater should be carefully recorded on the property person's expense sheet (see Figure 7-1). For bookkeeping purposes, the property person might be asked to record expendable and permanent items on separate sheets.

Program credits and/or complimentary tickets are sometimes given for the use of props. Be sure to check the producer's or management's policy and coordinate with the program editor. In some cases the lender definitely does not want a program credit. Be sure to clear this with the lender.

As soon as props are used in the rehearsals, you should remind the cast to cooperate with the property person by returning all props to the prop tables when they are carried offstage as part of the actor's business. Otherwise the property person finds her- or himself searching the dressing rooms and even the pockets of costumes.

As a safety factor, the stage manager is usually responsible for, and must carefully supervise, the firing of blanks, even though the weapon is a prop.

When the property person is also responsible for certain of the set pieces—those that will be bought, borrowed, or rented, as opposed to those that will be constructed—you must make absolutely certain that all staff members know which set pieces they are responsible for.

11

Supervision of Lights

You have checked all fuse boxes and circuit capacities, all lighting equipment and plugging locations (Chapter Five), you have worked out all light cues at the technical rehearsal (Chapter Thirteen), and you are ready to light up for the first performance. But before every performance, a light check must be run before the audience is admitted to the house.

To conduct this check, you normally ask the master electrician or lighting technician to bring all of the instruments used in the show to full. You then inspect the instruments to make sure that none are out. You must also see that the instruments are still properly focused. To do this you bring up one area of the stage at a time and check the effect against your area lighting diagram (see Figure 11-3). Then you check the focus of each special-effect instrument.

If *gel frames* are changed in the course of the show for special-effect lighting, you must inspect to make sure that the correct gel is set for Act I. (For instance, one spot may be used to produce both a bright sunlight effect flooding a window in Act I, and a moonlight effect at the same window in Act III by changing a gel frame during an intermission. You should inspect, as part of your light check, to make sure that the right gel is in place for Act I.)

The complete inspection of lights must be finished early enough to allow time to correct deficiencies without delaying the entrance of the audience. How long would it take you to bring in the ladder, set it up, trace a short in a cable, repair the short, and strike the ladder? That amount of time should be allowed between light check and the opening of the house. Yes, it means an early call for you and the lighting technician at every single performance.

Do you have on hand spare lamp bulbs ("bottles") of the appropriate base type and wattage for your instruments? Do you have on hand appropriate repair parts and tools?

Here are a few examples of mishaps that properly conducted light checks would have avoided.

Example A:

On Sunday mornings a small theater in Hollywood was used by a religious sect for meetings. During one meeting a screen was hung to show a movie—from the yokes of two instruments set for a performance that night. The stage manager later supervised the light check and found all of the instruments to be working. But he did not check focus against his area diagram (Figure 11-3). Result: an actor who was to give his final monologue illuminated by a single spot, delivered his speech in virtual darkness while a nearby table was lit beautifully. The actor could not move into the light without mounting the table.

Example B:

In another incident the light check was habitually late, conducted after the audience was in. The stage manager peeked through the curtains (extremely unprofessional) from his work area backstage to check the anti-pros (see Glossary), even though he could not replace burnt out lamps at this point without working over the heads of the audience. Then he checked instruments behind the curtains. Finding that one instrument on the first pipe was not working, he hurriedly brought in a ladder, checked the instrument by cross plugging, and concluded that there was a short in the cable. Quickly he replaced it with a spare cable and called "places." Unfortunately the play began with a coronation parade of the cast from the rear of the house. As they approached the proscenium, the curtain was to open revealing the throne. The stage manager cued the curtain. It opened two feet and stopped!

In his haste, the stage manager had run the replacement cable through the curtain rope. Subsequent repair had to be done in full view of the audience while the coronation parade looked on.

Example C:

The house lights dimmed, an actor delivered the first line of the script, and the director's voice came from the back of the theater: "We don't have any lights. Check out the problem and let's back it up and start again."

The stage manager had not only forgotten to perform the light check, he had failed to insure that the dimmers were on. The house, on a separate dimmer, went out all right, but when the lighting technician brought up the dimmer handles for the first light effect, there was no light. The first actor to speak was to start in darkness, taking his cue from a sound effect. When the lights failed to come up, the actor continued, assuming that the lights were late. So the director had to stop the show from the back of the house.

Embroider this on your sampler: an ounce of leisurely inspection prior to the opening of the house is worth tons of rushed repair.

In addition to conducting a thorough light check prior to half hour call, you must check each lighting effect immediately after you give the cue. (This will be discussed in Chapter Fourteen again.)

If you are fortunate enough to be working in a booth in back of the audience, you will have a good view of every effect. But if you are in the wings, you must arrange for a view, resorting to peepholes or mirrors if necessary.

If the cue is not immediately followed by the anticipated effect, you must be programmed as follows:

1. Don't panic.
2. Did the technician recognize and execute the cue you gave?
3. Is there a mechanical failure?
4. Is there anything you can do to alleviate this problem? If yes, do it. If no, restrain yourself.

In the case of a mechanical problem that cannot be immediately corrected, the most important principle to remember is the most basic and obvious one, that the audience must see the actors.

Example:

You give a cue to bring up an area. The area comes up slowly to full and the dimmer fuse pops. The actors who took their cue from the burn-in (first glow of the elements), continue their lines in darkness. What should you do? Answer: give the actors any light you can, short of shining your flashlight at them from the wings. You might bring up adjacent areas in the hopes that the actors will find some of it or gain from the spill. You might throw on the work light. At last resort you might even have to bring up the house lights. If and when the actors have enough light to continue the scene, then see if you can replace the fuse.

The continuance of the play takes precedence over the quality of the lighting.

Preparing a Lighting Sheet

Prior to the technical rehearsal, you should prepare written instructions for the individual who actually pushes the dimmer handles—the board man.

In a union theater the lighting technician is usually the master electrician, a member of the International Alliance of Theatrical and Stage Employees (IATSE).

In a nonunion theater the lighting technician is sometimes referred to as the board man or light tech. Sometimes you will be asked to serve as light tech, but this is not desirable. You should give the cues and should not actually handle the equipment.

The light tech does not need the entire light plot that you prepared to analyze the lighting problems of the play. He or she simply needs to know which dimmers to work for which cue, which direction, how far and how fast. You will probably want to tell him or her through the use of a lighting sheet (see Figure 11-1).

On your light plot, "light cue #9" may call for lights to come up in a small area around a doorway. To achieve this, the light tech will have to push up dimmer handles 6 and 13. The lighting sheet entry might look like this:

Col. One	Col. Two	Col. Three	Col. Four
9	6, 13	↑ 10	Bump up

Column one is the cue number. (It is advisable to reserve numbers one through fifty for light cues and number the sound cues from fifty-one up. This prevents confusion in warning and cuing.)

To eliminate confusion between light and sound cues I have always found it *much* more efficient to number the light cues and letter the sound cues.

Leonard Auerbach
Associate Professor, Department of Theatre Arts
State University of New York at Stony Brook

Column two tells which dimmer handles are to be moved. Dimmer handles are frequently labeled, each numbered or designated by the area or effect it controls, i.e., "Doorway special." The name or number of the dimmer is written on masking tape and placed beneath the dimmer handle.

In column three the arrow indicates the direction the dimmer handle is to move and the number ten tells how far it is to move. Many dimmers are graduated from zero to ten, with ten being full intensity, but there are other systems.

The fourth column indicates how fast the cue is to be executed.

You usually guess at your entries for columns three and four prior to the technical rehearsal, based on your observations at rehearsals. During the tech the director approves or refines each cue and you insure that the light tech makes corrections on the lighting sheet. At this point

Figure 11-1 Lighting Sheet Instructions for Technicians, Extracted from Light Plot

you rarely update your light plot; instead you write final cue factors in bold marking pen on each final horizontal cue line in your prompt script (see Chapter Fourteen and Figure 14-2).

Leave room between entries on your light sheet so that additional cues may be written in during the tech. If you number ahead (instead of during the tech) you will have to use fractions to indicate additional cues, i.e., "Warn 9 1/2."

Several cues that happen in a fast sequence should be numbered as a series:

Col. One	Col. Two	Col. Three	Col. Four
9a	6, 13	↑ 10	Bump up
9b	1, 2, 3, 4, 5	↑ 8	Fast
9c	6, 13	↓ 8	Imperceptibly

There is no time to give warns between cues. So you warn once with, "Warn series nine," and give your cues as, "Go A, go B, go C." When the light tech sees a series cue, he or she knows that he or she must execute the whole series without taking time to check each single cue between each execution.

The light tech usually takes the speed of the cue from your hand signal; that is, he or she moves the dimmer handle at the same speed as you move your hand in giving the cue. Entries in column four simply prepare the light tech for the speed that will be expected. Some commonly used terms are:

Bump up	Up as fast as possible, opposite of a blackout.
Fade up	Gradual.
Cross fade	Take two cues simultaneously, one coming in, one going out.
Lag fade	Start first cue, take second as soon as the first is perceptible.
Fade in (7)	Move dimmer handle on a count of seven.
Imperceptible fade	Move dimmer handle so slowly that change in effect is not noticeable.
Blackout	Take out as fast as possible.

Whatever words communicate your exact intentions to the light tech are the right ones to use.

> It is more precise to use cue counts (seconds) to control the speed of your dims. If you say, "Dim to zero on a five count," your crew knows exactly how fast to react. "Gradual" is too imprecise.
>
> Leonard Auerbach
> Associate Professor, Department of Theatre Arts
> State University of New York at Stony Brook

Entries in column four should correspond to the notes that you write in bold marking pen on the final cue lines in your prompt script to remind yourself of the desired effect.

Rather than using sheets of paper, some light technicians prefer to work from a deck of 3 × 5" note cards with one cue, or a series cue, on each card. You might discuss this with the lighting technician prior to making out the lighting sheet.

page ____ of ____ pages

RE-GELING PLAN / LIGHTING SCHEDULE

INST #	TYPE	AREA PLAYED	HANG POSN	lamp watt type base	GEL SIZE	GEL COLOR	PLGNG	DIMMER

Figure 11-2 Format for Re-Gelling Plan/Lighting Schedule

In some cases the lighting designer will prepare the lighting sheet if he or she is provided with the light plot or a script and thereby knows all of the cue lines and numbers. In some cases the lighting technician can prepare his or her own light sheet or deck during a tech call preceding the tech rehearsal, or even during the technical rehearsal (see Chapter Thirteen). If you do not actually write out the lighting sheet, you must insure that it is done properly.

Re-Gelling Plans/Lighting Schedule

You've just finished your light check, found one lamp out in an instrument and one gel in a special-effects instrument so faded that it needs to be replaced. So you climb up the ladder to remove the old lamp, find out what size it is, climb down the ladder, find a replacement lamp, and climb back up the ladder to put it in. Then you climb up the ladder to

Show: _____
Act: _____
Scene: _____

Platform (T)
12

(SP 1)

Orchestra Pit

11   1

7

4   1

9   3

5

SP 2   3   2

6

?   5

6
Platform (T)

Figure 11-3 Area Lighting Diagram for Round Stage

get the gel frame from the light instrument, climb down the ladder, hold the gel frame over the gel sheet, cut out the new gel, and climb up the ladder to replace the frame. Right?

Wrong. You completed your re-gelling plan/lighting schedule at the beginning of the season and you know the watts, base types, and gel sizes of every one of the seventy-eight instruments without climbing the ladder to find out. Your re-gelling plan/lighting schedule is indexed into your prompt script (see Figure 11-2). And you have gel patterns (see Figure 11-4) so that you don't need the gel frame as a pattern. You can take your replacement gel and lamp up the ladder the first time and save yourself a trip.

The main purpose of the re-gelling plan is to enable the lighting

SHEET METAL FRAME
(for 500 watt fresnels)

GEL PATTERN
7½" x 7½"
500 WATT FRESNELS
INSTRUMENTS *
26 - 50

CARDBOARD
GEL PATTERN

Figure 11-4   Gel Pattern Template with Complete Labeling

designer to tell the lighting technicians what color gels to put into what instruments. This form will expedite the turnover between shows. So you want to be sure that the form is on hand and filled in up to date.

You are usually responsible for supervising re-gelling for productions that run longer than the life of the gels, so it is desirable that you review the form with the lighting designer.

Area Lighting Diagrams

The area lighting diagram (see Figure 11–3) shows the areas on the stage where the instruments are focused. It may be expanded with notes and diagrams to remind you where certain focusing is critical, e.g., the lighting designer wants an instrument shuttered so that the light is exactly on a door frame and there is no spill on adjacent flats.

In re-gelling instruments, or during other work near instruments, technicians sometimes accidentally jar the instruments out of focus. Sometimes an instrument is simply not tightened sufficiently when initially focused and slips over a period of time. The area lighting diagram helps you to prevent such occurrences from affecting the quality of lighting in a performance.

The lighting designer usually makes a complex area lighting diagram for her or his own purposes. You can use the lighting designer's, or copy the important aspects of it. But for the sake of your familiarity with the lighting design, it is better if you make your own and then review it with the lighting designer.

Gel Patterns

Gel patterns are usually made of cardboard (see Figure 11–4). They are cut to the size of the gel frames used in your instruments. If you have spare gel frames on hand for all the different sizes used in your instruments, you may use the spares as patterns. The advantage of cardboard patterns is that you can easily write on them the numbers of the instruments that take that size. The cardboard patterns are also easier to handle.

12

Supervision of Shifts

Find a way, when working in the round, to coordinate a stage crew of fifteen in making scene shifts, striking an average of five props and eleven set pieces and setting as many—in thirty seconds—in the dark—every twelve minutes—for one hour and thirty-five minutes—for a total of fourteen shifts. This is the type of logistical problem that can make managers lose sleep and eat aspirins.

Shift Plot Charts

A shift plot chart (see Figure 12-1) is a device that will help you in planning and supervising scene shifts. Although this technique (and this example) is primarily applicable to productions in the round, it may also be used for complex shifts in any theater. The chart may be posted in the scene dock and prop area so that the crew may use it as a self-briefing aid.

Notice that the top row lists the scenes, the second row lists the cue that precedes the shift, and each row beneath describes an individual crew member's responsibility in each shift.

Make your shift plot chart BIG so that it is easily readable. Allow 2 1/2" high by 3" wide rectangles for each separate entry. This allows you to make corrections conveniently by posting halves of 3 × 5" notecards over entries that must be changed.

Notice that each entry gives the following information (for an "in the round" production):

A. Aisle traveled to reach the stage (e.g., 1st down *11*; the number 11 means the aisle at 11 o'clock if the stage is compared to the face of a clock with the orchestra pit at 12 o'clock).

Take Me Along – Act II	II-1 Barroom	II-1 Ballet	II-2 & 3 Miller Home
Warn CUE	PRESET	he reads book in bed. Thus spa Kezara-thustra Blackout	Ballet Ends... Blackout
George Ray IATSE 1	↓7 (4:00) Strike Piano, set birdcage (3) SET BIKBOX(9)	1st↓5 set ~~foot stool~~ Strike piano (w. Bill) ↑5	1st↓1 SET DESK (2:00) strike footpot(s) 1↑
Dennis IATSE 2	↓7 set bar (10:00) Strike porch (7) ↑7 W/Harold	1st↓11 Strike Bar w/ Harold ↑$ 11	1st↓5 SET Porch (5:00) W/HAL ↑7
Harold IATSE 3	↓7 10:00 Set bar (w Dennis) Strike porch (7) ↑7 W/Dennis	2nd↓11 Strike bar w/ Dennis 11↑	2nd↓5 SET porch (5:00) W/Dennis ↑7
BILL C.	↓7 w/Mike set Piano & stool Strike chair (2:0) TO Rch Hall	2nd↓5 strike piano w/George 5↑	3rd↓7 SET WINDOW St. (6:00) Strike chairs ↑#1
MIKE	↓7 (1:00) set 2 chairs Strike Table (3) TO Rch Hall	1st↓1 STriKE TABLE ↑1	3rd↓11 SET TABLE (11:30) & chair ↑7
Wally	GATE TENT	2nd↓1 STriKE 2 chairs ↑1	~~2nd↓11~~ ~~SET chair (5:00)~~ ↑ FLYMAN DroP BKT.
WAYNE	GUARD INSIDE TENT	SET DRY ice IN BUCKET (9:00)	3rd↓11 SET STEPS (11:00) ↑11

Figure 12-1 Shift Plot Chart for Several Crew Members

B. Order number on which to travel (e.g., *1st* down 11; if a crew member is preceded by two others she or he is "3rd down aisle"). Controlling order helps you to choreograph the change.

C. Set piece or prop carried on and location it is to be placed (e.g., "Set table at 11:00"). The location designator is not an exact one, but is used to refresh the runner's memory when used in conjunction with "before and after" diagrams described below.

D. Set piece or props to be struck, and destination if other than the scene dock and prop area (e.g., "Leave at top of aisle 11 for use in Sc. 5").

E. Aisle to exit.

II-4 BEDROOM	II-5 & 6 BEACH	II 7&8 Miller Home	AFTER PERFORMANCE
"Staying Young" reprise BLACKOUT	Hello, Operator PHONE Light out	SCRUMPTIOUS! Short: 9:00 reprise Blackout	WHEN AUDIENCE OUT
2ND ↓ 1 (2:00) STrIKE DESK w/WAYNE ↑1	3rD ↓ 1 set log ctr. ↑7	1st ↓ 1 SET DESK (2:00) WITH John ↑1	STrIKE LAMP (4:30) UNPLUG
2ND ↓ 7 SET PLATFORM w/HArOID (ctr.) ↑5	1st ↓ 11 STrIKE PLAT. W/HAL ↑7	1st ↓ 5 strike log w/Hal ↑5 During scene Move Trolley into posit.	strike lamp (11:30) UNPLUG
3rD ↓ 7 Set Platform w/Dennis ↑5	1st ↓ 3 Strike Platform W Dennis ↑7	2nD ↓ 5 Strike Log ↑5 Move Trolley to position	STrIKE PLUG (11:30)
4th ↓ 7 set bed open. w/Mike Strike F.PlACE ↑7	2nD ↓ 7 SET FIREPlACE (9:00) ↑11	2nD ↓ 5 set window seat (6:00) ↑5 Pull Trolley	
1st ↓ 7 Set bed w/ Bill COOK ↑7	1st ↓ 11 (11:30) set table & Chair (11:0) ↑7 AFTER WINDOW SEAT in	↓11 STrIKE F.PlACE (9:00) Pull ↑ Trolley 11	unplug (11:30)
4th ↓ 1 STrIKE LOG ↑1	3rD ↓ 11 (11:00) set steps ↑11	↓11 SET LAMP (11:00) Plug in ← STrIKE TABlE(11) ↑11	
1st ↓ 1 strike chair ↑1	3rD ↓ 7 Set 6:00 LWR. raiL w/HAL ↑7	↓11 Set small. plg. (11:30) strike chair ↑11	

Figure 12-1   (Continued)

F. Order to exit is designated rarely—when more than one large set piece must move up the same aisle, or when fast-traveling light pieces must precede slow-moving heavy pieces to expedite the shift.

G. If more than one crew member handles a single set piece, the names of the other crew members working on that unit are listed so that each crew member knows with whom she or he is to work (e.g., "with Roy").

H. If errors were made at any performance, you may put special cautions in an entry rectangle (e.g., "Watch out for hanging mike hit on opening night"). Other cautions might concern a false blackout or the rapid succession of two cues (e.g., "Hustle back to prop table for next shift").

Normally you wait until the take-in (see below) to make up the chart because you must know for certain exactly where the set pieces will play. Since the chart takes so much time to make, it is advisable to lay it out in advance, filling in the first column (crew members), the top row (scenes), and the second row (cues) well in advance of the take-in.

At the *take-in* (see below), you see all of the set pieces on stage for the first time. You should handle each piece. How much does it weigh? Should more than one person be assigned to carry it? Can it be picked up easily, or should handles be added? Should wheels be built onto it, or can it be moved on a dolly? Can it be carried in some other way than intended—upside down, sideways? Should it be cut in two, carried down in sections, and fastened together during the shift? Does it have sharp protruding edges that might be a safety hazard?

At the take-in you also make changes in your scene diagrams to indicate the exact placement of each set piece as determined by the set designer. There may be still more changes during the dress rehearsal, and you must continue to update your diagrams and call changes to the attention of the crew via the chart.

Immediately following the take-in you should be ready to make your chart. The best way to do this is by using cutouts of paper for the set pieces. Actually move the paper set pieces as you calculate who should move what and when. It is a fairly complex problem and errors are easy to make.

When there is time and money to allow for a crew rehearsal, all of the errors may be worked out by repeating shifts until they are "greased." (Also see below, "Crew Briefing.") But, as often happens, when crew rehearsal and dress rehearsal are simultaneous and the producer must justifiably use all available time for the cast and orchestra which the audience will see and hear, rather than for the crew, which the audience should not see or hear, shifts must be corrected and "greased" by debriefing, that awkward process of trying to talk through what happened and visualize what changes should be made. The shift plot chart and the scene diagrams are invaluable in this process.

What sometimes happens in a union situation is that after Act I and part of Act II have consumed the entire dress rehearsal call, the producer opts to finish the rehearsal by putting the cast and orchestra on overtime; but she or he sends the union crew members home in order to save money. You then carry out the remaining shifts with any hands available, and find yourself in the unenviable position of running some of the shifts with actual personnel involved for the first time on opening night—briefing union crew members during the scene for their moves

TAKE ME ALONG

SET/STRIKE
ORDER for Geor_g_e Spelvin (IATSE 1)

ACT SCENE CUE	ENTER	SET/STRIKE/DO	EXIT
Preset		Set desk 2:00 Lay trolley track.	
I-2 "Oh, Please" reprise!!!!! blackout	First down one	Set porch rail 3:00 Strike desk 2:00 with Wayne	Up One
I-3 "I wish we still belonged to England," blackout	Second down Five	Set Lamp 4:30 PLUG IT IN!!!!!!!!!!! Strike porch rail (to rehearsal hall, not scene dock)	Up One

Figure 12-2 A Set/Strike Order with Typical Entries

at the end of the scene. Can you imagine the pressured chaos? The preciseness and accuracy of your shift plot chart are really significant factors in running those "no rehearsal" shifts.

The chart should be posted prior to the first crew rehearsal and each member of the crew should jot down her or his moves from the chart so that she or he does not have to check the chart between each scene shift. This can save a lot of walking if she or he has two consecutive moves up and down an aisle that is 180 degrees away from the aisle leading to the scene dock.

If you desire, you may issue each crew member a complete strike/set order (see Figure 12-2). This order would take the place of the individual crew member's notes and theoretically make it unnecessary to post the shift plot chart. Unfortunately, this type of strike/set order gets lost or left in other pants. Then the crew member has to have some reference from which to copy. So you still need the chart.

Take-In

Coordinating with the scene designer and technical director, you share in supervision of the *take-in*.

The take-in is a procedure in which all of the set pieces and scenery are brought from storage, the shop, and the scene dock, and set up on stage for the first time. This allows the scene designer, technical director, and you to assess your progress and problems in turning the scene designer's sketches into illusion.

Your responsibility is to get enough hands out to move the scenery quickly so that the take-in may be completed as soon as possible without wearing out the participants. As usual, many hands make light work.

Your work during the take-in has been described above as part of your preparation for making the shift plot chart (Figure 12-1). Again, you must personally handle all of the set pieces and scenery so that you know what problems your crew members will encounter.

Crew Briefing

Generally you brief the whole crew prior to their first rehearsal. A hand-out to the crew is helpful in passing on important points that you've learned from experience (see Figure 12-3).

A. Introduce crew members to one another and explain that you expect them to work as a team.
B. Cite general problems.
  1. Audience moving during blackouts.
  2. Hitting mikes with set pieces.
  3. Too much talking among crew during scenes, thus distracting audience.
  4. Necessity of crew members staying out of tent or backstage area during scenes.
  5. Necessity of having all props, set pieces, and scenery in the scene dock prior to the show, during intermissions, and after the show so that everything is out of sight of the audience, and not a safety hazard.
C. Explain clock system (for round theater) or stage areas if necessary, set diagrams, and shift plot chart.
D. Review safety rules.
  1. Don't run.
  2. Pointed set pieces should be moved base first so as not to spear audience members.

ATTENTION CREW

1. Shake hands with your new crew members. The crew is a team. Everyone must know everyone else - and be able to depend on him.

2. Think of the stage as a clock. The orchestra pit is at 12 o'clock. Aisles 1, 3, 5, 7, 9, and 11 are relative - one o'clock, three o'clock, etc.

3. The Shift plot chart and diagrams of "before and after" positions of all props, set pieces and scenery are located above and on the prop table. Study them at your conv. If you don't understand, ask the SM, George Spelvin, or IATSE crew chief, Nate Spelvin, to explain it to you.

4. Follow these rules PLEASE!
   A. Don't run.
   B. Crouch at the bottom of aisles behind sight lines anticipating the blackout noiselessly.
   C. Watch out for audience moving on blackouts.
   D. Don't hit hanging mikes with tall units.
   E. Stay out of the tent when not doing your thing.
   F. Stash all props and units in scene dock prior to intermission and after show so that audience can't trip over them.
   G. Move pointed units base first so as not to stab audience members.
   H. Don't mingle with audience during intermission.
   I. Don't call attention to yourself.
   J. No talking or noise while you work or wait.
   K. Report any accident to the SM.

5. Please wear black polo shirts and black <u>full</u> length pants. Black tennis shoes and sox are available (free) from the costume mistress.

6. Maintain a clear aisle of 2' in front of the prop table. Don't set any units on that area painted yellow.

7. Report any damage to any prop or unit to the property master or crew chief as soon as practical.

8. Check each night for red markings on the shift plot chart. Changes in your strike/set duties are indicated by the entire rectangle outlined in red. Study the change and discuss it with the crew chief. Red X's indicate errors made;red cautions advise you how to prevent repetitions of the error.

9. You are expected to check in with the gate man at 7:45 pm SHARP! Don't be late. In case of emergency, call the theater, 268 3558, and leave a message with the box office.

Figure 12-3   Handout of Instructions to Crew

  E. Review dress and behavior expected of crew.
    1. Don't mingle with audience.
    2. Don't call attention to self.

Scene Dock

The scene dock is the area in which sets and props are stored while waiting to be placed on stage (see Figure 12-4).

During the first crew rehearsal you should delegate the responsibility for arranging the scene dock. Perhaps the crew chief or a particularly alert crew member can do it. Depending on the space inside the scene dock, the arrangement of scenery and set pieces must be controlled so that everything is accessible when needed. If a crew member needs a (extend to space needed) ↑   (extend to space needed) ↑

(extend to space needed) ↑

Set Pieces
I-5 to II-7

Crew Aisle

Staging Area for
One to Three Scenes

Set Pieces
I-3 & I-4

Set Pieces
I-2

Crew Aisle

Tent Wall

Aisle around Inside Perimeter of Tent

Audience Seats

Main Aisle
within Scene Dock
(used by audience in
emergencies only before
and during the show but
used as an exit aisle
after the performance)

Curtains Masking Scene Dock

Widest Aisle
to Stage

Curtains to Mask
Prop Table

Scene Diagrams

Current   Next

Prop Table

Crew Bulletin Board
with Shift Plot Charts

Curtains
to Mask
Prop Table

Half
Door

Control Booth

Window

Audience Seats

(area continues) ↓

Figure 12-4 Scene Dock Layout

set piece that is blocked by other units, she or he must climb over the other units and unnecessarily expend time and energy. The person placed in charge of arranging the scene dock should supervise the placement of returning sets just as carefully as you supervise their placement on stage.

Here are the factors to consider in designing your scene dock:

1. The main aisle within the scene dock should not be wider than the widest aisle down to the stage, but just as wide.
2. The width of the set piece staging areas should be just slightly less than the widest aisle.
3. The smaller aisles within the scene dock should be just wide enough for crew members to stand in.
4. Lines delineating the set piece storage areas should be painted on the ground.
5. Curtains masking the scene dock should open to the width of the widest aisle to the stage.
6. The scene dock should be as close as possible to the control booth so that the stage manager and crew chief can communicate rapidly.
7. Set pieces for Act I, Scene 1 may be stored outside of the tent and then brought into the main aisle of the scene dock if there are to be rehearsals on stage. Otherwise they may be preset for the next performance after the audience departs.
8. Depending on the size and number of set pieces, they may have to be stored as far away as the shop or other storage areas and then rotated into the scene dock during scenes.
9. Although outside of the main tent, the scene dock should be covered in case of rain.

Shift Inspection

During the shift you or your assistant should be on stage to supervise. If possible, do not assign yourself anything to carry in the shift. Keep your hands free to cope with emergencies. Attach your flashlight to your belt. Follow the crew onto the stage. Stay out from under their feet and watch carefully what they do. Check the placement of scenery, set pieces, and props. Make sure that every item from the previous scene is struck. Check that all actors who are to be discovered are in place. Check that all crew members have left the stage. For a round theater production, signal the booth, usually by blinking your flashlight from the stage that you are ready for light and sound. Dash offstage or up the aisle as the scene commences. You should be the last person to leave the stage before the performance resumes.

To stay neat and professional I would never suggest shining a flashlight from the stage in the round to cue the booth. Too many customers can see the effort. Find a way to cue that is hidden from the audience.

Leonard Auerbach
Associate Professor, Department of Theatre Arts
State University of New York at Stony Brook

A green gelled flashlight might be a bit less conspicuous. Or, if you can afford high tech, how about a voice-activated FM transmitter headset? Any other suggestions are welcome.

Do you think you can do all of that in less than thirty seconds? Practice.

Scene Shift Diagrams

Diagrams of every scene can help if there are many scene shifts and many crew members. These diagrams are a visual aid that will help prepare crew members for their journeys down and up the aisles in a theater in the round (see Figures 12-5 and 12-6) or offstage to the scene dock. These sketches allow crew members to check their next move and refresh their memories as to the exact location and specifications for the placement of props, set pieces, and scenery.

You should post these diagrams in the crew area so that only two at a time are visible. Rotating your diagrams in "current" and "next" positions, rather than posting all of the diagrams at once, avoids confusion.

Example:

The following discussion refers to a theater-in-the-round production of *Showboat*—Act I, Sc. 1, The Levee, (Figure 12-5), and Act I, Sc. 2, The Kitchen (Figure 12- 6).

The shift from Scene 1 to Scene 2 calls for the dropping of the hanging unit, the striking of two cotton bales, and the setting of a stool, table, and chair—not considering props. How will you assign your crew to accomplish this one shift? Study the diagrams for a moment.

Here are some considerations:

A. If there is an experienced flyman on the crew, she or he should drop the hanging piece.

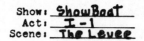

Show: **ShowBoat**
Act: **I -1**
Scene: **The Levee**

12

Orchestra Pit

11

1

10 o'clock bale

cotton
Bales

9

3

9 o'clock bale

7

5

6

to
scene
dock

Figure 12-5   Scene Shift Diagram: First Scene

B. Since the table is large, two men should be assigned to it and it should move down aisle 7, the widest aisle and the aisle closest to the scene dock, thus eliminating carrying the table around the outside perimeter of the theater.

C. It is generally most efficient for one crew member to both strike and set a piece. But in this situation since there are so few set pieces to be moved, there will be hands available to do the change more efficiently by having one crew member strike only and one crew member set only.

D. Usually the fewer crew members used for a scene the better, as they have a tendency to run into one another in the dark.

In this case a stool is to play where a cotton bale is now set. If one crew member is assigned to set the stool and strike the cotton bale, she or he has to do the following: (1) run the stool down the aisle, (2) set it

Show:_Showboat_
Act:_I-2_
Scene:_THE KITCHEN_

Figure 12-6   Scene Shift Diagram: Second Scene

down, (3) pick up the cotton bale and move it aside, (4) pick up the stool and put it in place, (5) pick up the cotton bale and run it up the aisle. Yes, the move could be made this way, but evaluate the time and noise factors.

Or, you might have two crew members take care of the above cited units, with an empty-handed striker going first to pick up the cotton bale ahead of the crew member who sets the piece that goes in its place. The striker might creep halfway down the aisle prior to the blackout and have the bale well offstage by the time the setter got her or his piece down to the stage.

Or, you may have the chair setter, not the crew member carrying the stool, place the chair at 8 o'clock and strike the 9 o'clock bale, to be followed by the crew member who places the stool. (Note that it is the 9 o'clock bale, not the 10 o'clock bale, that is blocking the placement of the stool. A set piece is designated as the "X" o'clock set piece according to its most easily discernible, if not exact, clock position. Finer designations, such as the "9:35 cotton bale," just don't seem to work.)

By now you can see that this simple-looking scene change needs thorough evaluation if it is to be done efficiently. These are the kinds of details that you will work out with diagrams and paper cutout set units as you make your shift plot chart.

The movement of cast members is still another problem with which you must cope. If at the end of I–1, the lights faded on two cast members standing next to the cotton bales, and if in I–2, two different cast members are discovered seated on the stool and chair, then there is the additional consideration of four traveling cast members during the blackout.

The general practice is to specify certain aisles or wing exits for cast exits whenever possible. For entrances, cast members usually follow crew members down the other aisles. During rehearsals you may remind the director to channel cast via aisles reserved for cast exits. When this is not possible for any special reason, you should note it and accommodate unusual cast exits in planning your scene shifts.

It is practical to select the narrower aisles for cast exits, as they are less convenient for moving large set pieces. Location of tent poles or other major fixtures in aisles would also be a factor to consider.

The importance of remembering exit blocking should be stressed to the cast. Obviously, a cast member who dashes up a darkened aisle in a rush to make a quick change only to find her- or himself blocked, does not need to be told twice.

Audience Caution

Members of the audience are usually cautioned in the program to remain seated during blackouts. In many theaters in the round the caution is repeated on the public address system prior to the performance. This responsibility usually rests with the house manager.

Distribution of Scene Diagrams

As soon as the scene designer has completed his or her design, scene diagrams should be made. Haste in this matter should take precedence over accuracy. In the course of building the set pieces and scenery there may be many changes. When the units are gathered all together on stage for the first time at the take-in and the scene designer sees what the set really looks like, as compared to the original perspective sketches, there are likely to be more changes, both in number and arrangement of units.

Yet if you wait until the take-in to make your diagrams, you might find yourself quite rushed. It is much more expedient to make corrections on diagrams with a bold marking pen than to wait for perfect initial copies.

The fastest way of getting the scene diagrams to those who need them is to have the scene designer draw the initial diagrams on spirit duplicator (Ditto) masters. The diagrams can then be used at staff meetings to help everyone understand the sets for the coming production. The scene designer, technical director, master carpenter, property person, stage manager, and assistant stage manager should all be issued a complete set. The producer's secretary tucks still another set into his or her files for coming seasons when the show might be repeated.

The property person uses her or his copies for preset diagrams of props.

The stage manager and assistant stage manager use their copies to help work out their shift plot chart. They note the cast members discovered in each scene and special-effects lighting that is initiated during rehearsals.

The technical director and master carpenter use theirs to augment perspective sketches and line drawings in understanding where units are to play.

The making of the diagrams is normally a responsibility of the scene designer (but they have been developed with the director's and your views in mind). You merely see to it that they are duplicated and distributed.

Upkeep of Sets

After opening night you are responsible for upkeep and minor emergency repair of scenery, set pieces, and lighting equipment. You are not expected to reupholster a couch or overhaul a dimmer, but you are expected to patch, shore up, glue together, and generally keep the set fit for the eyes of the audience and the comfort and safety of the cast.

You must always have the tools on hand to carry out this function. Check to see that you have access to appropriate tools.

In the absence of a staff technical director, you might find yourself responsible for the theater's tools. If so:

1. Provide a secure, locked area for storage. Disappearance and theft can thus be considerably reduced. Temporarily, the trunk of a car can serve for tool storage if there is no lockable space in the theater building.
2. No matter how small your tool collection is, it is desirable to make a tool board on which each tool is mounted and outlined or silhouetted. This allows you to determine easily which tools are not in place. It is also convenient since you can always expect to find your tools in the very same place (see Figure 12-7).

Photo courtesy of Mel Wixson and the Morgan-Wixson Theatre.

Figure 12-7 A Convenient Setup for a Tool Board. The toolboard above the workbench in the shop at the Morgan-Wixson Theatre, a community theater in Santa Monica. Note that the tools are silhouetted so that they may be returned easily to their correct places.

3. Painting all of your tools one color can also help to deter loss as there is no possible confusion as to whose tools they are.

Example:

When transient crews come in to work, they sometimes walk off with tools thinking that the tools are theirs. At an all-girls' school the tools were painted pink on the theory that no self-respecting transient male would steal a pink tool.

In nonprofessional companies where the actors are called upon to help build and paint scenery, you can save the company money by closely supervising the cleanup after work calls. This insures that tools are returned, brushes properly cleaned, and paint cans tightly closed. Close supervision in the proper use of tools can also prevent damage to the tools, and accidents.

You should keep on hand small quantities of the paints used on the set so that you can do touch-up work without having to buy fresh paint that matches the original. Sometimes this merely means having the wisdom to save nearly empty cans of paint until the close of the production.

13

Running the
Technical Rehearsal

The purpose of the technical rehearsal is to make a final confirmation and integration of all light and sound cues, special effects, scene changes, and curtain pulling. Every mechanical effect that should happen during the performance should happen at the technical rehearsal, and just the way it is to happen in performance.

It is during the "tech" that you will probably move from the director's side to your work area, usually in the wings, but possibly in a booth behind the audience.

Traditionally the tech is the time when actors stand around, holding positions while lights are refocused, or endlessly repeating cue lines until sound cues are tightened and sound levels are set. It is traditionally a rehearsal where overtime runs long and tempers run short. It need not be so.

The actors, who have rehearsed for weeks, meet the crew, who have possibly never rehearsed. The cast is impatient. They want to do their thing. They can't understand why the director, technical director, and stage manager are now giving their complete attention to the minutiae of mechanical matters that are totally insignificant compared to their performance. So think the actors. They can't understand why the crew can't get things right the first time.

You can most effectively shorten and sweeten the tech by holding a separate crew, and crew only, rehearsal of all the cues and scene changes prior to the tech—sometimes called a paper tech. Many of the problems of the tech can then be ironed out in advance. The crew will be able to do the work involved in smoothing out cues without the cast looking on.

Example:

On paper the light cue looks fine, but because of the design and arrangement of the equipment, it takes three hands on three dimmer handles to execute it. Who provides the third hand? It may take only a few minutes to resolve this situation by assigning another crew member to assist the light tech for that cue. But a few minutes at a "crew-only" rehearsal might save an hour for the cast, staff, and crew at the tech.

The real purpose of the technical rehearsal should be coordination and integration of light, sound, special effects, and scene changes, not the initial attempt at each. The tech should *not* be used to finish the design or devise the effects. If this distinction can be kept in mind, and if time, money, and union rules will allow you to hold a separate crew-only rehearsal prior to the tech, you will be doing a great service to the director, producer, and play by supervising that separate crew rehearsal.

If this is not possible, your burden increases with respect to planning the tech, anticipating problems, and briefing crew members.

The perfect tech is one in which the actors can have the benefits of a run-through while all technical aspects are polished as the play is in progress, or during breaks and intermissions.

This calls for good communications. If the director can talk to you, the technical director, lighting designer, costume designer, and other staff members without noisily interrupting the tech, it will go more smoothly.

Sometimes the seating arrangement of the staff can help. If staff members who do not absolutely have to be backstage will sit in the audience in the row in front of the director, she or he can simply lean forward to whisper comments. All staff members should have paper and pencil. You should provide them with adequate light so that they may take notes.

Since you have moved to your work area, be it backstage or booth, the director must be able to talk to you without running or shouting. You should try to set up whatever communications are necessary.

Many theaters do not have adequate communications. Sometimes you can improvise. Two prop phones in working order, sound wire, and a battery can be hooked up to give you some link. Of course, headsets would be an improvement.

You will usually need to talk to the lighting board technician, the sound technician, follow spot operator, curtain puller, and others during the tech and during performances (see Chapter Eleven). Ideally you should be able to talk to them via headsets. You should also be able to speak to the dressing rooms and the green room without leaving your work area. (A P.A. system that would allow you to reach the entire audience from your work area in case of an emergency, monitor equipment enabling cast to hear the performance in the dressing rooms and green room, and a phone would round out most of your communications needs.)

In our age of technology it is surprising that theater communications have been so neglected that these facilities are usually lacking or inadequate.

When planning for and scheduling your tech rehearsal, plan to give the staff, cast, and crew as much time as possible to work together. Any business other than the prime function of the tech should be relegated to other rehearsals. Directors should accept the fact that the tech is not the time to reblock or polish acting performances.

Cast members should be warned well in advance that they must expect to work late and that they must stay through to the end of the rehearsal.

There is a tendency for the crew to be concerned with their personal comforts and accommodations during the tech. Yes, it is important that the technician on the follow spot have a light in order to follow book. Yes, she or he should have a comfortable chair, since she or he has to sit there throughout the performance. Maybe she or he needs a pillow, too. And it would be desirable to run a phone line to her or him so that you can talk to her or him. But the period of the tech is not the time to take care of these things. They should be seen to before or after, but not while a cast of twenty and staff of ten are waiting to rehearse. Communications, lighting, seating, and other crew necessities and comforts should be anticipated and arranged. If these things cannot be worked out at a separate crew rehearsal, give your crew an early call for the tech and take care of these things before the cast and staff arrive. (See Chapters Eleven and Twelve.)

It is a good practice for you to run the tech by yourself, giving all cues to cast and crew as if it were opening night. If the show can be run as a run-through, do so, stopping only when technical problems make it impossible to go on. In the case of a very heavy technical show, you may wish to skip from technical effect to technical effect instead of running through. In either case, it is important that you have all of your cues clearly marked in your prompt script and all supporting paperwork—scene shift diagrams, shift plot charts (see Chapter Twelve), light tech's lighting sheet (see Chapter Eleven), etc.—distributed and reviewed with those concerned prior to the tech.

Few fledgling stage managers have the good sense to rig a fail-safe cue light—two bulbs at the receiving end of the cable so that if one blows the other will probably still function.

Leonard Auerbach
Associate Professor, Department of Theatre Arts
State University of New York at Stony Brook

In some cases, you may start your tech rehearsal as a run-through and then, seeing that you are falling behind, skip through the remainder of the show from tech effect to tech effect.

If time permits, it is desirable to schedule two technical rehearsals as a safety factor.

The technical rehearsal is one of the biggest tests of your ability, for it is the one single rehearsal where you can save the cast and staff the greatest amount of time and energy.

14

Running the Show

Now comes the easy part, the production phase.

The director tells you that it's all yours. There's an audience out there. All you have to do is run the show. You have some long-range responsibilities (see Chapter Sixteen), but your basic functions should now be firmly under control.

An interesting difference between new and experienced stage managers is that the new stage manager thinks of running the show as the most difficult and most demanding part of the job, whereas the experienced stage manager thinks of it as the most relaxing part. Perhaps the reason is that the experienced stage manager has built up work habits that make her or him so thoroughly prepared for the production phase that she or he just sits back during performances to watch that preparation pay off.

Checklists

Pre-curtain, intermission, and post-production checklists will help you to remember all of the little things you must do. These checklists should be placed into your prompt script facing the first page of dialogue, and following the last pages of dialogue, of each act.

A good approach is to think of someone replacing you immediately. Write out your list as if you were telling someone else what to do. Write the items in the sequence in which you perform them. Don't be afraid to be too detailed (see Figure 14-1).

Leave space between entries so that you can make last-minute additions in sequence.

When you arrive at the theater, open your prompt script to your

Pre-Curtain Check List

7 P.M.	turn on air conditioning
Dusk	turn on marquee
7:30	check crew present, call late ones
	conduct light, sound check (incl. bell, buzzer)
	unlock props, place on prop tables
	unlock stage door, sweep alley, empty butt cans
	unlock dressing rooms, turn on lights, check paper
	supplies
7:55	final check of stage: sweep it, all set pieces
	in place, all discovered props in place, set hands
	of clock (UR) to 3:45 and check wound
	check all set pieces and props in correct positions
	backstage, ready for changes
	turn off work light, masking tape over switch
	bring in curtain warmers, house lights, cue start
	of taped music
	turn house over to house manager
8:00	give half hour call, check sign-in sheet (post
	new one on Wednesdays), chat with cast, close
	curtain to green room
8:05	call late actors
8:15	turn on stage monitor, give 15 minute call,
	check monitor working in dressing rooms
8:25	give 5 minute call, blink marquee lights
8:30	await house manager's signal to call places (or
	give hold to cast) - call places

Figure 14-1 Detailed Pre-Curtain Checklist and Schedule

checklist and mentally check off each entry as you accomplish it. That way, when you call places, there won't be that aggravating question in the back of your mind, "What have I forgotten?"

> You must check off on an overlay or on a tear-off sheet or some other device. That way, if interrupted, you have a record of what you have not yet done.
>
> Leonard Auerbach
> Associate Professor, Department of Theatre Arts
> State University of New York at Stony Brook

In stock companies where you do a new show every week or two weeks, each day may bring both a rehearsal and a performance. Instead of pre-rehearsal and pre-curtain checklists, you will want to write out daily checklists covering your procedure for each day.

Your checklists, even if geared to a specific production rather than a season of plays, would be good material to pass on to the person who succeeds you.

A few items on your checklists deserve special comment.

Sweeping the stage, including the backstage walkways between the dressing rooms and the stage, is your responsibility. You may assign this task to someone, but you must make sure that it's done. Following the sweeping you should inspect for nails, screws, stage pegs, splinters, loose edges of rugs, or any other hazards. Only when you are willing to walk barefoot across the stage is the stage ready for the cast.

Besides checking to make sure that the worklight is off prior to curtain, you should check that it is on when needed, and that it is on as fast as possible in order to expedite scene changes and to enable the cast to leave the stage safely (see Chapter Twelve). Remember that the bright stage lights will leave the cast temporarily blinded and that they will need the worklight in order not to trip over set pieces on their way out. Even if the worklight is controlled by a separate switch, and not through the dimmer board, place the cue for it in your prompt script as if it were any other lighting effect. Call for it in the same manner that you cue all other effects.

Giving Cues

To run the show, you must signal or cue lights, sound, special effects (Chapter Eleven), and curtain, and thus coordinate these elements with the action of the play, making them happen at precisely the right time.

Your light pencil lines that identify cues (see Chapter Three) allow you to call the cues during rehearsals when you pinpoint them with the guidance of the director (see Chapter Eight). During the technical rehearsal, or just prior to it (Chapter Thirteen), you confirm the final cues in your prompt script with bold marking pen lines and number the cues (see Figure 14-2). Now you are ready to give the cues to lighting technicians, master electrician, sound technicians, curtain puller, and special-effects people.

Following your script through performance, just as you did at rehearsals, you give the cues clearly, firmly, and with certainty. If you do not feel clear, firm, and certain, pretend. The new stage manager may be compared to a person just learning to drive a car; she or he is afraid to step on the gas pedal. The experienced stage manager, on the other hand, gives her or his cues with the authority of a marine drill sergeant, but in a whisper.

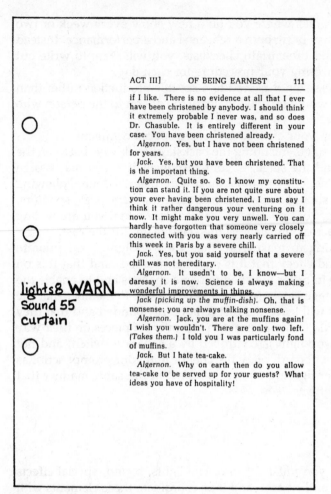

ACT III]   OF BEING EARNEST   111

if I like. There is no evidence at all that I ever
have been christened by anybody. I should think
it extremely probable I never was, and so does
Dr. Chasuble. It is entirely different in your
case. You have been christened already.

Algernon. Yes, but I have not been christened
for years.

Jack. Yes, but you have been christened. That
is the important thing.

Algernon. Quite so. So I know my constitution can stand it. If you are not quite sure about
your ever having been christened, I must say I
think it rather dangerous your venturing on it
now. It might make you very unwell. You can
hardly have forgotten that someone very closely
connected with you was very nearly carried off
this week in Paris by a severe chill.

Jack. Yes, but you said yourself that a severe
chill was not hereditary.

Algernon. It usedn't to be, I know—but I
daresay it is now. Science is always making
wonderful improvements in things.

Jack (picking up the muffin-dish). Oh, that is
nonsense; you are always talking nonsense.

Algernon. Jack, you are at the muffins again!
I wish you wouldn't. There are only two left.
(Takes them.) I told you I was particularly fond
of muffins.

Jack. But I hate tea-cake.

Algernon. Why on earth then do you allow
tea-cake to be served up for your guests? What
ideas you have of hospitality!

lights8 **WARN**
Sound 55
curtain

Figure 14-2   Final Cues and Warns Confirmed in Script
with Bold Marking Pen

Generally the cues are, "Warn," "Standby," and "Go." The warn
part of the cue is usually accompanied by the cue number so that the
technician will know which cue it is that he or she is to execute: "Warn
number nine."

If there are sound and light cues in the same general area, you might
want to clarify your warn: "Warn lights number nine." If a light cue
and a sound cue are to be simultaneous, the warn might be given as,
"Warn lights number nine, sound number fifty-three."

The warn is usually given one-and-a-half to two minutes before the
cue is to be executed. This is usually a half page to a full page before
the cue.

The warn should be given in enough time for the technicians to ready themselves and their equipment for the cue, check the cue on their plot or cue sheet, and give their total attention to executing the cue. If a cue requires extensive preparation—the patching of lines into a dimmer, the changing of reels on a tape recorder—then you might wish to write a separate tech cue into your prompt script to remind the technician to do this on the page prior to the warn, or immediately following the previous cue.

The standby portion of the cue should precede the go by five or ten seconds, giving the technicians enough time to place their hands in position, flex their muscles, and rivet their eyes and ears on you to await the go. Sometimes the verbal standby is accompanied or replaced by raising the hand.

The go may be given verbally or by lowering the hand.

The exact nature of your cues will depend on the communications equipment backstage, your proximity to your technicians, and their ability to see you and watch their equipment at the same time.

One of my pet peeves—only a strong personal preference—is the necessity of using "standby" in calling cues. Once the warnings are spaced correctly in good tech rehearsals, the next order should be "Cue 48......Go." The reiteration of the cue number should serve as a sufficient standby. There is much less room for misunderstanding.

Leonard Auerbach
Associate Professor, Department of Theatre Arts
State University of New York at Stony Brook

If several cues occur in a fast sequence and there is no time to warn in between them, you will warn and give standby for the series. Then give only your go, or signal for go, once for the whole series. If it is an extremely intricate series of cues, it is possible that you will want to rehearse it carefully, so that the technicians can get a feeling for the timing or rhythm of the series.

Again, all cues—warn, standby, and go—must be given clearly, firmly, and with certainty. Calling cues is another of your sacred duties, a sine qua non. You must be able to coordinate lights, sound, special effects, and curtain, and you do it by cuing.

Don't cop out on this responsibility. Don't delegate this responsibility. Even if the light and sound technicians can see and hear the cues and follow book just as well as you can, it is still your job.

Check the result of each cue that you give immediately. If you don't get what you expected, don't panic. Check it out calmly. The tendency is to reach over the technician's shoulder and pull a handle or throw a switch. But keep firmly in mind that the audience is much less aware of gradual changes than abrupt ones. Bringing in the correct effect slowly is usually more desirable than immediate correction of an improper effect.

Mistakes occur in every line of work. Don't allow an error on your part to prevent you from executing all subsequent cues correctly. Don't allow errors to compound. Get a hold on yourself and get the next cue right.

Musical Cues

In musical comedy, opera, and ballet it is often necessary that the stage manager read music and take light cues from a note in the score rather than from a word in the script.

In such cases the stage manager has a copy of the score and marks the cues in the score, spacing "Warn," "Standby," and "Go" as described above with respect to the time needed to alert the technicians. The stage manager might write a cue for her- or himself in the prompt script to go to the score for the next cue, including the page number of the score. Or the stage manager might place the score pages on which there are cues in the prompt script.

If you do not read music, tell your director and don't attempt to fake it. With the director's help you can sometimes get around your deficiency by using a stopwatch. Rather than listening for a note, you would time how far into the music that note occurs and then take the cue from the stopwatch. If there is a fast series of cues from subsequent notes, you would substitute mental counts for listening to notes. Sometimes you can look for concurrent cast movement rather than notes from which to take your cues. These are all cumbersome methods and learning to read music is preferable—and usually a prerequisite for stage management jobs in opera and ballet.

Equipment for Cuing

Should you use verbal and hand signals, or should you use a blinker light, hand-held? Or should you wire in sets of red and green lights with buttons at the stage manager's desk so that you can communicate with your technicians? Or should you wear TV-type headsets so that you can talk to, and listen to, your technicians?

There is no best system. It's a question of what will work best for your theater. Expensive headsets won't improve the quality of your performance any more than closed circuit TV in the dressing rooms so that offstage actors can watch the performance. More important than your cuing equipment is your consistency in using the system of cues described above.

Center stage

Shirley-May, Vicky, Dave, JoAnne, Terry, Jonas, Arlene, Rita, Sandy, Norma, Larry,

Enter from off   Move center on   Enter from off stage
stage right on   blackout.   left on blackout in
blackout in this   this order.
order.
                    Audience

1. Remain silent off stage while waiting for call. Move silently in
   final blackout. Join hands when in place.

2. Jonas is call leader. He will lead bows and give signal to break
   formation.

Figure 14-3 Curtain Call Order and Instructions

Timing Curtain Calls

You must learn to exercise your best judgment in timing the curtain call. You should insist on ample rehearsal of the curtain call so that it will be as professional as the rest of the play.

The director usually determines the curtain call order and the effect he or she wants to create in the process of having the actors acknowledge the audience's applause.

In some cases the producer or the management will have a policy on calls for every play performed in that theater. The policy may be, for instance, that the cast form a single line, in order of appearance, left to right. The policy may be that they should take only one bow, regardless of the audience response. This very professional or institutional form of curtain call is hard on the actors' egos, since the stars are not individually acknowledged by the audience, but it usually results in the house lights coming up while the audience clamors for more. This is quite desirable compared to the call where the applause dwindles as the cast takes its last bow.

The design of the call will vary with the taste of directors and producers, ranging from the absolutely simple, as above, to complexly choreographed. I once saw a fancy curtain call add some zest to an overwritten and dull last act of a musical, thus arousing some applause, but this is a highly unusual situation.

Often the planning of the curtain call is left for the very last moment and then done in haste. You can help by making a careful diagram of the call order as set by the director, and by posting this diagram on the callboard (see Figure 14-3).

The timing or running of the call is another of your sacred duties. You must decide how often to bring up the lights and how long to hold them up. Judgment in this matter can come only from experience. You will quickly learn to sense how long and hard the audience will applaud.

It is your good judgment that prevents the curtain closing to waning applause.

You should crank the curtain call cues into the lighting plot and rehearse these cues along with all others. It is disturbing to endure a long blackout following the final scene while the crew discovers that they must repatch before they can bring up the stage lights for the call. It is even more disturbing to see the house lights come up for the curtain call rather than the stage lights. We have all seen such incidents mar otherwise technically perfect productions.

When there is no curtain and the call is conducted with lights only, a cast member should be designated the "call leader" and given the responsibility of signaling the cast when to break their call formation and leave the stage. This will prevent a straggling exit that is discernible in the blackout. It also prevents cast members from breaking too early and being caught out of position when the lights come up.

Questions sometimes arise as to whether an actor is to appear in the curtain call and whether he or she must be in costume and makeup. Yes, he or she is just as obligated to appear in the call as he or she was to appear in the play.

"I have such a small part that the audience won't miss me." "I have a date after the show tonight and I don't want to keep her waiting while I get out of makeup." "I die in the first act and I don't want to hang around for two acts." There are many excuses, but no good ones. It is best for you to include a rule on curtain-call participation in the company rules (Chapter Four) and carefully explain to the cast what is expected.

Walking the Curtain

Sometime during rehearsals you should have the curtain pulled while you watch from the audience to see how it comes together. If there are no gaps when it is closed, there may be no need to have it walked. But if crew is available, it is always safer to have someone walk the curtain— walk out of sight behind the curtain to insure that it closes smoothly and completely.

Some of the familiar incidents you are guarding against by having the curtain walked are these:

Examples:

The man on the rope hits a snag and thinks the curtain is closed. The actors are hung, waiting for the curtain to close completely.

An actor accidentally jostles a set piece, moving it past the curtain line. The curtain drags the set piece and finally overturns it.

Access to the Control Booth

Only authorized personnel should be allowed in the control booth. Tampering with, or unintentional playing with, sound or lighting equipment by unauthorized personnel could detrimentally affect the running of your show. It is best to post a sign, and enforce it: "No admission," or "Authorized personnel only."

Is the director authorized? It's hard for a stage manager to tell the director to stay out, especially if the stage manager has not discussed this possibility with the director prior to opening night. There is the tendency for the director to want to talk to someone during the performance, someone who will understand his or her anguish, someone who will confirm that all of the actors are not doing what he or she told them to do. Worst of all, the director wants to give last-minute notes or make just a little change in some cue or effect.

If you and the director have done your work properly there is absolutely no reason for the director to be in the booth before, during, or after the performance. Make this clear in advance—that his or her presence would be a distraction. The same goes for cast members. Put this item in your company rules—you don't want anyone in the booth unless she or he is there to report a fire!

(Parenthetically, I don't feel that directors should give notes to cast members during intermissions. It's sometimes hard to convince a director that the urgent things she or he wants to say to the cast are not going to make that much difference in the second act. It's very hard to limit my comments about the director's behavior. I have to remind myself that this book is about stage management and not directing. From the stage manager's point of view, there is very little you can do to keep the director out of the backstage area during intermissions. You should discuss this behavior with the director in advance. "I hope you're not the kind of director who comes backstage at intermissions. I've found in the past that this seems to upset cast members more than anything else.")

15

Working with
the House Manager

The function of the house manager is to insure the audience's safety and comfort prior to a performance, during intermissions, and after the performance. You must understand the house manager's function and coordinate with her or him in the total effort of assisting the audience to see the production.

Normally, the most important item in your coordination is deciding how the house manager may notify you that the audience is ready to see the production. Will the house manager call you on a backstage phone or intercom and say, "It's all yours"? Or will you run the show at a prearranged time unless the house manager tells you otherwise? How might she or he tell you otherwise? Should you synchronize your watches?

There must be a very definite understanding between you and the house manager. It seems so obvious and yet it is frequently overlooked. How often does the audience return to their seats to find a scene in progress? How often does an audience return to their seats to wait several minutes before the curtain goes up? The audience resents being rushed or having to wait, and the actors resent playing to a moving audience. But it does happen and will continue to happen if you fail to coordinate with the house manager.

In large commercial theaters house managers belong to their own union, the Association of Theatrical Press Agents and Managers (AT-PAM), 165 West 46 Street, New York City, phone 212–719–3666. In a small company, the house manager may be one of the actors, and may have several other duties in addition to house managing and acting.

In some theaters the house manager is in charge of the whole theater plant, box office staff, ushers, custodial staff, etc. He or she turns the house over to the stage manager for the period of the play only, and resumes total responsibility during intermissions and after the final curtain.

In a small theater the house manager may double as usher, custodian, and assistant director. Halfway through the first act he or she may turn all of his or her responsibilities over to the stage manager and depart the premises.

In a showcase theater there might be a different house manager every night of the run, and it might be your responsibility to brief each new house manager.

The following discussion of a house manager's duties was written for a showcase theater.

Duties of the House Manager

The house manager acts as the producer's or sponsoring management's representative in greeting and seating the audience. He or she should be well dressed. He or she should wear a badge or ribbon to indicate his or her position. He or she should display his or her best manners. The house manager:

1. Obtains the reservation lists from the reservation clerk and brings them to the theater. This enables him or her to handle future reservations at the theater as well as the reservations for the evening's performance.
2. Arrives at the theater forty-five minutes prior to the curtain. He or she insures that both the sidewalk in front of the theater and the lobby are clean.
3. Checks the condition of the seats and the audience area. Insures that all fire exits may be opened easily and that alleys beyond them are not blocked. Answers the phones.
4. Greets and seats arriving audience, especially VIPs, and places reserved signs on front row seats for Helen Hayes, Mike Nichols, Rod Steiger, et al.
5. Prevents the audience from bringing food and lighted cigarettes into the theater.
6. Handles reservations problems: people arriving on the wrong night, overbooked audiences, etc. Holds people without reservations until all those with reservations have been seated. Helps people in wheelchairs to find the most convenient aisle space from which to watch the performance. Is alert to other handicaps among audience members and tries to assist if possible.
7. Watches for causes of audience delay—rain, freeway tie-ups, severe parking problems, etc.—and if he or she senses that the audience will be late, he or she asks the stage manager to give the cast a five-minute hold.

8. When the audience is seated, he or she closes the back doors, walks to the stage door, and tells the stage manager that he or she may, "Take the show."

9. After the curtain rises he or she returns to the lobby and seats people who arrive late, cautioning them that the curtain is up and asking them to be as silent as possible. (He or she tries to fill the house tightly from the front so that empty seats will be at the back for late arrivals.)

10. During the acts he or she again checks the sidewalks and lobby so that the audience will find these areas clean when they emerge from the theater during intermissions and after the show.

11. Finds time during acts to sit for a few minutes in the audience to check the temperature in the theater and to observe any audience distractions.

12. At intermissions he or she opens the back doors and outside doors to ventilate the theater. (Body heat and the lighting equipment may make the theater quite grim by the end of each act.)

13. Directs the audience to the rest rooms and the telephone. Insures that the rest rooms are clean and serviceable.

14. Makes any necessary announcements to the audience:
    A. "No smoking." (He speaks to those individuals who haven't read the posted signs and those who don't wish to comply.)
    B. Announces any unusually long delays in the curtain.
    C. "Lights on in car parked outside, license number EMR 223."
    D. "Is there a doctor in the house?"
    E. "Fire!" (The house manager knows exactly what to do to evacuate the theater. He or she knows the numbers to call for fire, police, and ambulance, and always carries emergency coins with which to use the pay phone in the lobby. Also see Figure 15-1.)
    F. Announces any cast changes and omissions in the program.

15. Times the intermissions and blinks the outside lights and/or strikes chimes in the lobby and/or announces, "Curtain going up," to bring the audience back in. Closes the back doors and the street doors at the end of the intermissions. Does not wait ten minutes to bring the audience back in, but starts them coming back after eight minutes so that they are seated and ready to go when ten minutes have elapsed.

16. If there are doctors on call in the audience, he or she takes their name and seat location and summons them if they should get a call during the performance.

17. Answers questions of departing audience, notes their complaints and suggestions, and passes them on to the producer.

18. Coordinates with the stage manager in securing the theater when everyone has left. Pushes up the seats and searches for

(Varsity. the Stage Daily. August. 1969)

**PROP BURSTS INTO
FLAMES AS PLAY
REACHES HIGHLIGHT**

Murfreesboro. Tenn., Aug. 15—Just as Mark Antony was about to deliver his "Friends, Romans, countrymen" speech in praise of Julius C   ̃ he was left speechless when a f   out on the stage of the And Theater during a Rebel Th& pany performance of the S ean play last night.

The blaze ignited a 1 foam and fiberglass bu which dominated the Ja' stage throughout the pl& veloped the stage prop the rest of the sevente ater before the eyes c tators.

Stage Manager nounced what specta . knew, that there was a fire, and asr.. patrons to leave as quietly as possible. More than a thousand spectators occupying three-fourths of the theater building managed to file out without panic. Shortly afterward four fire rigs arrived to quench the blaze. although stagehands and actors had already acted to douse the flames.

(Varsity, the Stage Daily. February, 1969)

FIRE DEPT HALTS SHOW

After a thirty minute delay, during which debris was removed and further precautions were taken against the outbreak of any other fire, patrons were permitted to re-enter the theater, still smoke-filled, and the play continued with Chuck Kitting as Antony resuming his eulogy of Caesar. Most of the audience waited out the firefighting efforts and returned to watch the end of the play. The biggest ovation of the evening went to five members of the Murfreesboro Fire Department as they marched out with full equipment shortly before the play was ready to resume.

FLAMES CALL OFF LIVING THEATER

(Los Angeles Messenger. February, 1969)

Performances of Living Theater at USC cancelled after fire this ola .

Figure 15-1   Onstage Fire Can Threaten Your Production Any Time, Anywhere

lost items. Before leaving the theater he or she must conduct a sniff test (fire inspection) of every row in the audience and every room and cranny of the theater and dressing rooms to insure that no burning cigarettes have been left anywhere.

19. Returns the reservation lists to the reservations clerk.

Problems frequently occur when you come to your job from one theater and the house manager comes from another. You have different expectations of one another based on different past experiences.

Talk it out. Give it a dry run. Anticipate problems together. What will you each do if it rains torrents, buckets, and cats and dogs on opening night? Who will roll out the heavy-duty mats in the lobby? Who

(Los Angeles *Bugle.* 1970)
LETTERS

Nuisance Noises

We recently attended the visiting St. Louis Opera Company's performance of "Aida" at the Municipal Opera Pavilion on December 5. In the middle of the opera we were severely distracted by pulsating drumbeats and musical sounds which seemed to come from the ceiling of the auditorium, as if they emanated from the restaurant upstairs. It was impossible for us to get a clear hearing of the last part of the opera. In order to be sure that the vibrations from above were not somehow imaginary, we turned to a neighbor for confirmation. "Good grief!" he said, "I've been fighting it since the second act." We wrote a strong complaint after the performance, but never received any acknowledgmer very poor taste on the part ment to permit conflicting this to be audible to patrons formances.

　　　　　Morris and Art Faye
　　　　　Northeast Cucamonga

Danny Bongo, public relations director for the Pavilion, admits there was no theater employee directly responsible for checking on such intrusive sounds beyond the first few minutes after the performance is under way. "Until somebody gives us the word," he said, "we have no way to be aware there's a problem." However, on December 5, a verbal complaint was made to a guard and, according to Bongo, the sound of the dance band was "totally sealed off" as a result by the end of the opera. Bongo denies that anybody involved received any written protest. But a similar complaint appeared in the Bugle's review of "La Gioconda" as performed by the St. Louis company during the same month here.

—The Editor

Figure 15-2　Plan Ahead to Handle Emergencies and Surprise Interruptions

will put down the planks in the gulley at the actors' entrance? How will the house manager tell you from out front that the rain has delayed the audience and that she or he wants you to hold the curtain an additional five minutes? Since there's no cloakroom, where can the audience store raincoats and umbrellas? Does the house manager lock up the theater? Do you? Or do you both share or alternate shut-down procedures? If you share or alternate, do you both know exactly what is to be done?

Anticipate emergencies together. Review what you each will do in the event of fire, civil disorder, air raid, flood, heart attacks among the audience, animals in the audience, incredibly loud noises emanating from places unknown (see Figure 15–2), and hysterical patrons begging to be let out.

ROSTER

	Thursday	Friday	Saturday	Sunday	Thursday	Friday	Saturday	Sunday
Albert Alvarez	A	B	C	D	E	F	G	H
Ben Blahzay	B	C	D	E	F	G	H	I
Charles Corn	C	D	E	F	G	H	I	J
Dave Dumpling	D	E	F	G	H	I	J	K
Earl Eastman	E	F	G	H	I	J	K	L
Frank Farley	F	G	H	I	J	K	L	A
Gina Glass	G	H	I	J	K	L	A	B
Helen Harvey	H	I	J	K	L	A	B	C
Ida Isely	I	J	K	L	A	B	C	D
Judy Jennings	J	K	L	A	B	C	D	E
Karen Kirsten	K	L	A	B	C	D	E	F
Louise Lehrer	L	A	B	C	D	E	F	G

A   Sweep front sidewalk

B   Strain sand in all four cans in lobby; move 2 outside

C   Sweep/mop lobby

D   Put all seats up; sweep/mop audience area

E   Clean men's room

F   Clean ladies' room

G   Clean dressing room tables

H   Sweep dressing rooms

I   Clean Green Room

J   Empty all waste baskets: rest rooms, dressing rooms, Green Room (trash can behind theater)

K   Resupply all paper to dressing rooms, rest rooms from supply cupboard

L   Dust lobby furniture, straighten

Figure 15-3   A Rotating Duty Roster

Rotating Duty Rosters

When there is no staff house manager and the cast must carry out the custodial duties, you may find it desirable to prepare a rotating duty roster (see Figure 15-3).

Example:

In a showcase theater situation where there was no budget for cleanup and maintenance of the theater, the cast was called to a discussion by the artistic director (one of the actors). They were asked how to solve the cleanup problem. All agreed that they were the only ones who could solve the problem, that they did not want to levy a tax to pay a custodian, and that their chief concern was an equitable distribution of the work. The artistic director then asked the stage manager (also an actor in the group) to set up a rotating duty roster.

The rosters were not posted in the dressing rooms or on the callboard, since cast members did not want their friends who visited after performances to see that they were expected to do chores. Instead, each cast member was given a copy of the roster. The stage manager supervised and also carried out his chores.

Cast members were given the option of carrying out their assignments fifteen minutes prior to the call, or after the performance. By doing two chores in an evening, one before and one after the performance, they could work on chores every two nights.

By inviting the cast to participate in solving the problem, the artistic director gained their cooperation. If he had simply ordered the roster posted, it might not have worked as well as it did. A few minutes of group consultation in advance can prevent a great deal of individual dissent later.

The stage manager also might take pains to explain where the cleanup materials are kept, how a mop wringer is used, and the importance of putting things back where they were found and reporting shortages of materials. (It was discovered, in the example above, that a thirty-year-old actor did not know how to use a mop! He had never used one. The stage manager demonstrated and the actor caught on. Unfortunately he became much more skilled at mopping than acting.)

Not all duty rosters need be of the rotating type if the cast is willing to distribute chores in another way.

Again, a group talk session in advance will help in the voluntary tapping of labor.

VIP Lists

A showcase theater's purpose is to attract to its audience producers, directors, agents, and other very important people (VIPs) who can hire the cast members for roles in movies, television, industrial shows, live theater, and other paying jobs.

Community, educational, and commercial theaters may function as showcases, even though it is not their primary purpose.

If the cast members know which VIPs have seen their performance, they can follow up the impression they've made by sending a résumé and phoning for an interview. They can ask agents who have attended to represent them on the basis of their performance.

So it is desirable that the cast know which VIPs have been in the audience. Posting a VIP list on the callboard is the easiest way to let the cast know (see Figure 15-4).

Posting such a list is not a mandatory function of the stage manager.

ONE FLEW OVER THE CUCKOO'S NEST

VIP LIST

Dale Wasserman	author
Charles Faber	critic - Citizen News
John Houser	critic - Herald Examiner
Phillip Scheuer	critic - L.A. Times
Jimmy Powers	critic - Hollywood Reporter
Dale Olsen	critic - Variety
Robert Lewine	agent V.P. C.M.A.
Milton Lewis	manager
Lurene Tuttle	actress
Jim Lister	cast. dir. Stalmaster-Lister Rawhide Gunsmoke
Boris Kaplan	producer
Gene Banks	casting ABC
Betty Garret	actress
King Donovan	actor-director
Meyer Mishkin	agent Mishkin Agency
Hy Sieger	agent Park-Citron Agency
Norman Pincas	producer
David Graham	agent
Bob Raison	agent Raison-Branden Agency
Harold Swoverland	agent Swoverland Agency
Eddie Foy, Jr.	casting Columbia Screen Gems (I Dream of Jeannie)
Jack Donaldson	agent Donaldson Agency
Bob Bowser	casting Universal
Bob Shapiro	agent William Morris
Naomi Hirshhorn	producer legit
George Pal	producer MGM
Dick Lyons	producer MGM
Al Trescony	casting MGM
Meryl Abeles	Desilu 20th
Dick Berg	producer Chrysler
Bert Kennedy	director MGM writer
Dale Garrick	agent Garrick Agency
Arthur Kennard	agent Kennard Agency
David Victor	producer Dr. Kildare
Russell Lewis	producer Sacremento legit
Sid Gordon	William Schuller Agency
Walter Grauman	director
Jere Henshaw	casting Revue
Bill Brademan	casting Revue
Walter Doneger	director Peyton Place
June Murray	casting Dr. Kildare
Olga Lee	agent Raison-Branden Agency
Paul Brandon	agent Raison-Brandon
Doug Benton	associate producer Dr. Kildare
Joe Swerling	producer Revue
Marc Miller	producer
Monte Hellman	director
E.J. Newman	director writer Mr. Novak

Lawrence Stern
Stage Manager
AN 8 4855

Figure 15-4   A VIP List for the Callboard of a Showcase Theater

Anyone who takes the time to check with the box office, house manager, producer, and director might make such a list. But it is one of the extra items that would demonstrate your interest in the welfare of the cast and the reputation of the theater.

16

Keeping the Show in Hand

The most difficult problem in a long-running production is keeping the quality of each performance as good as it was on opening night. If the director remains with the show, in attendance regularly and in communication with the cast, it is his or her burden. But if he or she says to you on opening night, "It's all yours," and means it, then you have your work cut out for you. It is your basic responsibility to strive toward retaining the director's artistic intent (see Chapter Eight).

In a short run there isn't much of a problem. But as the actors feel more at ease in their roles, especially if the show runs for two weeks or more without the director's presence, "improvements" set in.

Here are some examples of the things that happen in extended runs:

A. *New Business*: An actor sometimes feels "hung up" during the lines of fellow actors. During rehearsals and the first few performances he was busy thinking of coming lines and business, but with his new-found ease and self-assurance, he begins to feel that he is not doing enough. So he invents new business that he feels is appropriate to his character. He removes his shoe and darns a hole in his red sock with green yarn that he removes from his eyeglass case.

Or it just happens by accident. He trips on the set and hits his head on the door frame, severely shaking the flat, and the audience laughs, so at the next performance. . . .

B. *New Lines*: A late entrance prompts two actors to ad-lib some lines while awaiting the late-comer. Next performance the ad-lib lines are repeated on the entrance, and at the next performance the entering actor waits for the ad-lib lines.

Or, an actor throws in an ad-lib line on impulse and gets a laugh, so at the next performance. . . .

C. *Pauses*: The actor now senses that his big moment is being missed by the audience because he doesn't have focus. So he decides he needs a dramatic pause, big enough to drive a truck through. It just seems that long. Actually, his new dramatic pauses and those of his fellow actors only add up to one and a half minutes on your time sheet for the scene—of yawning and coughing in the audience.

D. *Handles*: Suddenly every other line in the script has as preface a new expletive ("Well"), an exclamation ("Wow"), or direct address ("You"). The actors start to make themselves "comfortable" with the playwright's lines. The crispness is gone, the pace is down, but each actor knows in her or his heart that the single word she or he has added is right, just the way the character would say it.

So you observe and listen carefully, and each time you hear new lines, handles or pauses, or observe new business, you make a caret in your prompt script at the place where it occurred and note the new addition carefully. After the performance you bring the changes and improvements to the attention of the actors, privately. (Important: in matters of acting performances, directors give notes to the whole cast but stage managers counsel individual actors privately.)

And that's when you hear wondrous things from the actors in justification and rationalization:

"I've grown in the part."

"It got a laugh."

"It just happened by accident but the audience bought it so why not keep it?"

"I'm experimenting. Don't want to get into a rut."

"Got to keep that magic, spontaneous, first-time quality so I decided to do it for the first time without warning him so he'd give me a response I could play off of, but the dumdum just gave me the same tired line reading he's always been giving me."

Et cetera ad nauseum.

What do you do in the face of such static? You bring as much friendly persuasion as you can to the situation. You remind the actor of the traditional discipline of the theater—that changes in lines, pace, the interpretation of lines, and the inclusion of business are all strictly the prerogative of the director, and that in the absence of the director, they are now the stage manager's prerogative, and you do not approve the changes and improvements the actor wishes to make.

You may or may not go on to explain your reasons for the undesirability of the change or improvement.

You may point out that an actor's reputation for self-discipline is more important in the long run than the change or improvement she or he feels is so important.

You may also point out that historically the worst performances of the best actors have occurred when they undertook to direct themselves.

You might also console the actor that the decision not to accept her or his changes and improvements does not in any way diminish your respect for the actor's excellent taste, inventive genius, great experience despite her or his youth, sagacious artistic judgment, and her or his manifestly sincere desire to improve the production. But cut it!

Finally, you simply do not argue about it. Your authority extends only as far as your persuasive influence in this matter. Never make the actor feel that she or he must apologize or even agree with you. If she or he gives you static after you have counseled her or him, simply leave her or him with a pleasant, "Why don't you give it some thought?"

You cannot control absolutely an actor's performance. You cannot run out on the stage and twist the actor's arm. Ultimately the actor must realize what you already know—that in live theater, the stage belongs to the actors, not the director or the stage manager. On the other hand, a production is a delicate balance of many performers' efforts, and any actor's reputation can suffer if she or he persists in upsetting this. For the really recalcitrant, the ultimate threat would be replacement with an understudy or a new actor, but this would be an administrative decision.

Cast Morale

Sometimes the gloom in the air at half hour call following a bad review is enough to make any stage manager feel that a comedy could not possibly be performed that evening, or that the tragedy about to be enacted on stage is nothing compared to the one backstage.

Here's how you handle the situation:
1. Don't overreact.
2. Get it out in the open.
3. Don't act elated when others are depressed.
4. Keep your own personal morale high.

It's never quite as bad as you imagine it will be before you get to the theater. Actors and actresses have a way of buoying up their own morale when they get together. Never feel that you must become court jester, or psychiatrist, backstage. This is not the time for a good show biz anecdote. Don't overreact.

Get it out in the open. A casual, "Rough break, Sam," to an actor who has been devastated by bad reviews might get it out from the sulking level to the verbal level and allow the actor to vent his choicest invective about the reviewers. But keep it casual. Show the actor that you don't attach too great importance to it.

Don't be elated when others are depressed. You should be sympathetic enough with the plight of a demoralized cast not to want to appear to be celebrating their disaster.

Keep your own personal morale high. Your morale is dependent on the fact that you are doing a difficult job very well. Continue to do your job very well. Let the cast know, by your deportment, that it is business as usual tonight, that you expect everyone to be on time and to acknowledge their calls cheerfully, regardless of the reviews.

Second-performance slump and "down" performances are other situations that you should be aware of.

The second performance of a run has a tendency to be a poor one. The cast, emotionally up for the opening night, experiences a letdown. The sense of urgency that attended opening night is gone. The second performance seems to be less important. Part of the challenge is missing. They know they can do it because they did it last night. And now they know how good they are. Didn't all of their friends tell them? So the cast relaxes, and the performance quality slips.

Sometimes you are simply not aware of the causes of a down performance. You observe the results. The first scene drags, the audience is unresponsive, and during the intermission it's very quiet in the dressing rooms. The cast is listless.

There is no one way to respond to second performance slump or other down performances. You must judge from your past experience how best to handle the situation. Do you give a pep talk to the cast during the intermission? Do you ask them for the old pzazz? Do you individually enlist the help of the old hands in the cast and ask them to pick up the pace? Have you developed the kind of rapport with the cast during rehearsals or on the tour thus far that enables you to give them the football coach's "You guys are letting me down" routine?

If you feel that you can be effective in fighting down performances, then you should try to do so. But you must not feel that it is an obligation. Simply make sure that you do not contribute to poor cast morale.

Finally, there is one other tradition in the theater with regard to morale that pertains to the stage manager. When a black-edged telegram arrives at the theater for a member of the cast, you hold it until after the performance.

Blocking Replacements and Rehearsing Understudies

Traditionally, as the closest assistant to the director, you are presumed to have the duty of blocking in replacements and rehearsing understudies. In reality, you rarely get to perform these duties. Sometimes the director wants to do it her- or himself. Sometimes other staff members step in. Sometimes there is simply no need to block replacements or rehearse understudies.

Of course, you should be ready and able to do it since you have the blocking notations in your prompt script.

Figure 16-1 Costume Tag. Tags with eyelets, and preferably wire ties, are available in stationery stores. When you have a large cast, it is important that you get the right costumes back to the right actor. Tags should be left in the dressing rooms and actors should be informed via company rules when and where they are to turn in costumes for cleaning or repair.

Rehearsing understudies or replacements is unlike original direction in that you should attempt to prepare the understudy or replacement to fit into the already mounted play. In most cases replacements and understudies have the opportunity to observe the cast and take their own blocking notation during a rehearsal or performance.

If working with an Equity company, you should review the rules concerning understudies with the producer. Some contracts require that understudies be present at the theater while other contracts require that the understudies simply be on call.

You should append the names and phone numbers of potential replacements and understudies to your cast list so that you are able to reach them when the need arises. Since you never can tell when you will need a replacement, it is a good idea to keep the résumés submitted during auditions with your notes of evaluation.

Upkeep of Sets and Costumes

On the very mundane level, the stage manager of a long run becomes responsible for the upkeep of the sets and costumes.

Every member of the cast should be encouraged to report to the stage manager any part of a set piece or set that is becoming worn or unserviceable. This might range from a door that is sticking, to a hole in a flat, to a loose cable backstage.

The stage manager should try to stay ahead of the cast by inspecting sets, set pieces, and costumes periodically and carrying out minor repairs before the cast members notice the need.

The stage manager is also responsible for seeing to it that costumes are laundered when necessary and repaired if necessary (see Figure 16-1).

17

Closing and Moving

When the show has completed its run, it is time to strike—tear down the sets and return or store the props and costumes. It is usually desirable to clean the stage area as soon as possible after the last performance.

In union companies the close of the show is announced two weeks in advance by a closing notice signed by the producer and posted on the callboard.

Strike Plan

To accomplish the strike efficiently, you might wish to write out and distribute a strike plan. This plan lets everyone involved know what is expected of them (see Figure 17-1). You should coordinate the plan with all concerned department heads.

Will the actors be involved in the strike or only the crew? In a union theater situation cast members do not participate in the strike. In educational, community, and showcase theater they usually do.

If you are working in the union situation, your strike plan will be very brief. It will advise the union crew of their call. Along with the producer, business manager, or production manager, you will want to evaluate the amount of time required and review the applicable union rules and pay scales to determine whether the strike can most economically be carried out during a night call following the final curtain, or delayed for a future date, even possibly the day that the next set is to be brought in. You will want to evaluate availability of storage space, storage cost, and trucking costs.

It is wise to review the strike plan with the union crew before finalizing it.

THE TORCH-BEARERS

STRIKE NIGHT PARTY*
Sunday, June 14, 1964
11 pm - 1 am

General
1. Strike can be completed in less than 2 hrs. with the cooperation of all.
2. Please bring hammer and/or crowbar plus at least one lge. corrugated paper box suitable for packing.
3. Please change out of costume and make-up and into work clothes as soon as possible.
4. Urging final night guests to leave as soon as possible will expedite.
5. Remove your own personal costumes, make-up, and prop. to your cars as soon as possible to facilitate cleaning of dressing rooms.
6. Stay off the stage unless specifically assigned there because of falling flats and flying hardware, tools, & crew members. (Use side doors to go between dressing rooms and aud.)
7. Upon completion of assigned tasks, see stage manager.

Assignments
Crew: Dick, John, Fred Barry (others):
    A. Strike front rows of chairs in aud.
    B. Bring in stairs, garbage cans, place in aud. near DSL.
    C. Remove sconces, place in one box;all furn. in aud. near DSR.
    D. Remove all portable lighting equip. to storage room, rear aud.
    E. Remove all flats, stage pcs., braces, rigging to aud. near DSL.
    F. When stage strike complete, replace curtains, move furniture to patio.
    G. Dick will be in charge of further refining crew assignments
Doug:
    A. Oversee removal of all items from stage.
    B. Supervise replacement of curtains front and rear.
Len & Hoke, Brett & Ben:
    A. Form 2 teams to work in aud. near DSL area to accept flats, rigging, stage pieces from crew.
    B. Remove hardware & break down to smallest desirable parts.
    C. Store all hardware in box.
    D. Remove all parts to patio & store as directed.
    E. Bring screw driver and/or pliers;work gloves desirable to avoid splinters.
Karl:
    A. Turn on patio lights.
    B. Organize patio area for quick future removal of all materials.
    C. Show Len, Hoke, Brett, Ben where & how to store flats & materials.
    D. When all materials stored, instruct crew to bring out furniture and supervise placement.
Jeanne, Barbara, Margaret, Evelyn, Marlene, Beatriz:
    A. Clean Dressing rooms. B. Store costumes to be ret.

Harvey and Randy: *see me for prop forms.*
    A. Pack all props in boxes.
    B. List contents of box on outside.
    C. Insure with completed forms that we will know what goes where & to whom on Tuesday, June 16th when furniture & props will be returned.

If you anticipate any strike night problems please see me.
Thank you all in advance for the swift, pleasant strike.

Figure 17-1 Strike Plan Handout

In a non-union situation it is usually best to accomplish the strike as soon after the final curtain as possible. Tools and transportation should be well planned so that your cast, staff, and crew will have everything on hand that they need to accomplish the strike. Be sure that you have enough bags and boxes to get all of the props and costumes properly packed and out of the theater, and enough back seats, trucks, and trunk space to accommodate all of the set pieces, scenery, props, and costumes. Cleaning implements should be in plentiful supply, too, so that the theater may be left clean for the next production.

Most cast members actually enjoy the strike if they know what is expected of them. There is usually a letdown that follows the closing performance, which is buffered when the cast members continue working together for the brief period of the strike. There is a sense of urgency, team play, and accomplishment present at the strike which makes it quite enjoyable.

During the strike don't tie yourself down with repetitive manual tasks. You should be free to observe and supervise. You should also delegate supervising authority to others, particularly when there is more than one area. Can an actor be put in charge of the shop area while you are on stage? Can one supervise an even smaller area, like a loading dock? Actors who suddenly remember long-lost hernias and war wounds at the mention of the strike have been known to do vast amounts of work when named supervisor.

You must be especially aware of safety problems during the strike, and take time to caution everyone about the most basic of potential dangers: watch where you step; don't step on nails and tools; don't fall into the pit; don't use power tools that you have not operated before until you have been instructed in their use; look above for falling scenery and tools.

Start the strike with a safety lecture and caution workers when you see dangerous practices.

The strike may well be the last chore that cast members see you do. Try to make a good final impression by carrying out the strike with the same calm and meticulous organization with which you managed the rest of the production.

Changeover Schedule

In cases where the theater will not have a dark night between two consecutive productions, it is necessary to prepare a changeover schedule. This schedule is actually a combination of strike plan, set-up plan, and rehearsal schedule which aids in smoothing out the transition from one production to another. It tells who has use of the stage space during the critical hours of transition. It coordinates the personnel of the out-

Friday	**July 15**	8 am to noon	electrics
		1-5 pm	carpentry props electrics
Saturday	**July 16**	open	
Sunday	**July 17**	1-6 pm	sound
		8 pm	half hour
		8:30	curtain Mathis show
		end performance	begin strike
Monday	**July 18**	12:00-3 am	strike/set
		3-6 am	full orchestra dress rehearsal
		6 am to 12 noon	as needed
		1-6 pm	technical cleanup (no performers)
		8 pm	half hour
		8:30	curtain TIJUANA BRASS

Figure 17-2   Changeover Schedule between Two Productions

going production, the incoming production, and the house staff (see Figure 17-2).

Before posting it, you should coordinate the schedule with the producer, business manager, production manager, and staffs of the incoming and outgoing productions.

During the changeover you must be on hand to supervise the on-the-spot adjustments that become necessary.

Examples:

When construction takes longer than anticipated, and it frequently does, you must keep the master carpenter from coming to blows with the choreographer of the incoming show who expected those all-important ramps to be in place at the beginning of the rehearsal period and not left for last.

You must be forearmed with the authority to make decisions as to whether or not ten members of a union will be paid for an additional four-hour call because their services are required for fifteen additional minutes (when the union requires a four-hour minimum pay period).

Discuss contingencies with the producer. Find out what authority you have to commit her or his money.

Send all personnel concerned a copy of the changeover schedule and post copies on the callboard, in the shop, and in the crew lounge area.

Moving the Show

All moves are alike and all moves are different. They require coordination of staff, crew, and cast in moving the cast, crew, and equipment.

A. You are moving your production from one theater to another. Your lease ran out but your advance sales are great so you have to find another house.
B. You tried out in Azusa and now you're opening in West Covina.
C. You are on a national tour, either via train and/or plane to major cities, or by truck and bus to the hinterlands.
D. Your children's play is traveling to all of the elementary school auditoriums in town.
E. Your industrial show will tour thirty-eight cities in two and a half months.

In any of these situations, here are some of the steps you will want to take:

A. Prepare and distribute an itinerary.
B. Caution the cast/crew on travel deportment.
C. "Mother-hen" the cast on the road.
D. Supervise the load-in, set-up, strike, and load-out.
E. Pave the way with letters to business agents, host theater owners, etc.

Itineraries

The first thing you need is an itinerary, whether you are moving across the street or across the nation (see Figures 17–3 and 17–4). What day are you making the move? What time? What is your destination? What's the new address (with zip code)? What's the new phone number (with area code)? What is the rehearsal and performance schedule during the period?

Planning the itinerary is not necessarily your responsibility, but you should contribute. Think through the moves in advance. Has enough time been allotted for set-ups? Try to anticipate problems. Have all of

LOST SHEEP PRODUCTIONS, INC.
12308 BRACKLAND AVE.
LOS ANGELES, CALIFORNIA 90033

ITENERARY - SPRING TOUR

AIR TRANSPORTATION		HOTELS
March 16	leave Los Angeles East. 72/4 PM arrive Miami 9 PM	Everglades Hotel 304 Biscayne St. Miami, Fla. 33101 FR 9 5461
March 19	leave Miami United 395/2:55 PM arrive Jacksonville 3:57 PM	Robert Meyer Hotel 514 Main St. Jacksonville, Fla. 33705 EL 5 4411
March 21	Leave Jacksonville TransFl. 151/1 PM; arrive Tampa 2:17 PM	Manger Motor Inn 200 Ashley Drive Tampa, Fla. 33164 813 223 2456
March 24	Leave Tampa National 462/12 PM arrive Pensacola 1:15 PM	Town House 16 West Cervantes St. Pensacola, Fla. 33225 904 438 4511
March 26	leave Pensacola Eastern 865/ 3:15 PM; arrive Birmingham 4:33 PM	Parliament House 420 18th Street Birmingham, Ala. 35445 205 323 7211
March 28	Leave Birmingham So. Air 285/ 8 AM; arrive Memphis 9:30 AM	Holiday Inn 200 W. Georgia Ave. Memphis, Tenn. 38103 901 525 0102
March 30	leave Memphis United 589/ 10:45 AM; arrive Chattanooga 12:28 PM	Towne House 831 George Ave. Chattanooga, Tenn. 37401 615 266 1255
April 1	leave Chattanooga Delta 736/ 8:30 AM; arrive Charlotte 10:45 AM	Manger Motor Inn 1187 Tenth St. Charlotte, N.C. 28202 704 332 3121
April 3	leave Charlotte Delta 710/2:40 PM; arrive Atlanta 3:33 PM	Marriott Hotel 47 Cain Street Atlantic, Ga. 30303 404 688 6500
April 6	leave Atlanta United 431/2:55 PM; arrive Cleveland 4:30 PM	Pick Carter Hotel 407 E. 9th Street Cleveland, Ohio 44107 216 771 7200
April 9	leave Cleveland American 257/ 11:25 AM; arrive Los Angeles 3:20 PM	

Figure 17-3 Itinerary for a Touring Company

the union rules been considered (i.e., union casts may not travel on their day off)?

It is your responsibility to make sure that every member of the cast and crew has a copy of the itinerary—perhaps two or three for family

BURT BACHARACH				NOVEMBER 1970		ITINERARY		
DATE	LEAVE	ARRIVE	HOTEL	PLACE OF ENGAGE- MENT OR REHEARSAL	TIME CONCERT	TIME RHRSL.	CALL NEXT DAY	NOTES
THUR. NOV 19 1970	NO GROUP TRAVEL		NONE	ATM RECORDS 1416 N. LABREA LOS ANGLEOS STAGE # 1-555-2711	NONE	7 P.M.	NONE	PARK IN BACK LOT
FRI. NOV 20 1970	NO GROUP TRAVEL		NONE SOUND PSL HOLIDAY IN HYLAND ST. 555-3714	LONGBEACH ARENA 270 E. LAKESIDE LONG BEACH CALIF.	8:30 PM	4 PM	NONE	BE AT AIRPORT ½ HR. BEFORE DEPARTURE
SAT. NOV 21 1970	PERSONNEL AUTO TO TERMINAL #116 (L.A)	ARRIVE 1:30 PM SALT LAKE BUS & LIMO	HILTON 200 W. SIXTH SALT LK.	SPECIAL EVENTS CTR. UNIV. OF UTAH 619-555-3719 SALT LAKE CITY	8:00 PM	5 PM	11/22 9 AM	NOON CKOUT. TRVL. W/SAL MONTE TO HOUSTON 11/22
SUN. NOV 22 1970	SLT. LAKE Wal 5 11:00 LAS VAGAS NAT 2 2:30	L. VAGAS 11:00 HOUSTON 6:50	check RIVIERA HOTEL THEN TO HOUSTON & SAME HOTEL		NONE	NONE	NONE	MERCER MC CUNE
SUN NOV 22 1970	SLT. LAKE WEST. A.L. 410 @ 1:31	DENVER 2:58	SHERATON 777 PARK 555-7010	NOTE: Wait in coffee SHOP FOR MERCER & MC CUNE & CAR	NONE	NONE	NONE	PUNCH BURNS

Figure 17-4   Itinerary for a Touring Musical Show

and friends who will wish to write or phone while the show is on the road.

Touring Agreement

You will want to caution the cast and crew about deportment expected on the road (see Figure 17-5). You are expected to be a model for the rest of the company. You must advise the company members if things get out of hand. In the absence of a regular company manager on the road you may be expected to do some "mother-henning." You should tactfully remind cast members that their health, as it affects their performances, is the first concern of the management, and it is for that reason that you are cautioning them to watch their health.

The most common occurrence for touring companies is simply making too much whoopee once out of town, resulting in reduced energy levels that bring down the quality of performances. You can't always prevent such things, but you can caution. If tactful influence fails and an actor's performance suffers as a result of his or her offstage activities, you must inform the producer or the management.

The packing, padding, and care of sets, props, costumes, and technical equipment concern every department head. You coordinate with them in planning every move. You are the overseer of the move.

It is particularly important that set diagrams be accurate and that all flats be marked with accurate butting guides so that crews who have never seen the assembled set can put it together with ease.

TO: LOST SHEEP PRODUCTIONS, INC.
     12308 Brackland Ave.
     Los Angeles, California 90033

Gentlemen

It is my understanding that all personnel employed by,
and who will travel with, the Lost Sheep road company
must agree to the following:

That while we are in the employ of Lost Sheep Productions, Inc., we will conduct ourselves in a manner that
will not bring any adverse criticism to Lost Sheep
Productions or its clients.

That our manner of dress will be businesslike, neat and
in good taste, particularly when traveling.

That we will travel with the group as assigned and ask
for no changes or deviations from travel schedules and
itineraries. All travel departures are final and no
changes can be made except by Lost Sheep Productions or
representatives who have been instructed that the only
change that can be made is a change for the entire group.
The reason for this is that changes affect price and
budget and will not be allowed.

It is our understanding that we are on a job and a
business trip and not on a paid vacation. The show and
any rehearsals are to take first consideration in any
planning of extracurricular activities.

That when technical rehearsals are called, all personnel
involved are expected to put the same effort into them
as into the performances.

That all personnel will be prompt at any and all calls
for fittings, rehearsals or performances as called by
the stage manager.

                    AGREED TO:_____
                                  (name)

                        DATE:_____

Figure 17-5   Touring Agreement for Cast and Staff

For the stage manager who travels and needs to focus a show quickly and
efficiently, I have found that it is most helpful to grid the stage by dividing
it into squares with numbers across the foots and up the center line. That
way positions and hot spots can be identified and recreated with great
precision. The only additional information needed is shutter information
and gel color.

Leonard Auerbach
Associate Professor, Department of Theatre Arts
State University of New York at Stony Brook

On arrival at a new location you first go to the theater. You inspect
the premises to insure that your set-up plans are workable (see Chapter
Five, "Information Packets"). You assign dressing rooms and make sure
that they are in serviceable condition. You supervise the set-up and
check your personal equipment. You greet the new crew members who
will run the show and review the running order, lighting sheet, sound
plot, and shift plot chart with them (see Chapter Twelve).

```
              LOST SHEEP PRODUCTIONS, INC.
              12308 BRACKLAND AVE.
              LOS ANGELES, CALIFORNIA 90033


Mr. Victor M. Otorino
General Manager
The Chechonovitz Civic Light Opera
2020 Himmelfarb Drive
Chechonovitz, California

Dear Mr. Otorino,

On November 18, 1970, we will be setting up the Lost Sheep
production of THE MAGNIFICENT EIGHT.  Our truck should
arrive on Thursday at 11 AM.

We would appreciate it if you would take the necessary
measures to clear any alley or passageway to allow our
truck access to your loading dock at that time.  Because of
a very tight schedule, it is essential that our truck be
allowed to unload immediately upon arrival and if elevators
are involved, that a man be placed on duty on a freight
elevator for our use at the time above until we have
finished carrying in our equipment.

Our stage manager will be Mr. Lawrence Stern.  Anything
he asks of you will be in the name of Lost Sheep Produc-
tions and your cooperation will be appreciated.

We would like your house electrician, when we unload, to
answer any questions of our technical crew.  Mr. Chris
Papadapoulos will be our carpenter.  We will be carrying
all of our own stage draperies, lights, PA system and
projection equipment.

We will be coming in on a yellow card and we will be
employing union stagehands.  Our carpenter will be in
touch with your local business agent concerning calls
for local men to assist us.

We will need a grand piano, tuned to 440 pitch, piano
bench and a 12' X 12' rug for the musicians at stage right.

Thank you for your cooperation.  We look forward to
working with you in your facility.

                    Sincerely

                    Sid Rosenwald
                    SID ROSENWALD
                    Executive Producer
```

Figure 17-6 Advance Letter to Host Theater Manager

Before leaving the theater, you post your local address and phone number on the callboard so that it is available in an emergency for the management of the theater and the local crew members.

You should then check with the cast to insure that their hotel accommodations are satisfactory.

Advance Letters

In very large companies there are sometimes advance people who go to a new location ahead of the company to prepare for their arrival. Sometimes an assistant stage manager may be dispatched in advance. But in many cases the problems of a traveling company can be anticipated and smoothed out via letter (see Figure 17-6 and Chapter Five, "Information Packets," and also Figure 5-6). Letters requesting specific support (to hotels for accommodations, to business agents of unions for local personnel, to host theater owners, etc.) are usually sent out over the signature of the producer or company management. You can contribute to these letters by letting management know what problems you anticipate or encounter, e.g., difficulty of hotels cashing checks for cast members on paydays, unavailability of an elevator during a load-in, etc.

Calling a special staff meeting to brainstorm a move or series of moves can save time and money on the road.

18

Organizing Information

We are in the midst of an information explosion. The availability of books, magazines, newspapers, radio and TV broadcasts, microfilm, Xerox copies, and computer printouts is almost overwhelming. As the amount of information available to every stage manager increases, she or he must decide on how to organize it so that she or he can make use of it.

Local Theater

You might want to start your personal acquisition of theater information by sending a postcard to every live theater in town asking to be placed on their mailing lists. Write to commercial, educational, showcase, community, and children's theaters. You will soon receive information in the mail about who's doing what, and you will receive more complete and accurate information than you can find in your newspaper.

Go to the theater as often as you can. Make notes in your programs as to outstanding acting and technical credits. Save your programs.

Newspapers and Magazines

Read local newspapers and national magazines regularly. Making a scrapbook of theater information is the easiest way of keeping abreast of live theater (see Figure 18-1).

Clip local reviews of plays. Note the technical credits. You may soon discover, for instance, that just a handful of people are getting all of the

(*Varsity, the Stage Daily,*
May, 1969)

LEGIT TECH MEN CONVENE IN L.A.

The United Institute for Theat
Technology will hold its ninth
conference at the Los Angtoday through Thursd
287 professionals
nected with
tending.

Th
Tota.
will b
and le.
week.
Between
and the Le.
panel chaired
fessor from N
tomorrow morn.

The next sessnoon, is "New Tecomputers in theatrbe discussed. Wedne.
tour the Music Cent.
"Building Codes and S.
sion at Ahmanson Theatnoon session will be "Pro,
ery," conducted at L.A. Ci
"Electronics in the The.
"Techniques of the Thrust Sta
be subjects of the final m
Thursday at the Hilton.

(*Varsity, the Stage Daily,*
December, 1969)

BROADWAY OPENINGS

Last of the Red Hot Lovers

New York, December 29—Neil
Simon does it again in this new
comedy, which opened last
night at the O'Neill Theater to a

(The Los Angeles *Bugle,*
January, 1970)

STAGE NEWS

Top Billing for Computer in "Tommy"

If you want information about
the production of the rock opra "Tommy," now playing at
 Roxy Theater as directed by
 Rosen and starring Teddy
 in the title role, then go
 the stage manager.
 's that? The stage manof 'ell, why not? Stage
the are in a pretty good
know what's going
 say, directors are
etter one—except
here some very
's recording the
is 'rector would
 's stage man
?.
nnel comger Dan
ammed
 . All
 ush-
 ide
?-

(Los Angeles *Messenger,*
February, 1969)

NEW THEATER GROUP IN EAST CUCAMONGA

Northeast Cucamonga—A new community theatrical group is forming
here to bring back the flavor of the
straw hat summer theater circuit to
this bustling area, long destitute of the
its former theatrical ornament. The
Greater Cucamonga Thespians'
ater Playhouse and Operatic Pavilion.
now dark.

The Cucamonga Caperers, a group
composed of theatrical people formerly active in Anaheim and Azusa,
under the leadership of Fred Freedley,
stage director, George Geomble, scenic designer, Louis Lumber, music director, and Archie Arkwright, legal
and business adviser. The non-profit
organization will provide talented locals with an outlet for their creative
energies, and visiting stage favorites
a chance to show their stuff to
with a summer audience.

Four plays are yet to be selected
as kickoff items to get the group moving, the first due to open in late May
or early June of this year.
ed by
d true mar
d technical art
acy of handling is
 you don't upstage your
ors. And we have just the
man to do the delicate handling:
our audio-visual programmer-
director, Jim McKie.

Figure 18-1   Likely Items for a Manager's Scrapbook

good lighting reviews. Even if you have never worked with these people, you will start to know who they are.

You will also be able to determine trends. What type of plays are being done by the many community theaters in your area? What types of plays are the educational theaters doing? The showcase theaters? The commercial theaters? The experimental theaters? By reading nationally published reviews of Broadway and off-Broadway openings, you can learn to anticipate which of these plays will later be done by certain local theaters.

Which local producers do consistently good work? By judging the type of plays they do and the quality of their work, which producers would you prefer to work for or learn more from? The largest, most plush plant in town may not be doing the kind of work with which you would want to associate yourself. By going to the theater and reading reviews, you can discover the theaters you would most like to be your own.

Also, clip articles on all aspects of production and reviews of new books about theater.

A subscription to one or more of the trade papers might provide you with good current information.

Variety
154 West 46th Street
New York, NY 10036
(212) 869-5700

Daily Variety
1400 N. Cahuenga Blvd.
Hollywood, CA 90028
(213) 469-1141

Hollywood Reporter
6715 W. Sunset Blvd.
Hollywood, CA 90028
(213) 464-7411

Drama-Logue Casting News
1456 Gordon
Los Angeles, CA 90028
(213) 464-5079

Drama
British Theatre Association
9 Fitzroy Square
London WIP 6AE England
01–387–2666

The Drama Review
(Tulane Drama Review)
MIT Press
NY University
Tisch School
28 Carleton Street
Cambridge, MA 02142
(617) 253-2889

Dramatics
International Thespian Society
3368 Central Parkway
Cincinnati, OH 45225
(513) 559-1996

Plays
120 Boylston Street
Boston, MA 02116
(617) 423-3157

Plays and Players
Brevet Publishing (UK) Ltd.
43B Gloucester Road
Croydon CRO 2DH England
01-689-4109

Theater
P.O. Box 2046
Yale Station
New Haven, CT 06520
(203) 436-1417

Theatre Crafts
P.O. Box 630
Holmes, PA 19043-0630

In addition to those listed above, *The Standard Periodical Directory* [Oxbridge Communications, 150 Fifth Ave., NYC 10011, (212) 741-0231] lists 160 separate entries of publications devoted to theater.

Guides to Goods and Services

A fast reference that you will want to index into your prompt script is the theatrical supply listings from the yellow pages of your local phone directory. You might enclose the listings in a mylar sheet protector for convenience.

Where can you get lighting supplies in a hurry? Where can you send someone to repair a damaged wig? Who has Max Factor pancake makeup in 7A on hand? Get the answers fast. Use your yellow pages.

How many times have you driven to a supply house only to find on arrival that they don't have what you need in stock? Call ahead.

Simon's Directory of Theatrical Materials Services Information is a national directory of theater information and should be in every stage manager's library. Unfortunately it has not been published since December 1975. A sixth edition is planned by Package Publicity Service, Inc., 27 West 24th Street New York City 10010, (212) 354–1840. In the meantime, you might want to look at *The Contact Book* [171 West 54th Street, New York City 10019, (212) 757–7979], which also lists many theatrical goods and services. In England, check *Contacts* [42–43 Cranbourn Street, London WC2H 7AP, 01–437–7631].

Collect catalogues from theatrical supply manufacturers throughout the country. You can learn a lot by studying catalogues. Here is a very small starter selection of manufacturers and suppliers:

Altman Stage Lighting
47 Alexander Street
Yonkers, NY 10701
(914) 476-7987
(212) 569-7777

Bash Theatrical Lighting, Inc.
3401 Dell Ave.
North Bergen, NJ 07047
(201) 863-3300
(212)279-9265

Colortran
1015 Chestnut Street
Burbank, CA 91506
(818) 843-1200

Eastern Costume Co.
510 N. Elm Street
Greensboro, NC 27401
(919) 379-1026

Electro Controls
2975 South 330 West
Salt Lake City, UT 84115–9860
(800) 453-7435

Kliegl Bros.
32–32 48th Street
Long Island City, NY 11101
(718) 786-7474

Olesen
1535 Ivar Avenue
Hollywood, CA 90028
(213) 461-4631

Package Publicity Service, Inc.
27 West 24th Street
New York City 10010
(212) 255-2872

Phoebus Manufacturing
2800 Third Street
San Francisco, CA 94107
(415) 550-1177

Rosco
36 Bush Ave.
Port Chester, NY 10573
(914) 937-1300

Strand Lighting
18111 South Santa Fe Ave.
P.O. Box 9004
Rancho Dominguez, CA 90224
(213) 637-7500

See *Simon's Directory* or *The Contact Book* for further selections.

Studying a few catalogues will help to make you aware of the industry that is ready to back up the theater. It will help you keep abreast of new products. What do you know about quartz lights? Black light? Foam scenery? Solid-state communications equipment?

You will want to send for samples, swatches, and gel books. Services and demonstrations are sometimes available from manufacturers who wish to promote their products. Can you get lighting equipment sales representatives to come out to your theater to help you analyze the problem of augmenting your lighting equipment for a particularly heavy show? Can he help you with the know-how to create special effects?

Before you buy, compare products carefully. Not all of the factors are always stated in brochures about the product. You will want to evaluate cost, durability, repair costs, availability of spare parts, capability of the product, ease of cleaning, ease of repairing or replacing worn parts, proximity to a repair facility, ease in use, unique advantages, and peculiar disadvantages.

Contact File

Use 3 × 5″ or 4 × 6″ note cards to assemble information: names, addresses, and phone numbers of people who may be helpful to you in your theater work (see Figure 18-2). You will want to keep cards for actors, producers, directors, designers, technicians, costume designers, suppliers of equipment, sources of props, unions, and others. You will want to alphabetize your cards and you might even want to use some sort of code—various color cards or flags—to help you pull information quickly.

A durable metal or wooden box to keep the cards in is a must.

You may be able to help in casting by keeping tabs on the various fine actors that you discover in plays that you see. Write a card for each actor whose work impresses you. Get his or her address and phone number. Get his or her agent's name and number, too, if he or she has one. Go out of your way to see him or her in the next play that he or she does.

Books

You should have available a few books on theater that can recharge your intellectual batteries, the type of book that you can read more than once and still find interesting and helpful. These might be considered your "clothesline" books, giving you the basic information that will allow you to assimilate other information, pinning it up on the "clothesline" in your mind.

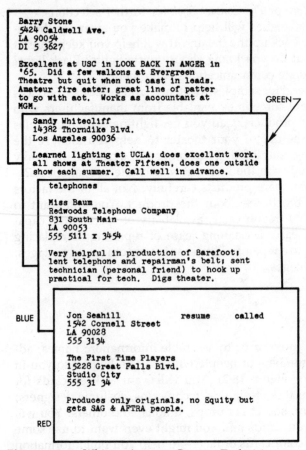

Figure 18-2 White, Actors; Green, Technicians;
Blue, Supplies; Red, Producers

What seven books would you take with you to another planet if you expected to establish a live theater there (see Figure 18-3)?

Perhaps these seven "other planet" books would be a good start for your own personal library. It is better to know seven books well than to own a huge collection of books with uncut pages.

Extensive bibliographies for every theater arts subject may be found in your local library.

In addition, if you are interested in a program of directed reading, many graduate schools of theater arts publish graduate reading lists. Contact the university nearest you.

Or you may wish to add your name to the mailing lists of the several publishers who specialize in books on theater arts.

"What Seven Books Would I Take to Another Planet if I Expected to
Establish a Live Theater There?"
(a small, prejudiced, but useful selection)

ACTING

Actors on Acting
Cole, Toby and Helen Krich Chinoy
Crown, New York, rev. ed., 1980

DIRECTING

Directors on Directing
Cole, Toby and Helen Krich Chinoy
Bobbs-Merrill, Indianapolis 1963

MAKEUP/COSTUMING

Stage Makeup
Corson, Richard
Prentice-Hall, 6th ed., 1981

Costume in the Theatre
Laver, James
Hill and Wang, New York 1964

SCENE DESIGN/SET CONSTRUCTION/LIGHTING

Scene Design and Stage Lighting
Parker, W. Oren and Harvey K. Smith
Holt, Rinehart & Winston, 4th ed., 1979

HISTORY

History of the Theater
Brockett, Oscar G.
Allyn and Bacon, 4th ed., 1981

PLAYWRITING

Playwriting: How to Write for the Theater
Bernard Grebanier
Barnes & Noble, div. of Harper & Row, New York 1979

Figure 18-3   Seven Titles to Start a Theater Library

Allyn and Bacon, Inc.
Longwood Division
7 Wells Ave.
Newton, Mass. 02159

AMS Press, Inc.
56 East 13th Street
New York City 10003

Cornell University Press
124 Roberts Place
Ithaca, New York 14851

Crown Publishers, Inc.
1 Park Ave
New York, N.Y. 10016

The Fireside Theater
501 Franklin Ave.
Garden City, New York 11530

Burt Franklin, Publisher
235 East 44th Street
New York City 10017

Indiana University Press
10th and Morton Streets
Bloomington, Indiana 47401

University of Miami Press
Drawer 9088
Coral Gables, Florida 33124

University of Washington Press
Box C-50096
Seattle, Washington 98145

Annotated Bibliography of New
Publications in the Performing
   Arts
The Drama Book Shop
723 Seventh Ave.
New York City 10019

Postcards sent to the publishers above will bring you the latest information about new books on theater as well as lists and mail order prices of hardcover and paperback editions of interest to you.

Police, Fire, and Municipal Regulations

You should be aware that there are police regulations, fire laws, and municipal codes that may control the operations of all theaters, if and when applied (see Figure 18-4).

These regulations vary with each city, and within cities, depending on the size of the theater. They are generally written in the form of ordinances and sections of the city code. The ordinances and codes are available in the offices of city administrators concerned, and in public libraries. Unfortunately, not all regulations pertaining to live theater are neatly grouped together. They may be found under such diverse headings as "Rules Governing Café Entertainment and Shows," "Assemblage Occupancies," "Safety to Life Requirements," and others.

Experts are usually available to assist theater owners and producers who may call to request inspections of their facilities, or submit plans for approval. The stage manager does not normally do this.

Occasionally, whether requested or not, fire marshals inspect theaters just prior to the opening of new productions to check fireproofing, exits, smoking signs, and other public safety features. Theaters have

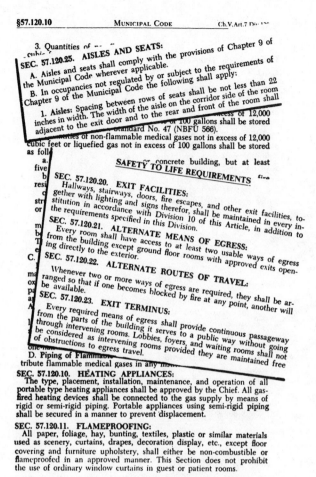

3. Quantities of ~~ ~~
SEC. 57.120.25. AISLES AND SEATS:
A. Aisles and seats shall comply with the provisions of Chapter 9 of the Municipal Code wherever applicable.
B. In occupancies not regulated by or subject to the requirements of Chapter 9 of the Municipal Code the following shall apply:
1. Aisles: Spacing between rows of seats shall be not less than 22 inches in width. The width of the aisle on the corridor side of the room adjacent to the exit door and to the rear and front of the room shall

~~... ess of 12,000~~ ~~~~ ~~100 gallons shall be stored
~~standard No. 47 (NBFU 566).
~~...~~s of non-flammable medical gases not in excess of 12,000
cubic feet or liquefied gas not in excess of 100 gallons shall be stored
as foll

a.
five
b
resi
c
str
or

SAFETY TO LIFE REQUIREMENTS

SEC. 57.120.20.   EXIT FACILITIES:
Hallways, stairways, doors, fire escapes, and other exit facilities, together with lighting and signs therefor, shall be maintained in every institution in accordance with Division 10 of this Article, in addition to the requirements specified in this Division.
SEC. 57.120.21.   ALTERNATE MEANS OF EGRESS:
Every room shall have access to at least two usable ways of egress from the building except ground floor rooms with approved exits opening directly to the exterior.
SEC. 57.120.22.   ALTERNATE ROUTES OF TRAVEL:
Whenever two or more ways of egress are required, they shall be arranged so that if one becomes blocked by fire at any point, another will be available.
SEC. 57.120.23.   EXIT TERMINUS:
Every required means of egress shall provide continuous passageway from the parts of the building it serves to a public way without going through intervening rooms. Lobbies, foyers, and waiting rooms shall not be considered as intervening rooms provided they are maintained free of obstructions to egress travel.
D. Piping of Flamm~~...~~
tribute flammable medical gases in any ~~...~~

SEC. 57.120.10.   HEATING APPLIANCES:
The type, placement, installation, maintenance, and operation of all portable type heating appliances shall be approved by the Chief. All gas-fired heating devices shall be connected to the gas supply by means of rigid or semi-rigid piping. Portable appliances using semi-rigid piping shall be secured in a manner to prevent displacement.

SEC. 57.120.11.   FLAMEPROOFING:
All paper, foliage, hay, bunting, textiles, plastic or similar materials used as scenery, curtains, drapes, decoration display, etc., except floor covering and furniture upholstery, shall either be non-combustible or flameproofed in an approved manner. This Section does not prohibit the use of ordinary window curtains in guest or patient rooms.

Figure 18-4 Typical Theater Safety Regulations

been closed and performances postponed as a result of such inspections (see Figure 18-5).

You should review public safety requirements with the staff of your theater. The entire staff should take the time to review plans for emergencies.

Frequently in small theaters, scene designers and technical directors build into the audience, covering exit lights and no-smoking signs, and blocking exit aisles with scenery. You should prevent this by calling their attention to the rules.

If you are involved in opening a show in a building that has been newly converted into a theater, you should ask the producer or management if local regulations have been checked. The number of people allowed in the building, the number of off-street parking spaces necessary, and even the amount of lavatory space, are all the subjects of city regulations.

(Los Angeles *Bugle*, July, 1969)

STAGE NEWS TODAY

*

The Awareness Theater, recently closed by the fire marshall, has relocated temporarily at the Psychiatry Center Auditorium at the UCLA Medical Center where Bella Harpman is directing two one-acts by Harry Rose on Friday and Sunday nights. The plays are "Big Sol" about an aging convict who fantasizes about the blonde he murdered so effectively that he has his cell seeing things, and also "Time Charlie" which deal an opium addict who d peddling dope on hors

Mrs. Harpman say versity will reinstate ness Theater, start other members Students' Guild o while the ther duction on r cal Center ovation theater

(Los Angeles *Messenger*, February, 1969)

USC LIVING THEATER CALLED OFF

Performances of the Living Theater Saturday night and tonight were canceled at USC following apparent violations of fire safety regulations.

Police called a tactical alert on the campus Friday evening after learning that fire safety laws had been violated and that too many ersons were occupying the ized stage at once in regulations.

executive director, university rela-d that the per-had been can-cause the theater, staff were "inade-to assure that the ssary compliance with safety codes and audi-nce safety would be carried out in accordance with municipal regulations."

Refund information is available by telephone at the following numbers: 555-7834, 555-6093, 555-8427.

(Varsity, the Stage Daily, February, 1969)

FIRE DEPT HALTS SHOW OF LIVING THEATER

Performances of the Living Theater at USC were cancelled this weekend after fire safety code violations were alleged by the marshalls. A tactical alert was called by police Friday after notification that fire safety codes were apparently being ignored and that too many people were being allowed on stage. Refunds were made available.

Figure 18-5 A Theater in Violation of Safety Laws Can Be Closed Down

If you are working in an Equity company and feel that the producer is failing to comply with regulations, thus endangering public safety, and you have discussed it with him, then take the issue to your union and let the union take up the issue with the producer.

If you are in a non-union theater situation and can't convince your management or producer to make the theater safe, quit first. Then call for fire, police, and building code inspections as a concerned citizen.

People die in theaters as the result of negligence—failure to know and obey the law. As a stage manager, the lives of your cast, crew, and audience may depend on your knowledge and application of the law.

Getting to Know the Unions

"You can't join Equity until you have a job in an Equity company, and you can't get a job in an Equity company until you are a member of

Equity." This seeming paradox is often quoted but quite misleading. As soon as you can convince an Equity producer or director that you should be his or her stage manager, the doors of the union will open to you. Equity is not one of the closed unions where nepotism reigns or where "blood is thicker than talent."

If it is your intent to become an Equity stage manager, don't wait for an Equity job to get acquainted with the union. Try to understand the benefits and disadvantages of union membership. Go out of your way to meet a union stage manager. Engage her or him in conversation about her or his work and union. If you live in a city with an Equity office (N.Y.C., L.A., S.F., Toronto), visit it and get to know the people in the office. The union office is not a placement service, but the union staff is in a good position to know what producers are anticipating productions or casting. Bulletin boards in the union offices frequently display information useful to stage managers. Sometimes the union has available handouts, such as lists of union-approved theaters where you might apply for work.

If you accept a job as a stage manager with an Equity company, you must join the union. Thereafter you may never legally work in a non-Equity company without first getting a waiver from Equity.

An Equity card is what one should strive towards, not start with. We recommend that stage managers (and actors) get as much experience as they can before accepting an Equity contract. An AEA card does not guarantee you work. This is attested to by the high unemployment of both actors and stage managers in our union. There are from one to three stage managers in any given production, as compared to whatever the number in the cast. So jobs are even harder for a stage manager than an actor. Stage managers limit their experience possibilities by getting their Equity card because they cannot work non-Equity once they join the union. Experience is the only way for a stage manager to perfect his/her craft. I recommend that a stage manager get as much experience as possible before accepting a job as an Equity stage manager. I cannot stress enough that experience is a most important aspect of a stage manager's future potential.

Martha R. Jacobs
Stage Manager
New York City

Martha is currently working in an administrative position in live theatre in New York City. Her work as a stage manager led to her current position.

Once in a union position, you may quickly find it necessary to deal with members of other unions, depending on the size of your theater staff:

Screen Actors Guild (SAG)
American Federation of Television and Radio Artists (AFTRA)
American Federation of Musicians
American Guild of Variety Artists (AGVA)
International Alliance of Theatrical Stage Employees (IATSE)
Association of Theatrical Press Agents and Managers (ATPAM)
Theatrical Wardrobe Attendants
Treasurers and Ticket Sellers Union
Musicians Union
Teamsters

As closely related unions for performers, SAG, AFTRA, and AGVA have reciprocal agreements as to when and how their members may perform in jurisdictions of the other unions. The producer normally handles arrangements with the unions and insures that all members of his cast are members of Equity, or have been cleared by Equity to work in the production.

Union composition of a staff varies from theater to theater, depending on size and on the arrangements that producers have made with union locals. In a small union house all of the cast may be Equity and there may be only one non-Equity union member, an IATSE master electrician.

In another larger house there may be three IATSE members (carpenter, lights, props); two Theatrical Wardrobe Attendants members; five Treasurers and Ticket Sellers members in the box office; two members of ATPAM (publicist and house manager); and five musicians from the AFM (who are paid to play bridge in the wings during a play in which there is no music).

In a huge outdoor theater Teamster truckers may refuse to leave their trucks and enter the stage area to pick up scenery, insisting that the scenery be loaded out by IATSE stagehands and handed to them on their truck, while IATSE stagehands will refuse to get on a truck, insisting that Teamsters must be present to stack the scenery.

In still another tent theater four well-paid IATSE crew members may work right alongside six non-union "apprentices" who are not paid at all; both union and non-union crew members do the same work, but at the end of the union work call period, the union men go home while the non-paid "apprentices" continue to work to the end of the rehearsal period.

The stage manager need never feel that he or she must contest the inequities of union regulations. This is a responsibility of management or the producer.

The stage manager should do his or her best to understand the rules that apply to other union members with whom he or she must work: hours, minimum calls, overtime rules, and working restrictions and jurisdictions.

165 WEST 46th STREET
New York, N. Y. 10036

DEFINITION OF THE DUTIES AND OBLIGATIONS OF A STAGE MANAGER

A Stage Manager under Actors' Equity Contract is, or shall be obligated to perform at least the following duties for the Production to which he is engaged, and by performing them is hereby defined as the Stage Manager:

1. He shall be responsible for the calling of all rehearsals, whether before or after opening.

2. He shall assemble and maintain the Prompt Book, which is defined as the accurate playing text and stage business, together with such cue sheets, plots, daily records, etc. as are necessary for the actual technical and artistic operation of the production.

3. He shall work with the Director and the heads of all other departments, during rehearsal and after opening, schedule rehearsal and outside calls in accordance with Equity's regulations.

4. Assume active responsibility for the form and discipline of rehearsal and performance, and be the executive instrument in the technical running of <u>each</u> performance.

5. Maintain the artistic intentions of the Director and the Producer after opening, to the best of his ability, including calling correctional rehearsals of the company when necessary, and preparation of the Understudies, Replacements, Extras and Supers, when and if the Director and/or the Producer declines this prerogative. Therefore, if an Actor finds him/herself unable to satisfactorily work out an artistic difference of opinion with the Stage Manager regarding the intentions of the Director and Producer, the Actor has the option of seeking clarification from the Director or Producer.

6. Keep such records as are necessary to advise the Producer on matters of attendance, time, welfare benefits, or other matters relating to the rights of Equity members. <u>The Stage Manager and Assistant Stage Managers are prohibited from the making of payrolls or any distribution of salaries.</u>

7. Maintain discipline, as provided in the Equity Constitution, By-Laws and Rules where required, appealable in every case to Equity.

8. Stage Manager duties do not include shifting scenery, running lights, operating the Box Office, etcetera.

9. The Council shall have the power from time to time to define the meaning of the words "Stage Manager" and may alter, change or modify the meaning of Stage Manager as hereinabove defined.

10. The Stage Manager and Assistant Stage Managers are prohibited from handling contracts, having riders signed or initialed, or any other function which normally comes under the duties of the General Manager or Company Manager.

11. The Stage Manager and Assistant Stage Managers are prohibited from participating in the ordering of food for the company.

12. The Stage Manager and Assistant Stage Managers are prohibited from signing the closing notice of the company or the individual notice of any Actor's termination.

RJB:dmt
Rev. 6/84   Mis. #39

Figure 18-6 Definition of the Duties and Obligations of a Stage Manager (Courtesy Actors' Equity Association.)

Examples:

A union property master may be prohibited from moving any lighting equipment, so he looks on while the master electrician, his friend and a member of the same union, toils.

A union carpenter may be paid to be on hand for a show in which he has no duties other than pulling the curtain, but his union rules will not allow him to use that paid time to work on the sets of the next show which follows in the same house for the same company.

Start by asking the producer or administrative manager for the information you will need to know about union calls to enable you to plan work calls most efficiently.

If she or he cannot give you sufficient information, request permission to call the business agents of the unions to get this information. Usually the producer or business manager will want to handle this for you.

Discuss work rules with the individual union members concerned. In informal chats find out what union members feel are their obligations to their employer, as well as what they consider the benefits of their union membership.

In the long run, the more you know about the work rules of the other unions, the more money you will be able to save the producer in scheduling calls.

Union rules cannot be summarized here, since they vary from local to local, and since they are also dependent on agreements that each producer makes with each local business agent. It is a mistake to infer that wage scales, hours, and work restrictions are not locally negotiable, regardless of nationally distributed union literature. Stage managers do not negotiate, but producers and business managers do.

Inexperienced stage managers are frequently apprehensive about working with IATSE personnel for the first time. Perhaps this is because the veteran IATSE members are often much older than the new stage managers. There is nothing to fear. Treat members of all other unions with professional courtesy. Give them the same respect for the job they are doing as you expect for yours. Assume that they are trained specialists who know exactly how to carry out their work once you have scheduled it.

It is wrong for a stage manager to harbor contempt or resentment for a member of another union simply because his or her union prevents his or her exploitation by the producer.

19

Correspondence

The stage manager has little need to write extensive correspondence, but you will want to consider writing a letter to the next stage manager, critiques, letters of recommendation, and thank-you notes.

A Letter to the Next Stage Manager

Turnover of stage managers is very frequent. Sometimes they are there for a season only, and next season a new person is holding the clipboard, starting anew, running into the same problems that you ran into last season. Sometimes stage managers are replaced in the middle of a season, and sometimes a theater has a different stage manager for every single production.

No matter what your length of service, you have found out some things that your replacement can only learn by time-consuming research, trial, and error.

Where did you take the tape recorder to be serviced last time it broke down? When was the last time it was serviced? How frequently should preventive maintenance be done?

Where is the key to the metal bulb protectors for the dressing room lights?

Who services the air conditioning units?

What ceiling outlets are on what lines into the booth?

What mistakes did you make that the next stage manager should avoid?

What working diagrams and templates, applicable to this theater only, can you turn over to your replacement?

There are many little things that only you know. When you leave, the staff cannot be expected to pass this information on to the new stage manager. Some of it may be trivia. Some is important. But all of it would help the new stage manager to adjust to the job more easily.

If you are not going to be around to break in the new stage manager, why not leave a letter to make the adjustment easier? Simply write the same kind of letter that you would like to find if you were coming to the job instead of leaving.

Critiques

The purpose of a written critique is to help you to improve your work on future productions. It is intended to remind you of mistakes you made, problems you solved, and methods you devised. It need not be formal and it need not go anywhere. Don't feel that you have to turn it over to a producer or director because you wrote it. It is for you.

Experience is a great teacher. If the critique reminds you of your experience it will be a great self-improvement aid. As history students know, mistakes of the past are too soon forgotten and too often repeated.

In your theater career what seems unforgettable to you today will be just a hazy, useless memory tomorrow unless you write it out, review it, and apply it.

As you start into your next production, review your old critiques and try to see how you can contribute more effectively to better theater.

It is the exceptional theater than holds critiquing sessions following productions or seasons. If you should be asked to contribute to such a critique, select one significant item from your written critique to present. Using your most tactful manner, present that one item from the point of view of how best to improve the next production or season. Make sure your suggestions are concrete. Don't offer vague censure or praise. Remember the effective critique should be concerned with locating the "curse" rather than the "culprit." Be hesitant of giving adverse criticism on techniques or devices that have produced desired effects.

Letters of Recommendation

You can help capable people with whom you work by writing a letter of recommendation for them (see Figure 19-1). It will help their morale to know that their work was appreciated, and it may help them to secure better jobs in the future.

Use the theater's letterhead stationery when available.

In your letters of recommendation (1) cite the exact work that the individual performed, (2) give your evaluation of his or her work, (3) state whether or not you would wish to work with him or her again in the same capacity, (4) evaluate the individual's potential for doing other

THE CHECHONOVITZ CIVIC LIGHT OPERA

CHECHONOVITZ, CALIFORNIA

August 29, 1969

To Whom It May Concern
c/o Mr. George Spelvin
335 Ostrova Drive
Bialistok, California

During the 1969 season I had the pleasure of working with
George Spelvin. He was the company "gopher", a title
given in summer stock to the first person called upon when
there is work to be done.

As a member of the stage crew George set and struck
scenery up and down the aisles of our theater in the round,
seven nights every week. During the day his duties varied.
He assisted me as shipping clerk, errand runner, truck
driver and typist. He helped the property master in collecting and returning props. On loan to the technical director,
he helped build sets. He painted scenery, properties and
the stage.

It was always a pleasure to assign George to a job, because you knew it would be done right -- the first time. He
always accepted assignments cheerfully and was alert in
seeing if there was a better way to do a job. Despite his
long hours George was always willing to do a little more,
and often recognized and did work before I could assign it.

George earned the respect of the production staff and cast
members for his dependability and quiet, courteous, un-
assuming ways.

I would be very pleased to work with George again. I feel
that he is ready for an assignment of greater responsibility.
He would make an excellent assistant stage manager.

Sincerely

Lawrence Stern

LAWRENCE STERN
Production Stage Manager

LS:1h

Figure 19-1   Letter of Recommendation from a Manager

related work, and for advancement, and (5) be sure to give your title and relationship to the individual.

If she or he was property master this season, do you think she or he might make a good assistant stage manager next season? If she or he was assistant stage manager, do you think she or he is ready for stage manager, business manager, or technical director?

If you feel that you have performed well in your position, don't be reluctant to ask for a letter of recommendation from your immediate supervisor.

Copies of letters of recommendation may sometimes be enclosed with résumés when applying for a job.

Thank-You Notes

Don't forget to write thank-you notes, letters of thanks, or letters of appreciation. Let the capable people with whom you worked know that you cared.

20

Festivals

Festivals and *tournaments* are two terms used to describe drama events in which more than one group presents work to an audience or judges, or both. Sometimes *tournament* is used to describe a competitive event and *festival* a noncompetitive event, but generally this distinction is not observed. *Festival* is used below for both.

Purpose of Festivals

Festivals promote the improvement of theater. They give theater people the opportunity to meet to present their dramatic skills and to see what their fellow theater workers are doing (and how well). They offer opportunities for exchange of ideas, competition, and social contact. Participants get a chance to "go on the road," to play in an unfamiliar environment. They have an opportunity to evaluate themselves by the reactions of judges and a new audience. Participants may also measure themselves by comparison to the other groups entered.

The festival may be used as a marketplace, bringing together groups and individuals who can hire the groups for appearances at other locations.

A festival should have all the values of a traditional play. In addition, it should give the festival audience a chance to experience a wide variety of theater in a single day. Audiences become more discerning as a result of attending festivals.

Festivals often result in joyful, stimulating, exciting, and rewarding experiences.

Festival Format

Here are four basic ways to organize a festival. There are a great many variations on these formats.

Plan A

All of the participants prepare a production with a time limit of about forty-five minutes. Usually each company chooses its own material, but sometimes the festival rules specify the work to be performed. It may be a scene from a play or musical, a one-act play, or an original script written for the festival, depending on the festival rules. One at a time, each group presents its work to a panel of judges and an audience composed of other festival participants and invited guests. A single auditorium and a single panel of judges are used.

This system is the simplest and works well if the number of entrants is limited. With a dozen entrants, using a schedule that grants forty-five minutes to each group, fifteen minutes between groups to change sets and to allow the audience to stretch, and forty-five minutes to an hour for lunch and dinner, such a festival might start at 9 A.M. and end—by the time the judges had conferred, tabulated their evaluations, and awarded trophies—at midnight. It's a long day for the judges and the festival managers. It is also a long day for any audience members who want to see the entire festival.

In its favor, however, it must be said that this plan is very fair to entrants; they all get to present their work under exactly the same conditions. (But do impatient judges give the last performers the same consideration they give the early ones?)

Plan B

Entrants invite festival judges to see their work at their home theater. From all the entrants, a few are selected to present their works at the finals held in a central location. With just a few plays to be evaluated in the finals, cuttings from each play may be performed during one evening. Or the complete plays may be presented on three successive days, with afternoon and evening performances at a centrally located theater. Or the top three groups may present their complete plays on three successive evenings in competition and the next five groups may present cuttings during the mornings and afternoons, not in competition but as showcase. The judges in the preliminary rounds need not be the same ones who judge the finals. Although initially some entrants may have material advantages (lighting, sets) by performing in their own theaters, judges can compensate for this in their evaluations. In the final rounds, all entrants are on an equal footing.

Award categories may have to be limited or adjusted. For example, if there is usually an award for best lead actress, judges may agree that the finest performer in this category was not invited to the finals. Either they give an individual award on the basis of points during the initial home ground evaluation or they leave out this category and make only group awards. Such a festival might also elect to give no trophies or awards, but rather offer the entrants an evaluation and possibly souvenir pins for participation.

Plan C

The festival is composed of many different five- to ten-minute events—individual pantomime, group pantomime, individual humorous, individual serious, group humorous, group serious, group special event, etc. Each school may enter as many events as it chooses. Teams of judges watch the events in rounds and submit ratings. At the end of the first two rounds, after each group in each category has been seen in competition with other entrants by two sets of judges, the ratings are tabulated and the winners proceed to the semifinals.

In the semifinal round another panel of judges rates each entrant, and those with the highest ratings go on to the finals. In this round, entrants are evaluated by still another panel of judges, and winners are selected. The winners then perform for the entire festival audience composed of guests, entrants, and judges.

As complex as this plan is, it can work smoothly and effectively and allow some seventy schools in a metropolitan area to take part during a single day with a schedule that may run from 8 A.M. to 5 P.M. Winning entrants have to repeat their scenes five times during the day, but since the scenes are short and there is much time between performances, this is not too much of a hardship. Those eliminated during the early rounds have a chance to watch the work of those still in competition.

Plan D

Plan D must be held at a large facility such as a university or multitheater art complex. Ten to twenty-five participating groups perform one-acts, children's theater, or cuttings in a carnival atmosphere. Each entering group presents its selection two to five times during a period of one to three days. There may be ten to fifteen different "theaters" operating simultaneously, with starting times overlapping. Audience groups may be scheduled to see specific performances, or they may arrive at the festival at any time during the day, examine the schedule, and then go to see the entrant that is performing next or wait and see another group that is scheduled to perform fifteen minutes later. In this type of festival the entire audience is not expected to see every entering group, but it is hoped that there will be something for everyone. Entering groups do not usually compete for trophies, but judges may submit written evaluations or critique orally.

Planning

Regardless of the format you choose, organization and long-range planning are absolutely essential to its success. Festival planning should start with a meeting of the festival staff, at least six months to a year before the festival. It is important to allow enough time to organize the festival and to do all the supporting work.

The number of participants and the size of the audience should be carefully estimated at the initial meeting. The number of invitations, programs, judges, etc., will depend on this estimate, and very little advance work can be done without it. The date(s) of the festival, the host campus or theater, and the overall festival theme, if any, should also be determined at that meeting, because all publicity from then on should emphasize the date(s), place, and theme.

Here are some of the individuals and committees usually needed to make a festival run smoothly:

1. Producer (Executive Director, Chairperson)
2. Rules
3. Registration
4. Judges/Evaluators
5. Tabulations/Evaluations
6. Programs
7. Publicity
8. Guests/Hospitality
9. Facilities (Technical Director, Room Chairperson)
10. Stage Crew (Stage Manager)
11. Associate Producer or Reviewers
12. Food/Refreshments
13. Business Manager/Trophies

Some of the committees may be combined (such as rules and registration, business manager and trophies, and judges and evaluation). But it is desirable to break up duties as much as possible so that individual chairpersons can do a small job very well rather than accepting a lot of responsibility and carrying it out marginally.

It is also usually preferable to have one individual responsible for the work of each committee rather than appointing cochairpersons. Each chairperson may recruit a deputy chairperson and should recruit as many committee members as are needed to carry out the work of the committee.

Following are brief descriptions of the work of individuals and committees, with some discussion of the problems that must be faced. Since the specific work of individuals and committees varies with the type of festival, letters A–D are used following each entry to denote the types of plan to which it applies.

Festival Producer (A, B, C, D)

The top executive officer, regardless of title, coordinates all committees, troubleshooting any problem that they cannot resolve. He or she presides over festival planning and critiques and serves as figurehead for the festival.

The producer's most difficult problem is delegating authority to individuals and committee chairpersons. An effective producer motivates capable individuals to accept responsibility.

The producer does not get bogged down in the actual work of the committees. If a committee chairperson becomes ill during a critical period before the festival, the producer finds a new chairperson; the producer does not take over the sick person's work.

A producer's effectiveness is not measured by how much he or she does, but by how much he or she gets done by others. (Before you accept a job as a festival producer, embroider that last sentence on a sampler.)

The initial planning meeting is very important for the producer. He or she should review the production calendar or schedule with all the chairpersons and ask them to determine deadlines for the completion of their work.

Three important principles should be applied in setting up the production calendar:

1. Plan delays! Play the "What if . . . ?" game. Example: What if it takes the registration chairperson two more days than planned to get in all the names of the entrants? How will this delay affect the work of the program chairperson? After answering such questions, space deadlines so that there is room between interdependent deadlines. You now plan a three-day period between the registration deadline and the deadline for the program chairperson to get the names to the printer.
2. Set up minor checkpoints with each chairperson. Instead of establishing one deadline for each chairperson's completed work, set up deadlines or checkpoints for small parts of that work. Example: Instead of establishing a single deadline for the program chairperson, establish deadlines for artwork completed, copy edited, material to the printer, etc.
3. Plan deadlines as far in advance of the festival as is comfortable. Example: At the initial planning meeting, decide on the type of trophies. What deadline should be established for obtaining the trophies? Two weeks before the festival? Three? Four? When

possible, schedule deadlines so that they do not coincide with other deadlines. This will allow you to deal with one item at a time.

Applying these three principles allows the producer the comfort of checking on minor problems throughout the organization stage rather than facing total panic the day before the festival.

Committee chairpersons should be encouraged to submit an information copy of all work to the producer as it is completed. The producer should also call and meet with chairpersons periodically to insure that they have not run into snags or delays.

The producer also works with the chairpersons, especially the publicity chairperson, when a figurehead is needed. If a newspaper runs a picture headed, for example, "Mayor Presents Festival Proclamation," the smiling, relaxed individual accepting the proclamation is likely to be the producer.

After the festival the producer should hold a critiquing session with all committee chairpersons. Each chairperson should discuss the major problems he or she encountered. Emphasis must be placed on what the chairperson had not been adequately prepared to do. The chairpersons should then write brief notes to their hypothetical successors (even if they plan to be around next year). They can attach samples of their work, such as the illustrations in this chapter. With the materials gathered into a festival procedures file or book, the next year's chairperson can start planning with the benefit of past years' experience.

The person who is appointed festival producer should be someone who has had experience as chairperson of one or more committees during prior festivals. It should be clear to all committee chairpersons that their work will be considered when staff appointments are made for future festivals.

The work of a festival producer is unquestionably time-consuming. Principals and department chairpersons must recognize this fact. If possible, they should reduce the teaching hours or other responsibilities of producers to allow them adequate time to devote to their festivals. In some cases student teachers, teaching assistants, or students can be recruited to assist producers. Above all, however, producers must delegate authority and not overcommit their own time.

Rules (A, B, C, D)

The rules chairperson is responsible for writing, updating, and distributing the rules of the festival. At some Plan C festivals, the rules committee holds session during the entire festival to make judgments on reported infractions.

Some rules that have worked for various festivals in Southern California are included here as examples: Figure 20-1 gives the rules used by the Adult Drama Association of Los Angeles in a Plan A festival; Figure 20-2, the Southern California Educational Theatre Association, Plan B; Figure 20-3, The Drama Teachers Association of Southern California, Plan C; Figure 20-4, the Southern California Educational Theatre Association, Plan D.

Rules should be reviewed prior to the initial planning meeting for the festival. Any proposed revisions should be brought to the attention of the entire committee—and sometimes to the attention of the entire membership of the sponsoring organization—before they are made.

Complete rules should be mailed out with the invitations to participate. You might want to send out two copies with instructions that the second copy be signed and returned with the registration forms. This might promote study of the rules and compliance. It is also helpful to underline or use asterisks to call attention to rules that have been changed since the last festival.

One possible system for handling infractions at a Plan C festival is as follows: Anyone (participant, judge, or observer) may report an infraction to a room chairperson. The room chairperson then fills out an infraction form (Figure 20-5) and sends it to the rules committee. The event is allowed to continue, but after the event, the rules committee summons the parties involved and decides whether a participant has indeed violated a rule and whether the participant is disqualified.

In Plan C tournaments, possible violations can also be examined by dispatching judges to observe in subsequent rounds.

Registration (A, B, C, D)

The registration chairperson is responsible for soliciting entrants. He or she mails to potential entrants flyers announcing the festival along with registration forms (Figure 20-6). When mail response is not adequate, the chairperson follows up with phone calls.

The registration chairperson is also responsible for collecting entry fees, photographs, and other entry requirements.

ADULT DRAMA FESTIVAL

WHERE:	Bing Theatre
	Los Angeles County Museum of Art
	5905 Wilshire Boulevard
	Los Angeles, California
WHEN:	Saturday, March 19, 1977
	10:00 am to 11:00 pm
	NOTE: If more than fifteen (15) groups apply, we shall extend the Festival to Friday, March 18, 1977, 7:00 pm to 10:00 pm.
WHO:	All community theatre groups are eligible to participate.
WHAT:	Community theatre getting together to present their best.
WHY:	To promote and promulgate proper community theatre.

Figure 20-1 Rules for a Plan A Festival—Adult Drama Association. (Courtesy of Los Angeles County Department of Parks and Recreation.)

RULES AND REGULATIONS

PARTICIPATION
1. Theatre groups must be members of the Adult Drama Association in order to compete in the Festival.
2. Participation is limited to theatre groups in Los Angeles County.
3. Audience: admission is free, but no one will be allowed entry while a production is underway.

PRODUCTION MATERIAL
1. Scripts can be one-act plays, one act from a larger play, or adaptations. Rights and royalties for copyrighted materials are the responsibilities of the individual theatre groups.
2. Maximum time limit for a production is 30 minutes, curtain-to-curtain. A total of 15 minutes is allowed for set-up and strike; the 15 minutes can be divided between set-up and strike at the discretion of the theatre group. The 30 and 15 minute time limit are separate units.
   PENALTIES for time overruns are as follows:
   A production is "downed" one level (e.g., from first place to second place) for a one minute overrun, two levels for two minutes overrun, etc. and disqualified for anything over five minutes.
   Penalties apply to production and direction categories, but not acting categories.
3. In fairness to all participants, it is recommended that participating groups try to stay relatively close to a 30-minute production time. We can thus stay "on schedule" for the total time of the Festival.
4. Material should be selected on its potential for demonstrating acting and directing capabilities of the participants, for these are the sole criteria upon which the productions will be judged.

   Friday evening, March 18, has been reserved so that groups may make a visual inspection of the Bing Theatre. It is hoped that the technical crew will be at their stations to demonstrate the capabilities of the theatre, e.g., how a sound system might be patched in, a curtain pulled, or a light dimmed. No rehearsals will be allowed at this time. Each participating group will be sent a floorplan of the Bing Theatre stage when their entry is received, so that they may rehearse accordingly. However, Friday, March 18, may be used as part of the competing Festival if more than 15 groups participate. If so, another evening will be designated for inspecting the theatre.
5. Simple risers, chairs, tables, couch and cubes will be provided. Should a group wish to rely on specific furniture units that hold a play together, the transport and storage of these materials must be their responsibility.
6. The theatre is beautifully equipped to brightly light the stage (or moodily dim it). Special lighting plots cannot be accommodated.

ENTRY PROCESS
1. Send in the NOTIFICATION OF ENTRY as soon as possible to get the time slot of your choice. The non-refundable entry fee of $10.00 must accompany this Notification. Details such as cast members are not required when you send in this Notification.
2. When your Notification of Entry is received, you will be mailed an entry packet which includes (1) The Bing Theatre floor plan, (2) A form to fill in with program information, i.e., name of play, cast members, director, publisher, and selection of scene, (3) A complete list of flats, risers, furniture that you will need. The form must be returned by February 15, 1977, to get your information in the program.
3. THE DEADLINE FOR RECEIPT OF THE NOTIFICATION OF ENTRY IS FEBRUARY 1, 1977. It is important that your prompt attention be paid to this deadline, because Los Angeles County insists that you adhere to these rules.
4. The Notification of Entry must be accompanied by an application form for membership in the Adult Drama Association if you are not already a member group. The membership fee is $10.00 per year. Enclose the check with application.

MISCELLANEOUS
1. Three to five judges from the field of professional theatre will critique performances; these will be written and presented to participating groups at an A.D.A. meeting.
2. Awards of Best Production, Second Place and Third Place, Honorable Mention, Best Director, Best Actor, Best Actress, Best Supporting Actress, and Best Supporting Actor will be made at the conclusion of the festival.
3. The first fifteen (15) entrants will perform on Saturday, March 19, 1977. Should more than 15 groups enter, latecomers will perform on Friday, March 18, 1977, and awards will be made after the Saturday performance.
4. As many of you know, the best way of getting to know other members of the A.D.A. is by working with them. How about volunteers for house management, backstage coordination, etc.? We need you.

Figure 20-1   *(Continued)*

In some cases the chairperson is responsible for assigning entries a code. In competitive festivals some entrants feel that judges will be influenced by the name of the school rather than the performance of the actors, particularly in cases where that school has won the past competition or several past competitions. Codes (like X, Y, Z, 25MM;

RULES FOR HIGH SCHOOL THEATRE FESTIVAL 1975

I. **Eligibility:**
   1. Any secondary school in Southern California is eligible to enter. (See Section VI)
   2. Members of the company must be duly enrolled in the entered high school. (Exceptions: A production requiring children's roles incapable of being played by high school actors, i.e., the boys of Medea and Jason in Medea, may be included.)
   3. Only one play may be submitted by each high school.
   4. Productions must be directed by an accredited faculty member within the entered school.
   5. Each production must adhere to the rules and regulations as herein stated or be disqualified. Evaluators may report possible violations which the Committee will investigate and determine whether disqualification is necessary. Entry fees will not be refunded.

II. **Type of Play:**
   Any type of full length play of educational value that is generally intended for adult audiences, i.e. not child audiences, is acceptable.
   Musicals and original material are not acceptable.
   Music may be included if it is incidental to the production, leaving a production that is clearly recognizable as a drama rather than a musical comedy or musical play.

III. **The Company:**
   The company must be limited to thirty students including cast and crew.
   The company screened by the evaluators must be that which is used at C.S.U.N.

IV. **Production Requirements:**
   To avoid difficulties in executions at C.S.U.N., plays must be produced for or adaptable to the proscenium stage. Weight and size of scenery should correspond to the limitations specified by the American College Theatre Festival. Simplicity in setting and technical effects is recommended. (1,000 cubic feet)

V. **Evaluations:**
   The Festival Committee will provide qualified evaluators to screen the production during the play's scheduled run at its campus site.

VI. **Costs:**
   1. Entry fee is $35.00 and membership in SCETA. Each school provides its own production costs.
   2. The Festival Committee will provide, through entry fees, ticket sales, the following to the shows selected for reproduction:
      a. Costs for the play's reproduction, i.e. additional royalty, additional rental of costumes and props(not to exceed Festival revenue).
      b. Transportation costs for the companies and their theatrical baggage.

VII. The Festival Committee reserves the right to refine, expand, or adjust the rules of the Festival if circumstances demand such action.

VIII. Directors must participate in Festival Activities.

IX. **Deadlines:**
   1. The deadline for Festival entries is October 20th.
   2. Productions must be presented by December 13th. No evaluations will be made after that date.

X. Each Director & School is responsible for 10 tickets to each of the three performances at C.S.U.N.

Figure 20-2 Rules for a High School Festival (Plan B). C.S.U.N. stands for California State University, Northridge. SCETA is the Southern California Educational Theatre Association.
(Used by permission of the Southern California Educational Theatre Association.)

FALL DRAMA FESTIVAL--1975

EVENTS	TIME LIMITS	POSSIBLE ENTRIES
I Individual Pantomime	5 min.	1
II Group Pantomime	5 min.	2 to 8
III Individual Humorous	5 min.	1
IV Individual Serious	5 min.	1
V Group Special Event	9 min.	2 to 8
VI Group Humorous	9 min.	2 to 8
VII Group Serious	9 min.	2 to 8

SCHEDULE

8:00-8:30	Registration
8:30-8:45	Assembly
9:00-10:20	Round I
10:25-11:45	Round II
11:45-12:15	Luncheon
12:15	Assembly: Semi-finalists announced
12:30-1:40	Semi-Final Round
1:45	Assembly: Finals announced
2:00-3:15	Final Round
3:15-4:15	Awards Assembly

ENTRY FEE

Entry fees are $2.50 per participant up to $50.00 maximum fee per school. This entry fee includes programs for each participant up to 20. To order more programs, 25¢ per additional program must be sent. (A limited number of programs may be sold at the festival for 25¢ each.) DTASC MEMBERSHIP DUES ($6.00) must also be sent with entries unless paid earlier this school year.

ENTRY DEADLINE

SENIOR HIGH: Entries and fees must be postmarked or delivered not later than MIDNIGHT, WEDNESDAY-OCTOBER 15.
JUNIOR HIGH: Entries and fees must be postmarked or delivered not later than MIDNIGHT, WEDNESDAY-OCTOBER 8.
LATE ENTRIES WILL NOT BE ACCEPTED. ANY HARASSMENT REGARDING THE ENTRY DEADLINE SHALL BE REFERRED TO RULES COMMITTEE WHICH CAN DISQUALIFY ENTRIES FOR THE NEXT FESTIVAL.

TIME LIMITS

TIME LIMITS WILL BE STRICTLY OBSERVED. PARTICIPANTS WILL BE STOPPED WHEN TIME HAS EXPIRED, BUT WILL NOT BE DISQUALIFIED.

GENERAL STANDARDS FOR JUDGING OF ACTING EVENTS

1. Manner of approach to the audience.
2. Use of appropriate speech and acting techniques.
3. Characterization.
4. Theatrical effectiveness and general excellence of performance.

SPECIFIC RULES

1. A memorized introduction is recommended though not required. If it is given it must be included in the time limit.

Figure 20-3   Rules for a High School Festival (Plan C).
(Used by permission of the Drama Teachers Association of Southern California.)

40ZZ) replace school names in programs and the judges' ballots, thus lessening the possibilities of prejudice.

In Plan C festivals, to handle registration of several different events, registration forms for each event (individual humorous, individual pan-

2. Where an introduction is used, the student making the introduction is considered a participant. In individual events the participant must make his own introduction if he chooses to have one.

3. Selection is to be memorized.

4. No participant may perform in more than one event. However, a participant may portray more than one character and may enact a character of the opposite sex.

5. Sound effects are permissible but only through the use of a participant's hand, feet, or mouth. No manufactured devices may be employed.

6. No director, parent, or student may attempt to influence the decision of any judge or discuss in the hearing of a judge the merits of any participant.

7. No director or parent may act as a judge in a section in which he has a participant.

8. The opinion of the judges as to the excellence of the performance and the judges' decision as to the ranking of the contestants should not be challenged. Any protest regarding rules violations should be made to the Rules Committee.

9. Only published or professionally produced material is to be performed in any event, except pantomime.

10. No Shakespearean material may be used. Verse drama is acceptable.

11. The terms "serious" and "humorous" refer to the mood of the selection performed, not necessarily to the form of the work from which the cut is taken. (That is—a humorous scene or monologue might be cut from a tragedy, for example.)

12. No properties may be used except available classroom furniture, such as a table and chairs. They may be used in any manner, except in pantomime.

13. Participants shall wear acceptable school clothing, including shoes, but no costumes may be worn. It is permissible to color coordinate and to dress in the mood of the scene. Special footwear (i.e., tennis shoes, ballet slippers, etc.) is acceptable for all events.

14. Clothing may be used (example: hands in pockets) but not removed or put on.

15. Each participating director must serve either as a judge or on a committee. The Rules Committee is given the authority in extreme circumstances to disqualify all entries of an entire school for unsportsmanlike conduct and/or discourteous behavior by the director, students, or parents.

Figure 20-3   (*Continued*)

tomime, group pantomime, etc.) should be color-coded.

The registration chairperson schedules the entrants and in some cases mails back to them confirmation of their entry along with their specific performance schedule (see Figure 20-7) and a festival information packet.

16. Students are not to be notified of placement in any rounds. Semi-finalists and finalists will be announced at the scheduled assemblies.

17. A school with only boys or only girls enrolled in its student body may join with one other school which has only the opposite sex enrolled to enter as a "team" in competition. Rules and fees will apply to such a team as to a single school.

18. Specific events, such as pantomime and the Special Event, have specific rules which are given herein following the standard rules.

19. All entries must be directed and/or supervised by members of DTASC.

20. In a four-year school, 9th grade is considered part of the junior division, while 10th, 11th, and 12th grades are part of the senior division.

RULES FOR PANTOMIME

1. Pantomime is defined as a dramatic (either humorous or serious) performance by actors using only dumb show.

2. No music is to be used in pantomime.

3. The pantomime is to be prepared and to have an introduction consisting of a title which is not more than ten words.

4. The pantomime is not to exceed five minutes.

5. Words may be mouthed in pantomime, as long as there is no vocal utterance.

6. Chairs are allowed in pantomime. No other furniture or property is to be used. No chairs may be moved during the pantomime.

7. Each performer may pantomime any number of characters and may pantomime characters of the opposite sex.

SPECIAL EVENT RULES

1. To honor the Bicentennial, DTASC chose Carl Sandburg's poem, The People, Yes. A composite or straight cutting may be taken from any part or parts of the poem.

2. Participants may number 2 to 8 and the time limit imposed is nine minutes.

3. Humming or chanting of any music may be used as background, but no lyrics may be used from any other source.

Figure 20-3 *(Continued)*

Judges (A, B, C, D)

The judges (evaluators) chairperson is responsible for obtaining the judges, or evaluators, needed for the festival. The number of judges will depend on the type of festival and the number of entrants.

DRAMA TEACHERS ASSOCIATION OF SOUTHERN CALIFORNIA

IMPROVISATION

RULES -- STANDARDS -- PROCEDURES -- EXAMPLES

1. Four participants must be entered, no more, no less.
   May be four boys, or four girls, or three and one or
   two and two. The sex does not matter, nor does the
   combination.
2. Spectators will be allowed to watch all rounds of
   improvisations, including semifinal and final. They
   must, however, remain in the room until the round is
   over.
3. In rounds one and two, and in the semifinal round, the
   participants will be in the room and may watch because in
   the first three rounds the situations will be different.
   In other words, the same situations will not be given
   to each group in a room in Rounds one, two, and semifinal.
4. Situations will be in a sealed envelope for each room.
   Participants will select their own envelope.
5. Improvisation introductions will consist of a title of
   not more than ten words.
6. In the final round, the participants will not be
   allowed to watch. They will be placed in another room,
   well out of hearing distance, and will perform one
   group at a time. After performing, the group may watch
   the others perform. The order of the final performance
   will be determined by drawing numbers.
7. Up to two minutes of preparation time will be allowed
   within the five-minute time limit. Less time in
   preparation may be taken and the entire five minutes
   does not have to be used up in Rounds one, two, and
   semifinal.
8. A visual warning will be given to all performers at
   the end of three minutes and at the end of four minutes.
9. At five minutes, if the improvisation is not completed,
   the group will be told to stop.
10. In the final round, the improvisation must be (including
    the preparation time) over three minutes.
11. In the final round the situation, as in the first three
    rounds, will be in a sealed envelope. However, in
    the final round there will be two sealed envelopes
    for each group. The four finalists in each group must
    choose a member who will not be involved in the
    situation until the final two minutes. This member
    will have the second sealed envelope, which may be
    opened once the other three begin. The fourth member
    who has the second envelope will act as the _deus ex_
    machina, the surprise element. He or she will enter
    the situation during the final two minutes (at the time
    the three-minute mark is reached).

Figure 20-3   (*Continued*)

The chairperson should be aware of a common tendency of entrants to accept decisions more readily when there are more judges for each round. For instance, entrants would prefer to be rated by five judges rather than three. But if some fifty sections are to be judged simulta-

```
                    CHILDREN'S THEATRE FESTIVAL
                 PHILOSOPHY, RULES AND EXPLANATIONS
                         (ABBREVIATED FORM)

 I. Statement of Philosophy

    Recognizing a continuing need to raise the standard of
    theatre for the child audience, the Southern California
    Educational Theatre Association has established the
    following goals for their annual Children's Theatre
    Festival:

       A. To encourage educational, commercial, community
          and recreational theatre for the child audience,
          to enrich the lives of children and to contribute
          to the development of discerning audience members
          of the future.

       B. To bring selected professionals in contact with
          one another and their productions in order to
          promote sharing of talents, techniques, and goals.

       C. To provide a showcase for productions and focus
          the attention of the media and the public on the
          productions created by professionals from the
          educational, commercial, community and recreational
          theatres.

       D. To strive to obtain sufficient profits and subsidies
          in order to underwrite the expenses of all festival
          participants, thus eliminating artist exploitation.

       E. To provide a weekend of family entertainment at a
          reasonable cost to the public.

    Since the festival strives to create an atmosphere of mutual
    support, no awards or ratings will be given to the participants.
    A board of reviewers will evaluate each performance in order to
    encourage each member of each production company to improve his
    theatrical skills.  Critics from the commercial media will be
    invited to review each production.


 II. Eligibility

       A. Any Children's Theatre Producer in Southern California
          who is invited by the Festival Committee and whose
          producer or director is a member of SCETA.

       B. Members of the acting company must be of college age
          or older.  Exception: an occasional child's role,
          i.e., Tiny Tim in "A Christmas Carol."
```

Figure 20-4   Children's Festival Rules (Plan D).
(Used by permission of the Southern California Educational Theatre Association.)

neously (Plan C), an increase in the number of judges required can involve recruiting 100 extra judges!

Qualifications for judges should be set up within the festival rules; for example, a judge for a high school festival should be at least four years out of high school.

The judges chairperson should look for theater-knowledgeable people. Schools and theaters can each recommend several judges. High

---

2

III. Size of Company

The company must be limited to a maximum of 20 persons.

IV. Type of Play

Any type of full length production, scripted or improvisational, including scripted puppet theatre.

V. Production Facilities

The Executive Producer of the 1976 Festival will supply technical details to invited companies.

VI. The Executive Festival Producer will forward application forms to producers selected by the Festival Advisory Committee. All companies will be reviewed. The Festival Advisory Committee reserves the right to refuse participation to companies whose shows do not meet the expected criteria.

January 18.......Deadline for receiving application forms, plot synopsis, background information on Company, 8 x 10 action shots of group (rehearsal pictures or shots from previous productions) and $35.00 deposit. $25.00 is refunded if Festival commitments and deadlines are met.

March 15........Deadline for sample program (printed by individual producer) 8 x 10 glossy black and white photographs from production, for newspaper publication and media. 35mm color slide for TV. Glossy pictures are not acceptable for television.

VII. Expenses

A. The Festival Committee will provide theatre facilities for the individual and collective companies participating in the 1976 Festival.

B. The host campus will provide minimum technical assistance without cost to the producer.

C. Participating producers will pay their own production costs and author's royalties and provide transportation for their company and their theatrical baggage, including scenery.

D. When Festival revenues permit, companies may be assisted in defraying expenses.

Figure 20-4 *(Continued)*

school drama teachers may judge junior high festivals, and college instructors may judge high school festivals.

The chairperson should also try to bring in VIPs as festival judges—the artistic director of a local resident theater, the manager of a television station, actors and actresses from the community, newspaper critics and

3

E. Each participating producer will provide a sufficient number of programs for each performance -- delivered to the house staff upon arrival.

F. Companies seeking financial assistance must submit detailed estimates 30 days in advance of the festival dates.

G. The $35.00 entry fee will be considered a deposit guaranteeing appearance at the festival. If the company exhibits its production and meets scheduled deadlines for sample programs, pictures, etc., $25.00 will be refunded. If the $5.00 process fee was included with indication of interest form, the entry fee is $30.00.

VIII. Liability

The Festival liability waiver must be signed by the chief administrative officer of the production organization or his designee. If the policy of the individual company requires release or field trip permission forms for its members, all arrangements relating to those forms are the sole responsibility of the producer.

IX. Board of Reviewers

A. The appointed Director of the Reviewing Board will select a panel of reviewers from the educational and professional theatre community to review each show presented. Although no prizes or awards will be given, a written critique will be presented to each producer by a minimum of three reviewers. Specific procedures and evaluation forms will be provided by the Director of the Board of Reviewers.

B. Each producer is expected to serve as a reviewer for at least one production other than his own.

X. Registration

A. The producer must submit the final registration form along with the thirty-five dollar($35.00) check by January 18, 1976.

B. Make checks payable to: Children's Theatre Festival.

Mail to: Children's Theatre, Executive Producer
Dr. Pam Woody
Department of Speech, Communication and Drama
California State University, Los Angeles
5151 State University Drive
Los Angeles, California 90032

Figure 20-4   (*Continued*)

editors, etc. Sometimes VIP judges may also serve as presenters of awards at the conclusion of the festival. If so, they should be advised in advance, not on the day of the festival. A postcard invitation with a mail-back reply card attached (see Figure 20-8) is a handy way to recruit new judges and invite former ones.

CRITERIA FOR PLAYS FOR CHILDREN
PARTICIPATING IN THE SOUTHERN CALIFORNIA
CHILDREN"S THEATRE FESTIVAL

All children's theatre productions entered in the Southern
California Children's Theatre Festival will be previewed by
members of the Festival Advisory Committee or an approved
evaluator. Shows may not be changed between preview performance
and the Festival, except for changes approved by the Festival
Advisory Committee. The Festival reserves the right to refuse
participation to companies whose shows do not fulfill the criteria stated below.

A. Shows should be designed to appeal to children rather than
   adults and should be intended for a <u>stated</u> age range.

B. Shows should demonstrate an integrity of style, whether it
   be audience participation, formal theatre, improvisational
   theatre, or story theatre.

C. If a show is audience participation oriented there must be
   built in audience controls and the actors must work with
   and listen to the children.

D. The direction should demonstrate an understanding of pace,
   reasonably creative movement, the necessity for variety,
   appropriate casting, and respect for children.

E. The acting should be consistent and the actors should appear
   to enjoy performing for and working with children. The
   illusion of the first time is vital, particularly with shows
   that tour and do many performances.

F. The literature should not show characters rewarded for evil
   or include unnecessary violence. The play should treat all
   characters fairly and not poke fun at any race, religion,
   nationality, sex, color or way of speaking with the exception
   of regional accents.

G. The costumes, sets and makeup should be executed with some
   style and unity and should be appropriate for the production. They must be in good condition.

H. The length of the show should be appropriate to the style of
   the show.

   Audience participation plays for K-3   30 - 50 minutes
   Formal play for 2-6 grade   60 - 75 minutes

I. No intermissions are allowed.

Figure 20-4   (*Continued*)

The chairperson should keep a file of willing and capable judges,
listing their names, addresses, and telephone numbers on 3 × 5″ or 5
× 8″ cards. Such a file can shorten recruiting time for each successive
festival.

NOTE: The Festival Advisory Committee reserves the right
to refine, expand or adjust the rules of the
festival, if circumstances demand such action.

The participating producers agree that all interpretations of regulations and decisions of the Festival
Committee are final, including the selection of participating companies, and that no recourse will be
initiated against the Executive Festival Producer,
the Festival Advisory or Working Committees or SCETA.

I have read these rules and criteria and agree to abide by them
and return one copy with my entrance fee to the Executive Producer,
by the stated deadline:

Signed _____

Date   _____

Figure 20-4   (*Continued*)

A code is useful for making concise notes on the file cards. For
example, as the returns come in, the chairperson should indicate
whether or not each person is coming, along with the date the reply
was received. The letter *R* would indicate that the judge sent regrets.

```
┌──────────────────────────────────────────────┐
│           Report of Suspected Rule            │
│                 Infraction                     │
│                                                │
│   School Code Number:_____           │
│                                                │
│   Room Number:_____            │
│                                                │
│   Category:_____            │
│                                                │
│   Reported by:_____            │
│                                                │
│   Date/Time:_____            │
│                                                │
│   Suspected Infraction:_____            │
│                                                │
│   _____         │
│                                                │
│   _____         │
│   - - - - - - - - - - - - - - - - - - -        │
│                                                │
│   (for rules committee use:)                   │
│                                                │
│   Judges:_____            │
│                                                │
│   Findings:_____            │
│                                                │
│   Action Taken:_____            │
│                                                │
│   _____         │
└──────────────────────────────────────────────┘
```

Figure 20-5 Rule Infraction Report Form.

After a few regrets from the same individual, that chairperson would know not to invite him or her again.

If any judges accepted the invitation and then did not participate, the chairperson would mark their file cards "NS" for "no show" and might not invite them the next year. Some judges chairpersons find it necessary to invite more judges than are needed to make up for the few no-shows. If there is a surplus of judges, some may be asked to observe the first rounds and then be held for use in later rounds, when other judges may be dismissed.

Those judges who have proven their dependability at prior festivals

```
                  SCETA HIGH SCHOOL THEATRE FESTIVAL
                         REGISTRATION FORM
(PLEASE PRINT OR TYPE)
    1. _____
       Name of person to whom all correspondence should be addressed
    2. _____
       Street                   City                 Zip
    3. _____
       Telephone (including area code)
    4. _____
       Name of entering school
    5. _____
       Street                   City                 Zip
    6. _____
       Title of play

       _____
       Playwright               Adaptor or translator
    7. _____

       _____
       Dates and times of local performances
    8. _____
       Name and address of theatre if different from participating school
    9. _____
       Name of director          School phone (including area code)
   10. Enclose five copies of maps to your school indicating freeway exits and
       location of your theatre on campus.*
   11. Form letter will be sent at a later date to be signed by the appropriate
       administrative officer giving your school permission to participate and
       releasing the Festival and C.S.U.N.** from liability.
   12. Please have black and white 8 x 10 glossy photographs available for newspaper
       publication and photographs for the "all schools" display at Northridge.
   13. List below the names and addresses of local newspapers, TV, radio stations,
       and drama editors.
   14. The participating school agrees that all interpretations of regulations and
       decisions of the Festival committee are final, including the selections of
       participating schools, and that no recourse shall be initiated against the
       Festival committee, SCETA, or the sponsors of the Festival.

       _____
       Signed

       _____
       Title          Date
       Please send registration form, maps, and entry fee of $35.00 to:

              H.K. Baird                  (Make check payable to SCETA.
              144 So. 1st Avenue          If not a member, you must
              Covina, Calif.  91723       join SCETA.)

       *One copy is sent to each judge.
       **C.S.U.N.: California State University, Northridge
```

Figure 20-6   Festival Registration Form.
(Used by permission of the Southern California Educational Theatre Association.)

should be given a coded mark on their file cards (e.g., "X") so that the judges chairperson will schedule them for all the rounds. Those so coded should be programmed first, for all rounds. Unproven judges should be assigned only to preliminary rounds (when more judges are needed).

The 3 percent problem: When you mail out double postcards to prospective judges to request their participation, you will find that

```
John Actor
1437 Broad Street
Santa Monica, California  90404


Friday, April 23


TIME                    EVENT                   PLACE

10:00 A.M.              A & J Storytellers      Outdoor Theatre #5
                        Story Theatre

11:00 A.M.              A & J Storytellers      Reader's Theatre
                        Story Theatre

12:30 P.M.              A & J Storytellers      Outdoor Theatre #3
                        Story Theatre


Saturday, April 24

 1:00 P.M.              A & J Storytellers      Reader's Theatre

 3:30 P.M.              A & J Storytellers      Reader's Theatre


Sunday, April 25

 3:30 P.M.              A & J Storytellers      Reader's Theatre


On Saturday, April 24, and Sunday, April 25, I intended that the story-
tellers might stroll around and gather their own small groups to tell
stories to.
```

Figure 20-7 Registration Confirmation and Assignment Used in a Plan D Festival.
(Used by permission of the Southern California Educational Theatre Association.)

roughly 3 percent will return their postcards and fail to write their names and addresses on their return postcard tearoffs. (See Figure 20-8.) Some of them will show up at the festival even though you didn't send them final instructions in the mail. We call them "mystery" judges.

There are two ways to prevent this minor annoyance: (The hard way:) print two sets of address labels and place one set on the return

The Drama Teachers Association
of Southern California
would be honored to have you as a

Judge

at their 56th Annual Shakespeare Festival
(Hamlet, Much Ado About Nothing, The Winter's Tale)

on Saturday, April 24, 1976
8:30 o'clock in the morning

Please R.s.v.p.
before April 17

Beverly Hills High School
241 Moreno Drive
Beverly Hills, California

☐ I will be able to attend

☒ I will not be able to attend
   ☐ but wish to remain on list
Are there any events you prefer not to judge ?

_____

_____
    Name   (Please Print)

_____
    Address
_____

Figure 20-8 Postcard Invitation to Prospective Judges. The card
was perforated so that the two sections could be easily separated.
It was folded and stapled for mailing. The reverse side of the top
part is addressed to the judge; the reverse side of the bottom part
is addressed to the judges chairperson.
(Courtesy of DTASC.)

tearoffs. This requires a lot of work. (The equally hard but less expensive way:) number your list of judges and write each judge's number on his or her return tearoff; then look up the names and addresses of the mystery judges on your list when you get their blank responses.

If a judge is assigned to several rounds in a Plan C festival, it is desirable that the rounds be in a variety of categories, to make partici-pation more interesting. Instead of judging four rounds of individual pantomime, for example, the judge should be given one round of group serious, one round of individual comedy, one round of individual pan-tomime, and one round of group special event.

About ten days prior to the festival a reminder note should be sent to all judges who have accepted the invitation, asking them to phone in last-minute cancellations (see Figure 20-9). It is a good idea to enclose a rough map showing how to get to the festival, with a note on where to park.

Upon arrival at the festival, each judge should be greeted by the judges chairperson and presented with the festival rules pertaining to judging (see Figure 20-10), an envelope containing ballots and evaluation forms, a nametag, and an identification ribbon. The judges chairperson should then address the judges as a group, thank them for their partic-ipation, and review the procedures with them.

Some method should be set up for getting feedback from judges. Either they should be provided with a festival evaluation form (see Figure 20-21) to encourage their suggestions, or they should be debriefed orally by the judges chairperson. Example: At one Plan C festival judges felt that it was too difficult to render evaluations in the improvisation cat-egory. They did not feel comfortable in applying the rules. As a result, the category was dropped in subsequent festivals. Perhaps the rules should have been changed or clarified.

In some cases there will be honoraria for the judges, ranging from travel and hotel expenses to a free lunch pass. The judges chairperson should take responsibility for distributing such honoraria.

Tabulations/Evaluations (A, B, C, D)

The tabulation chairperson is responsible for tallying the ballots of the judges during a competitive festival. The chairperson should design the judges' ballots (Figure 20-11) and prepare tally forms (Figure 20-12) in advance so that ballots may be quickly processed at the end of each round. Last-minute, roughly drawn tally sheets can lead to confusion in adding the judges' votes.

The chairperson recruits a tabulation committee to work during the festival.

The tabulation chairperson may also distribute a summary of votes (Figure 20-13) to interested teachers immediately following the festival so that they may see how their students fared in various rounds. Some-

THE DRAMA TEACHERS ASSOCIATION OF SOUTHERN CALIFORNIA

Thank you for accepting our invitation to judge at the 56th
annual Shakespeare Festival to be held on Saturday, April 24, 1976.

Enclosed please find a map to Beverly Hills High School, located
at 241 Moreno Dr., Beverly Hills, California.

Please plan to arrive by 8:30A.M. and report to the library.

If for any reason your plans change and you cannot attend,
please call me at Burbank High School, 555-3138, and leave a
message, or in the evening at my home number 555-6904. (Area
code 213)

Again thank you for taking the time to make our festival a
worthwhile experience for our students.

Deane Wolfson
Deane Wolfson
3rd Vice-President
DTASC

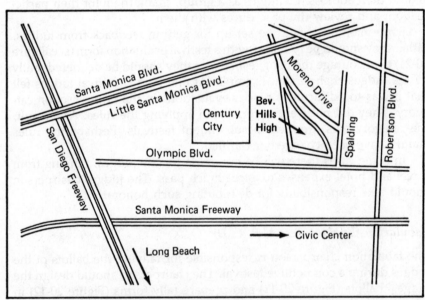

Figure 20-9 Reminder Note. This is sent to judges about ten days prior to the
festival. A map and parking instructions can be helpful.
(Courtesy of DTASC.)

SHAKESPEARE FESTIVAL - INSTRUCTIONS TO JUDGES

1. Room chairpersons will list the code numbers of contestants on the blackboard in the order in which they are to perform. PLEASE COPY THESE CODE NUMBERS, IN ORDER, ON YOUR BALLOT. Note the character name, if you wish.

2. Room chairpersons will time each performance and will stop the performers at the expiration of the allotted time. Contestants must stop when time has expired whether they have finished or not. Please evaluate each performance on the basis of its quality, even if performance has been stopped. DO NOT DISQUALIFY ANY CON-TESTANTS. (It is assumed that an unfinished performance may have an effect upon its quality and upon your rating.)

3. PLEASE DO NOT CONFER with other judges or others in the room before marking and sealing your ballot. We want your private judgment.

4. Please do not announce your ratings to ANYONE. Winners will be announced in the assembly at the close of each round.

5. Please report to the chairperson of judges any attempt by students, teachers, or parents to influence or dispute your judgment.

6. At the close of each round, give your SEALED AND SIGNED ballot to the room chairperson, who will deliver it to the Tabulations Room.

7. Please stay available in the judges room in case of questions and we need to find you.

FESTIVAL RULES

   *All selections are to be memorized.
   *Students may portray more than one character and may play characters of the opposite sex.
   *No props are to be used.
   *Classroom furniture, such as tables and chairs, may be used with no limitations.
   *Clothing worn may be used (i.e., hands in pockets) but may not be removed or put on during the scene.
   *A memorized introduction is recommended but not required.
   *Introductions may be either dramatized or narrated.
   *Directors, parents, and students may not discuss performances with judges or attempt to influence decisions.
   *Protests or questions must be handled by the Rules Committee. This committee can be contacted by room chairperson.

RULES FOR SPECIAL SCENE - WINTER'S TALE

   *This scene must be done exactly as cut. No deletions or changes of any kind will be allowed.
   *No introduction at all may be given, not even the title of the play.
   *This scene will not be timed.
   *All other general festival rules apply to the special scene.

VIOLATIONS OF RULES

   Please report any suspected violation of rules to the Rules Committee as soon as possible. DO NOT DISQUALIFY CONTESTANTS! Only the Rules Committee may dis-qualify an entry.

PLEASE SIGN YOUR COMPLETED BALLOT!

Figure 20-10 Rules for Judges. These should be an abbreviated form of the complete festival rules. They should be reviewed orally before the festival. (Courtesy of DTASC.)

times it is desirable that teachers show these results to their students so that they may see just how subjective the judging was. (Example: An entry that does not even take third place in the final rounds of a Plan C festival may have had several first-place votes from judges in earlier rounds.)

It is desirable that the tabulations room be near the stage or room

BALLOT

Drama Teachers Association of Southern California

Event: VI   Section: —   Room Number: 212

Round (Circle one:)   I   II   Semi-final   Final

Order	Code Number	Notes	Placement
1	HH	C	6
2	C	A	2
3	VV	A+	1
4	BB	B−	5
5	T	B+	3
6	A	B	4
7	P	EXCESSIVE SHOUTING	
8	LL	DROPPED LINES	
9			
10			
11			
12			

Winners' code numbers: only six places are to be listed,
other performances need not be rated.

First place: VV

Second place: C

Third place: T   Please do not list ties
                              for any places! Ties must
Fourth place: A   and will be broken by
                              tabulation!
Fifth place: BB

Sixth place: HH

Judged by: CAROL KATO   *Carol Kato*
            (Please print your name.)

Please give this ballot, in a sealed envelope, to the
room chairman who will deliver it to tabulations. Thank
you!

Figure 20-11   Judges Ballot for a Class C Festival.
(Courtesy of DTASC.)

where the winners of rounds are to be announced. This can eliminate some footwork.

In noncompetitive festivals (Plan D) an evaluations chairperson may be appointed to design evaluation forms (Figure 20-14), supervise the collection of the forms from judges or evaluators, and distribute the forms to the participants. At children's festivals, children may be asked to serve as evaluators, in which case evaluation forms should be espe-

TALLY

Event: __VI__   Section: __—__   Room Number: __212__   Round: __F__

Code	Judges							Total	Place	Sweep
	1	2	3	4	5	6	7			
HH	6	7	7	3	7	6	6	42		
C	2	3	7	5	6	7	3	33		
UU	1	1	5	6	4	4	1	22	2	4
BB	5	4	6	4	7	7	7	40		
T	3	2	4	1	1	2	4	17	1	6
A	4	7	1	2	2	5	5	26	3	2
P	7	6	2	7	5	3	7	37		
LL	7	5	3	7	3	1	2	28		

Figure 20-12 Tally Form for a Plan C Festival. The placements awarded to an entry by each judge are totaled, and the entry with the least number of points is awarded first place in the place column. If a sweepstakes trophy is to be awarded, winning entries are given sweepstakes points. First place in a group event (one in which two or more actors participate) wins six sweepstakes points; second place, four points; and third place, two points. In an individual event (one in which a single actor participates) first place gets three points toward sweepstakes, second place gets two points, and third place gets one point. In Event VI, Group T took first place, Group UU took second place, and Group A took third place. Since this was a group event, Group T earned six points toward the overall festival sweepstakes.
(Courtesy of DTASC.)

cially prepared for them (see Figure 20-15). If oral critiques are held, the evaluations chairperson is responsible for scheduling and moderating the sessions.

Programs (A, B, C, D)

It usually takes at least two months to write, rewrite, proof, and publish a festival program. The following items should be included:

1. Statement of the festival's philosophy
2. History of the festival or the host institution

```
                        FINALS
Event II                                  Event III

UU 20 7757776   C 20 777 2775             C 30 4277727    P 302672475  ②
BB 20 7475674                             L 30 3376754    P 357777177
 R 25 5777777                            YY 30 7771277   JJ 301417577  ①
 X 20 1113227  ②                         RR 35 7124776 ④ DD 307735667
CC 20 352IIII  ①                         ZZ 30 6553771 ③
 P 20 4267352  ③                          C 35 7777313
 K 20 7336747                            GG 35 7747732
LL 20 6644537  ④                         LL 305767747
 P 25 7777777
 C 25 2777463
                                         Event V
Event IV
                                         LL  142IIII    ①
LL 40 4777376                            CC  6566544
 E 40 3121433  ①                          Y  5674256
 X 45 2734224  ③                          P  2374465    ③
 W 40 1242542  ②                         RR  773772
LL 45 7567717                             M  4242677    ④
 Z 40 7677777                             B  775777
CC 45 7415171  ④                         WW  3113332    ②
OO 40 7776777
 C 40 5353655                            Event VII
WW 40 6777767
                                         XX  2115345  ②
Event VI                                 LL  4242231  ①
                                          L  7437456
HH 6773766                               CC  7564667
 C 2375673                                E  3376777
UU 1156441   ②                            Y  5623122  ②
BB 5464777                                G  1751513  ④
 T 3241124   ①                            A  6777774
 A 4712255   ③
 P 7627537
LL 7537312   ④
```

Figure 20-13 Duplicated Summary of Votes. This may be distributed to teachers after the final rounds of a Plan C festival to allow the teachers to point out to their students just how subjective the judging was. Note, for instance, that in Event VII Entry LL was judged best by only one judge, but came in first; Entry XX was judged best by two judges, but came in second; and Entry G was judged best by three judges, but came in fourth! Because there was a tie for second place, no third place was awarded.
(Courtesy of DTASC.)

3. Statement of the festival's theme
4. Schedule (see Figure 20-16, Plan C, and 20-17, Plan D)
5. Map of grounds and room maps of the larger buildings
6. List of officers of the producing association and festival committee chairpersons
7. List of participating schools, theaters, etc.
8. Program of events with room assignments for Plan C (see Figure 20-18)
9. Background information on plays and playwrights whose works are to be presented
10. Background information on groups participating, with synopses of the works they will present (see Figure 20-19, Plan D)
11. Page with blanks on which to record names of festival winners (see Figure 20-20) (List continues on page 257.)

```
              FOURTH ANNUAL CHILDREN'S THEATRE FESTIVAL
              California State University, Los Angeles

                   Reviewer's Evaluation and Critique

Reviewer_____ Production_____

Date and Time Reviewer saw production_____

Style of Production_____
(formal, audience participation, musical, improvisational, educational, other)

Please rate and/or comment on the following aspects of the production.  Suggested
ratings are:  excellent, very good, good, adequate, needs improvement.

1.  ENTIRE PRODUCTION

    a.  Overall rating of relative success
        of production                               _____
    b.  Audience response                           _____
    c.  Consistency of style                        _____
Comments:
    _____
    _____
    _____
    _____
    _____
    _____


2.  DIRECTING

    a.  Appropriateness of production concept
    b.  Development and execution of production      _____
        concept                                     _____
    c.  Development of ensemble                      _____
    d.  Casting and role development                 _____
    e.  Blocking and design of space                 _____
    f.  Respect for and ability to control and
        entertain an audience of children           _____
Comments:
    _____
    _____
    _____
    _____
    _____
    _____
    _____
```

Figure 20-14 Evaluation Form for a Plan D Festival.
(Used by permission of the Southern California Educational Theatre Association.)

12. Decoration (an artistic cover design can make the program a valuable souvenir; designing a children's theater festival program as a coloring book is a clever idea)
13. A tear-out feedback form, addressed to the festival producer, that will encourage constructive criticism (see Figure 20-21)
14. Acknowledgments

3. ACTING

    a. Development of characters
    b. Clarity of speech
    c. Control of movement
    d. Ability to relate to other actors and
        the audience
    e. Illusion of the first time
    f. Flexibility

Comments:

_____
_____
_____
_____
_____
_____

4. DESIGN ELEMENTS

    a. Overall reaction

Sets_____   Costumes_____

Lights_____   Makeup_____

Sound_____   Props_____

Comments:

_____
_____
_____
_____
_____

5. SCRIPT

    a. What age child is the script appropriate for?
    b. Consistency of style of script
    c. Integrity and validity for an audience of
        children

Comments (particularly appropriate if script is original):

_____
_____
_____
_____
_____
_____

Figure 20-14   (*Continued*)

Most of the items listed are self-explanatory, but a few need further comment.

The artwork for the program cover might take more time than the other items. The program chairperson should recruit an artist well in

```
                        SOUTHERN CALIFORNIA
                    CHILDREN'S THEATRE FESTIVAL, 1976
                    California State University, Los Angeles

                    JUNIOR REVIEWER'S PLAY EVALUATION FORM
```

Reviewer_____ Production_____

Date and time reviewer saw production_____

1. The first questions are about how you liked the play. (Circle your response.)

    Did you like the play?   Yes   No   Parts of it
    Was the play interesting?   Yes   No   Parts of it
    Was the play fun to see?   Yes   No   Parts of it
    Could you follow the story?   Yes   No   Pretty well
    Would you like to see this play again? Yes   No

2. Circle the comments below that describe the way you felt about the play.

    Great!!   Pretty good   Too noisy   Too fast

    Exciting   Dull   Too violent   Too long

    OK   Scary   Too slow   Too boring

    Hard to understand   Easy to understand   Part good,part bad   Too scary

3. Give short answers to the following questions about the play.

        What did you like best about the play?

        What did you like least about the play?

        What did you learn from this play?

Figure 20-15   Evaluation Form for Use by Children at a Children's Festival.
(Used by permission of the Southern California Educational Theatre Association.)

advance of other production work on the program.

The program chairperson should tell other chairpersons (registration, room chairperson) the deadline for submitting information for the program. Late entries are a major problem for the program chairperson; therefore, a definite deadline should be determined at the first planning meeting.

4. What age kids do you think this play is best for?

    (Circle one age group)   3 - 6   6 - 9   10 - 14

    Would this play be fun for grownups, too?   Yes   No   I don't know

5. Please answer the following questions about the actors and the acting.
    (Circle your response)

    Did the actors have fun?   Yes   No   I don't know

    Were the actors nervous?   Yes   No   I don't know

    Did the actors have lots of energy?   Yes   No   Some of them

    Were the characters believable?   Yes   No   Some of them

    Could you hear the actors well enough?   Yes   No   Some of them

    Could you understand what they were saying?   Yes   No   Sometimes

    Which character did you like best?_____

    Why?

    Which character did you like least?_____

    Why?

Figure 20-15   (*Continued*)

Illegible names and partial names on registration forms also create problems for the program chairperson. He or she should remind the registration chairperson to insure that the forms ask entrants to print clearly and to submit complete names.

After cost, proximity is the most important factor in selection of the

6. If this was the kind of play where the actors ask the audience to answer questions or do things on the stage, please answer the following questions. If it wasn't, skip #6 and go on to #7.

   Did the actors talk <u>to</u> the audience?   Yes   No   Sometimes

   Did the actors listen to the answers the   Yes   No   Sometimes
   audience gave?

   Do you think it was a good idea for the   Yes   No   I don't know
   actors to ask the audience's help with
   this particular play?

7. Please answer the following questions about the scenery and costumes. (Circle your response.)

   Was the scenery practical for the play?   Yes   No   I don't know

   Did you enjoy looking at the scenery?   Yes   No

   Was the scenery easy for the actors to   Yes   No   I don't know
   work with?

   Did the scenery take away from the play?   Yes   No   I don't know

   Did you enjoy looking at the costumes?   Yes   No

   Were the costumes easy for the actors to   Yes   No   I don't know
   work in?

   Do you think the scenery and the costumes   Yes   No   I don't know
   went well together?

8. Is there anything else you would like to say about this play?

Figure 20-15   (*Continued*)

printer because the program chairperson will have to visit the printer often. An ideal arrangement is for the program chairperson to work with the school printshop.

To determine the number of programs to be printed, the chairperson should add the estimated number of entrants, judges, festival workers,

FAIRFAX HIGH SCHOOL
7850 Melrose Avenue
Los Angeles

NOVEMBER 15, 1975

SCHEDULE FOR THE DAY

8:00 a.m. .... Hospitality in Library for directors and judges

Judges meeting in Library

Rules committee meets in Library

Room Chairmen meeting in Student Cafeteria

General registration and distribution of programs in foyer of auditorium. (Each school must be registered by its director who will receive programs.)

8:30 a.m. .... Assembly in auditorium

General announcements by festival chairperson, Mr. Alan R. Josefsberg

9:00 a.m. .... Round 1. (Participants proceed to assigned rooms as indicated in festival program.)

10:25 a.m. ... Round 2. (Participants proceed to assigned rooms as indicated in festival program.)

11:45 -- 12:15 ... Luncheon

12:15 p.m. ... All participants will meet in the auditorium for the announcements of the semi-finalists

12:30 p.m. ... Semi-final round. (Semi-finalists as announced in the auditorium will report to assigned rooms.)

1:00 p.m. .... Improvisational Workshop in amphitheater during semi-final and final rounds

1:45 p.m. .... All participants will meet in auditorium for the announcements of the finalists

2:00 p.m. .... Final round. (Finalists as announced in the auditorium will report to assigned rooms.)

3:15 p.m. .... Awards assembly

Presentation of guests

Presentation of awards

Figure 10-16   A Festival Schedule. Four rounds are scheduled during one day. (Courtesy of DTASC.)

Saturday April 24	Main Stage	Arena Theatre	Trident Theatre #1	Trident Theatre #2	Union Theatre #1	Union Theatre #2	Union Theatre #3	Union Theatre #4
10:30	SO. COAST REP. - A Bicentennial Salute to Orange County	MAGIC CARPET Kid's Writes			CSU-NORTH RIDGE Story Train			THE HAPPY HANDFULS Deaf Theatre
11:00			RENEGADE THEATRE Sacramento 50 Miles			PYRAMUS & THISBY Oh Rubbish	UCLA The Saturday Night Afternoon Wild Bunch	
11:30								THE HAPPY HANDFULS Deaf Theatre
12:00		MAGIC CARPET Kid's Writes			CSU-NORTH RIDGE Story Train			
12:30	ITP Colonel Montana		RENEGADE THEATRE Sacramento 50 Miles			PYRAMUS & THISBY Oh Rubbish	UCLA The Saturday Night Afternoon Wild Bunch	
1:00								
1:30								
2:00		SYNTHAXIS THEATRE Phantom Tollbooth			MIME THEATRE PLAYERS Mime Show		TARADIDDLE TRAVELERS Sleeping Beauty	
2:30			SCORPIO RISING THEATRE The Blue Light			MAGIC CARPET Kid's Writes		
3:00	ITP Guns							
3:30					MIME THEATRE PLAYERS Mime Show			LA MAMA HOLLYWOOD Killer Fleas
4:00		San Diego Jr. Theatre A Thurber Carnival					TARADIDDLE TRAVELERS Sleeping Beauty	

Sunday April 25	Main Stage	Arena Theatre	Trident Theatre #1	Trident Theatre #2	Union Theatre #1	Union Theatre #2	Union Theatre #3	Union Theatre #4
10:30	PYRAMUS & THISBY Oh Rubbish	THE GIVING TREE Just So Stories	Tales from the EAST WEST PLAYERS					
11:00					RIO HONDO COLLEGE The Journey			MAGIC CARPET Kids Writes
11:30						J.P. NIGHTINGALE Celebrates America	UCLA- The Saturday Night Afternoon Wild Bunch	
12:00		THE GIVING TREE Just So Stories						
12:30	CREATIVE ARTS The Wierd & Wacky Game of Time				RIO HONDO COLLEGE The Journey	J.P. NIGHTINGALE Celebrates America		

Figure 20-17 A Festival Schedule. This shows one day of a three-day schedule.

expected audience, and guests, and then add a large number of extras. It is better to order too many than not to have enough.

Publicity (A, D)

The publicity for a festival requires all the effort that would be expended on a single production and then some. The publicity chairperson should devise a schedule of publicity releases starting five weeks before the festival and building to a peak the weekend before the festival. (Some large annual festivals start their publicity work nine to twelve months ahead of the festival date.) The chairperson should attempt to obtain coverage from all media in the area of the festival and all media in the

EVENT 2 -- GROUP PANTOMIME

Semi-finals in Rooms 110, 112, 114

Finals in Room 112

Section 6		Round 1	Round 2
AAA	20	. . 110	. . 110
MMM	20	. . 110	. . 111
SS	20	. . 110	. . 112
S	20	. . 110	. . 112
B	20	. . 110	. . 114
R	20	. . 110	. . 115
CC	20	. . 110	. . 110
TT	20	. . 110	. . 111
Z	20	. . 110	. . 113

Section 7		Round 1	Round 2
N	20	. . 111	. . 113
LLL	20	. . 111	. . 114
FFFF	20	. . 111	. . 115
BB	20	. . 111	. . 114
JJ	20	. . 111	. . 113
K	20	. . 111	. . 112
SSS	20	. . 111	. . 115
A	20	. . 111	. . 111
Y	20	. . 111	. . 110

Section 8		Round 1	Round 2
H	20	. . 112	. . 111
C	20	. . 112	. . 112
YYY	20	. . 112	. . 114
RRR	20	. . 112	. . 113
TTT	20	. . 112	. . 110
NN	20	. . 112	. . 112
XX	20	. . 112	. . 111
JJJ	20	. . 112	. . 112
F	20	. . 112	. . 110

Section 9		Round 1	Round 2
EEEE	20	. . 113	. . 113
EEE	20	. . 113	. . 115
ZZZ	20	. . 113	. . 110
PPP	20	. . 113	. . 113
LL	20	. . 113	. . 115
NNN	20	. . 113	. . 114
UU	20	. . 113	. . 115
E	20	. . 113	. . 111
UUU	20	. . 113	. . 110

Section 10		Round 1	Round 2
AAAA	20	. . 114	. . 110
L	20	. . 114	. . 115
HH	20	. . 114	. . 112
J	20	. . 114	. . 115
AA	20	. . 114	. . 114
BBB	20	. . 114	. . 111
OO	20	. . 114	. . 111
X	20	. . 114	. . 110
OOO	20	. . 114	. . 113

Section 11		Round 1	Round 2
ZZ	20	. . 115	. . 112
GG	20	. . 115	. . 114
CCC	20	. . 115	. . 114
CCCC	20	. . 115	. . 113
DD	20	. . 115	. . 114
P	20	. . 115	. . 113
U	20	. . 115	. . 112
DDDD	20	. . 115	. . 111
FFF	20	. . 115	. . 115

Figure 20-18   Room Assignments for First Two Rounds of Plan C Festival. These rounds are scheduled in advance, letting entrants know in which rooms they will perform. Room assignments for later rounds are announced as judges eliminate entrants from competition.
(Courtesy of DTASC.)

THE TWELFTH NIGHT REPERTORY CO.

12732 Moorpark Street   Studio City, Calif. 91604   (213) 760-2112

GREEK MYTHOLOGY

On October 18, 1974 we first presented GREEK MYTHOLOGY to
Vintage Street School, in Sepulveda. The performance was for
the Los Angeles City Schools Principal's Cultural committee.
This committee rated GREEK MYTHOLOGY as "Excellent," and we began
a massive tour of the Los Angeles City Schools.

This tour resulted in establishing Twelfth Night as a major
source of educational theatre in Los Angeles. We played GREEK
MYTHOLOGY to over 75,000 youngsters during the 1974-1975 school
year. It remains one of our most requested presentations. In
December of 1974, members of the Office of Multicultural Education
for the L.A. City Schools came and saw GREEK MYTHOLOGY. They were
very enthusiastic about the potential of using this same theatrical
format as a means of multicultural education, and they proceeded to
help us secure a $30,000.00 grant from HEW for that purpose.

In short, GREEK MYTHOLOGY was the start of something very good
for Twelfth Night.

THE CAST

STEVE MUNSIE (pantomimist) is a founding member of Twelfth Night,
                and was the first to perform in GREEK MYTHOLOGY.
                Although his role has been successfully repeated by
                Don Lewis and Michael Ross Oddo, much of GREEK MYTHOLOGY
                has always been Steve's inspiration. Steve has taught
                at ISOMATA (Idyllwyld School of Music and the Arts), an
                extension of USC.

SCOTT CATAMAS (narrator) first founded Twelfth Night in June of 1973.
                Scott has played many leads, directed, and produced
                numerous productions. He was the original narrator for
                GREEK MYTHOLOGY in 1974. Scott is the President of
                Twelfth Night.

AARON HASSMAN (musician) MA in educational psychology, BA in Theatre
                Arts, BA in Music. Aaron first joined Twelfth Night
                in January 1975. He is currently performing every
                day for us with his MUSICIAN'S SEMINAR program. Aaron
                also teaches Creative Dramatics and Creative Guitar to
                Los Angeles City School teachers (through the In-Service
                Workshop program).

GREEK MYTHOLOGY was written and produced by Scott Catamas.

The Twelfth Night Repertory Company is an independent, Non-Profit
Organization.

Figure 20-19 Description of a Group Participating in a Plan D Festival. This
information may be printed in the program or on a flyer distributed to the
audience.
(Courtesy of the Twelfth Night Repertory Co.)

areas of prospective audiences. Releases to junior high, high school,
college, and teacher organization newspapers will be especially useful
(see Figure 20-22).

The publicity chairperson might issue releases on the following subjects (separately or in combinations):

AWARD WINNERS

Event 1 — Individual Pantomime

_____
Third

_____
Second

_____
First

Event 2 — Group Pantomime

_____
Third

_____
Second

_____
First

Event 3 — Individual Humorous

_____
Third

_____
Second

_____
First

Event 4 — Individual Serious

_____
Third

_____
Second

_____
First

Event 5 — Group Special Event

_____
Third

_____
Second

_____
First

Event 6 — Group Humorous

_____
Third

_____
Second

_____
First

Event 7 — Group Serious

_____
Third

_____
Second

_____
First

Event 8 - Group Improvisation

_____
Third

_____
Second

_____
First

Sweepstakes Trophy

_____
Third

_____
Second

_____
First

Figure 20-20   A Page for Listing Award Winners in the Program.
(Courtesy of DTASC.)

1. Dates, places, chairperson, and intended audience for the festival
2. History of the festival
3. Judges named for festival
4. Participants listed for festival

FESTIVAL EVALUATION FORM

What did you like best about the festival?

_____
_____
_____
_____
_____
_____
_____
_____

What could we do to make it better or different?

_____
_____
_____
_____
_____
_____
_____

Were you well provided for in terms of facilities and courtesy?

_____
_____
_____
_____
_____
_____
_____

_____ I am willing to work on a committee for next year's festival.
_____ I would like to serve as a reviewer for next year's festival.
_____ I would like to be invited to bring a production next year.

What day or days did you attend the festival?_____
In what position did you attend the festival? (Circle one) Producer, Director,
Reviewer, Performer, Audience member, Other_____

Name_____ Position_____
Address_____ City_____ Zip_____
Home Phone_____ Office Phone_____

Figure 20-21   Festival Evaluation Form.
(Used by permission of the Southern California Educational Theatre Association.)

5. VIPs planning to attend festival
6. Trophies, scholarships, and future competitions announced for festival winners
7. Winners selected and trophies presented

Sometimes it is better to divide the work of the publicity committee between two or more people. For example, the publicity chairperson

Children's theatre festival '76

The spring of 1973 marked the beginning of a rather special theatrical enterprise: Immaculate Heart College of Los Angeles hosted the initial outing of the Children's Theatre Festival.

Appreciative of the concept which launches the American College Theatre Festival, members of the Southern California Educational Theatre Association hoped to bring together a diverse group of performers specializing in entertainment for children. It was of equal importance to provide good examples of Children's Theatre fare being produced throughout Southern California, and to present such programs at a reasonable cost to Southland families. An opportunity for children's theatre artists to meet and see one another's work (and a chance to broaden the audience for such artists) was also of special interest to festival planners.

The gathering at Immaculate Heart joined a dozen producing companies and an enthusiastic audience nearing a thousand people. The 1974 Festival held at Cal Poly, Pomona doubled the 1973 attendance and last year's festival, produced at California State University, Northridge, drew an audience of over 8,000. Since the beginning of the festival, many innovations such as strolling players on the grounds, a playwrighting contest, and premiere performances of a number of original plays have been introduced to the weekends activities.

Children's Theatre Festival '76 will be presented on Friday, April 23rd; Saturday, April 24th; and Sunday, April 25th at California State University, L.A. Over forty companies of performers will provide entertainment on Friday from 9:00 a.m. to 2:00 p.m. and on Saturday and Sunday from 10:30 a.m. to 5:00 p.m. Admissions will be $2.00 for adults, $1.00 for children. Families are again encouraged to picnic in a lovely campus setting — refreshments will be available at convenient locations — while enjoying the most diversified theatrical afternoon available at the price.

New representation in this years festival of educational, professional and community theatre groups will include a presentation of *Colonel Montana* by the Improvisational Theatre Project from the Mark Taper Forum; San Francisco's Magic Carpet presenting the critically acclaimed production of *Kid's Writes: Multicultural Mythology* produced by The Twelfth Night Repertory Co.; the L.A. Mime Company; a zany production of *Castle Hassel At Rainbows End* presented by the Trobadoor Puppets; and an exciting production of *Winnie-the-Pooh* produced by the University of Nevada.

Musical theatre, always a part of the festival, is represented this year by productions such as *H2O Where Are You?* produced by the Space Place Players in conjunction with the California Museum of Science and Industry and *Sacramento Fifty Miles* from Bakersfield College.

Among returning favorites are Betsy Brown in *Carnival of the Animals*. A salute to Orange County from the talented South Coast Repertory, John and Pam Wood as *J. P. Nightingale*, and *Macaroni Feathers* by McKerrow and McClelland produced by San Diego State University.

An exciting line-up, and only a part of all the entertainment to be staged in the theatres and on the lawns of the Cal. State L.A. campus.

Executive producer Pam Woody of the Cal. State L.A. faculty is busy collecting a distinguished group of theatre experts to act as production reviewers; for, though the festival remains a noncompetitive event, a basic part of its philosophy is the improvement of quality and communication in children's theatre. However, the most expert of opinions may be provided by a panel of junior reviewers also being assembled. This year we will agains ask young people of the general age of the festival audience to express their thoughts and preferences to the performance companies and to the festival committee.

Plays, improvisational adventures, creative dramatics, clowns, strolling singers and dancers: a lively two-day presentation of theatre arts for children. Sponsored by the Southern California Educational Theatre Association, the 1976 Children's Theatre Festival presents its fourth annual gathering — a reflection of the unprecedented growth in theatre for children in California.

Further inquiries may be directed to Pam Woody at (213) 224-3342 or 224-3350, or to:

The Children's Theatre Festival
c/o California State University, L.A.
5151 State University Drive
Los Angeles, California 90032

Figure 20-22 A Festival Publicity Release Placed in a Teachers' Newspaper. (Used with the permission of United Teachers–Los Angeles.)

can handle all public relations (face-to-face and telephone contacts) while the deputy or assistant chairperson handles all written releases to the media.

All public relations contacts should be logged and copies of all media releases should be filed so that successive publicity chairpersons can build on the work of their predecessors.

Guests/Hospitality (C, D)

The guests, or hospitality, chairperson is responsible for guides. Ways to obtain guide services include the following:

1. The host campus is asked to provide guides from one of its service organizations (Honor Society, ROTC, etc.).
2. Each entering school is required to bring one student to serve as a guide.
3. Students in the drama department earn classroom points by serving as guides (usually on college campuses).

The guest chairperson briefs the guides before the festival, explaining the layout of the host campus and taking them on a quick tour of important locations. Each guide receives a map to keep, some handout maps, and an identifying ribbon.

The guest chairperson might want to establish an information (and lost-and-found) booth, at the main entrance or in the central corridor, to which guides can direct people whose problems they can't resolve.

The guest chairperson should have ready emergency information—phone numbers for police, fire, and ambulance.

The guest chairperson is also responsible for personally greeting and hosting VIPs.

For a Plan D festival the hospitality chairperson might also want to plan social events for participants (such as a welcoming cocktail party). If many of the festival participants are from out of town, the hospitality chairperson might provide a memo to each on accommodations, entertainment, and points of interest in the vicinity of the festival.

Facilities (Technical Director) (A, B, C, D)

Generally, the responsibility of the facilities chairperson (or technical director) is to insure that the participants can perform comfortably in the space assigned to them.

For a Plan D festival the facilities chairperson drafts stage plans or floor plans for every production area of the festival. He or she consults with the technical director of each entry to insure that the stage or room scheduled for use by that entry can accommodate its scenery and lighting requirements.

It is best to set up separate appointments with each technical director to inspect the site before the festival and review the production requirements. Arrangements can be made for any necessary adjustments to the allotted facilities. Sometimes this will simply mean finding an extension cord. But in other cases more serious steps must be taken. For example, background flats that won't fit through the door to the stage area may require rescheduling of two presentation areas.

If entrants will have to travel a great distance to participate and technical directors cannot inspect sites in advance, the facilities chairperson must make special efforts to insure that complete floor plans are reviewed through the mail. Incoming groups should be advised of the height of the playing area, the diagonal length of the largest door (for entering scenery), the number and capacity of electric outlets and their distance from the playing area, and any other limiting factors.

Another especially important function of the facilities chairperson is checking with the host campus early in the planning stage to insure that there is adequate seating capacity for the expected participants and audience. For a Plan C festival, for example, there must be enough large rooms to accommodate the group events.

The facilities chairperson is also responsible for negotiating with the supervisor of the host campus for any special requirements—space, telephones, custodian time, etc. Therefore, it is convenient for the chairperson to be on the staff of the host school.

The chairperson, the festival producer, and the supervisor of the host campus should also discuss facility problems that arose during past festivals to determine how to prevent similar problems during the current festival.

Example 1

A home football game and a high school Shakespeare festival were scheduled at the same time. No conflict was expected, but the blare of the public address system from the field drifted through the open windows on that hot day and interrupted every Shakespearean scene. Can the host campus be persuaded not to schedule any event other than the festival? If an athletic event must be scheduled, can the volume of the public address system be limited?

Example 2

On the weekend of a three-day children's theater festival, the host state college also scheduled national debate finals, a national piano competition, and a gymnastics event. The resulting parking situation was impossible. Many people who might have attended one of those events were discouraged when they could not find parking within three city blocks of the campus. Can the facilities chairperson convince the campus supervisor to limit the number of events scheduled? Can a separate parking area be set up for the festival with large signs at the theater directing drivers to the lot and a shuttle bus to run drivers from the lot to the festival?

The chairperson should insure that notes are written to the faculty and staff of the host campus, letting them know that guests will be on their campus and in their rooms.

Room Chairperson (C)

The festival room chairperson sees that the host custodian unlocks the schoolrooms on time. The festival room chairperson organizes student room chairpersons to serve in each room to monitor and time events.

Usually each entering school is required to bring along with its participants two or more students to serve as room chairpersons. They insure that the judges and participants are present, time events, and supervise the running of the festival within each room.

The festival room chairperson should brief the student room chairpersons just before the festival by orally reviewing a written handout (Figure 20-23). He or she is also responsible for distributing stopwatches, instructing students in their use, and recovering them. The festival room chairperson should number the stopwatches and have the room chairpersons sign for them.

Stage Crew (Stage Manager) (A, B, C, D)

The stage crew chairperson, or festival stage manager, is responsible for the stage and backstage areas before, during, and after the festival. He or she insures that the stage, lighting equipment, and scene-changing facilities are ready. The chairperson also meets with the technical directors and stage managers of each entry to insure efficient use of the stage.

In a Plan C festival the stage is used primarily for the presentation of trophies and sometimes for the performance of winning entries. Another important use of the stage in a Plan C festival is the announcement of winners of the preliminary rounds. The use of an overhead projector for this is highly recommended. So much screaming and yelling follows the announcement of each preliminary winner that the reading of the entire list will be delayed without the use of a projector. With a projector, winners and their room assignments for the next round can all be projected at once. The projector operator is warned to wear ear plugs!

Associate Producer or Reviewers (D)

In festivals where groups are invited to perform, the festival producer might insist that the group's work be seen and evaluated prior to a formal invitation. In this case, an associate producer may recruit committee members (reviewers) to preview, individually or as a committee, the work of prospective entrants.

INFORMATION FOR ROOM CHAIRPERSONS

8:00 - 8:30	Registration	
8:30 - 8:45	Assembly	
9:00 - 10:20	Round 1 - Prelim	
10:25 - 11:45	Round 2 - Prelim	
11:45 - 12:15	Lunch	
12:15 - 12:30	Assembly - Semi- finalists Announced	
12:30 - 1:40	Semifinal Round	
1:40 - 1:55	Assembly - Finalists Announced	
1:55 - 4:00	Final Round	
4:00 - 4:30	Awards Assembly	

Important Rooms

Room Chairpersons	-	Room 52
Judges	-	Library
Tabulations	-	Faculty Lounge
Rules	-	Cafeteria

1. Report to Room 52 on Saturday at 8:00 to get instructions and materials which will include program.
2. Go to your assigned room.
3. List code numbers for the entrants on the board.
4. Check to see that all entrants are there by calling numbers.
5. Be certain to start each round at the time indicated, if possible. If late entrants arrive they may perform when others are finished. Cross out code numbers of entrants who do not participate.
6. Check to be certain that the indicated number of judges is present. If not, send a runner to the library. (Preliminary round --- 3 judges; semifinals --- 5 judges; finals --- 7 judges.)
7. Explain that if anyone feels there has been a rules violation he or she should speak to the room chairperson as soon as the scene in question has finished. Send a runner with a rules infraction slip to the cafeteria. A member of the rules committee will review the situation and determine whether it has been disqualified. Important: no judge or room chairperson can disqualify a scene for any reason.
8. There is to be no talking during scenes and no applause or comments which could influence the judges. You may ask anyone who misbehaves to leave the room.
9. Time each scene from the moment the players begin. (Individual pantomime, group pantomime, individual humorous, and individual serious --- 5 minutes; group special event, group humorous, and group serious --- 9 minutes; improvisation --- 5 minutes.)
10. If a scene runs over, you must say "time," and stop the scene. The entrant is to be judged on what was performed, not penalized for running over time.
11. At the end of the round, try to hold people in the room until the end of the time period to avoid noise in the halls.
12. When judges have finished voting, take their ballots immediately to the tabulations room.
13. Thank judges and participants and proceed to your next assignment.
14. At the end of the final round, or before if you do not have an assignment, return your stopwatch to Room 52.

Thank you!

Figure 20-23 Room Chairperson's Briefing Form.
(Courtesy of DTASC.)

Food/Refreshments (A, B, C, D)

The food/refreshments chairperson is responsible for food services at the festival. In some cases service will be limited to providing coffee and doughnuts for the judges and festival staff. In other cases, the host campus cafeteria will be set in operation to provide lunch for all participants in the festival. In still other cases, the chairperson might supervise a string of concessions for from one day to a week.

At one large, three-day children's festival the food chairperson decided to sell a box lunch of sandwiches, potato chips, and fresh fruit to the audience and provide the same, free, to participants, workers, and judges. The price was kept low. The overall cost of the food program was not entirely covered by sales, but most felt that the program, though simple, was adequate and desirable.

In all cases the chairperson is advised to confer with the supervisor of the host campus cafeteria and to check on local government regulations concerning food services.

Business Manager/Trophies (A, B, C, D)

It is desirable that the treasurer of the organization sponsoring the festival serve as the business manager of the festival. The business manager is responsible for all income and expenditures. He or she approves payment of all expenses, makes out the checks, and receives income from the registration chairperson and the food/refreshment chairperson (assuming a profit from concessions).

The business manager submits a written report on the festival's finances (Figure 20-24) at the critique following the festival.

The business manager may be given the additional responsibility of obtaining trophies, or that duty may be assigned to a separate chairperson.

Consideration should be given to awarding special trophies to individuals who have worked especially hard in mounting the festival over a period of years and to the individual or institution that hosts the festival.

To Compete or Not to Compete

Many teachers with whom I've spoken resent competitive festivals. They state that they don't want to put their students in pressured situations. Some feel that competition is alien to art. Some say they don't want to attend festivals where year after year the same few schools win trophies both in events and in the festival sweepstakes (most points earned by a school in all events). Some feel that returning from festivals year after year without trophies reflects poorly on their teaching, and others say that they simply don't have the student talent to make their schools competitive. It feels good to win and it feels bad to lose, and at every competitive festival there are many more losers than winners.

On the other hand, those who favor competitive festivals say that they merely reflect our society. Our students live in a world of Olympic Gold Medals, Emmys, Tonys, Obies, and Oscars. Outstanding talent

```
                          DTASC
                    Financial Statement
                    September 20, 1975

Balance--February 1, 1975                                    $3129.53
    (Last Financial Statement)

Receipts

      Entry Fees--Shakespeare Festival

          Sr. High      $1819.00
                         1024.50
                                                              2843.50
                         TOTAL BALANCE & RECEIPTS TO DATE    $5973.03


Expenses
      General
          Coffee & Food Services
                  (Planning Meetings)          77.45
          Art Work & Printing                  221.64
          Programs                             849.54
          Queen's Costume Rental (Jr. & Sr.)   100.00
          Trophies & Ribbons                   923.53
          High School Theatre Festival (SCETA)1000.00
          Rental, CTA Auditorium                37.50
          Postage, Supplies, Phone             146.60
                                                             $3356.26

      Shakespeare Festivals--Facilities, etc.
          Sr. High
              Judges Inv. & Postage        65.00
              Postage, Fest. Question.      8.20
              Luncheon & Food Services    196.18
                                                  269.38

          Jr. High
              Lunches & Food Services     173.36
              Custodial                   105.28
              Photography                  52.84
              Supplies                     11.00
                                                  342.48
                                                              611.86
                         TOTAL EXPENSES TO DATE              $3968.12


Balance in Bank, September 20, 1975

      Savings    $2000.00
      Checking       4.91
                                                             $2004.91
(TWO SCHOLARSHIPS AWARDED, BUT NOT PAID AS YET.)
```

Figure 20-24 Festival Financial Statement.
(Courtesy of DTASC.)

should be rewarded. Students must learn to win and to lose, to live with success and failure, to rise above setbacks, and, most important of all, to rise above accolades. The first time students go to an open reading at a community theater, they will be competing. Why shouldn't we prepare them?

Some teachers find that their students, particularly the shy and the overconfident, benefit enormously from the experience of competitive work.

"I love to take my students to festivals," one drama teacher told me. "They get off their high horse when they see so much talent at other schools. They go with such exaggerated ideas of their own importance and they return with such wondrous humility."

Festivals can also be run on a noncompetitive basis. Instead of trophies, all entrants get medals for participation. Instead of points, judges render evaluations that are forwarded to the students' teachers. Following the festival, each teacher reviews the evaluations and decides which items would be useful for the students. This takes massive amounts of paper shuffling and sorting. Participants still gain the major rewards of a festival—playing in a different environment to a different audience, sharing experiences, and measuring their own work against the work of others. But there are no winners or losers.

Drama teachers should make their feelings on the matter of competing known to festival planning committees. Festival planners must be responsive to the majority of their constituents. If teachers simply return their registration forms with a statement that they are not entering this year, the festival is likely to continue as it always has. But if they state their reason for declining, they may get some response.

If you are going to compete, prepare your students for it. Tell them how you feel about competing. Ask how they feel about it. Discuss what behavior they expect of themselves during and following the festival. Ask what they expect to gain by competing, and follow up afterward by asking if they got out of it what they expected.

One teacher has his entrants present their work to an audience of parents the night before the festival. Another drama teacher has his entrants tour selected classrooms to present their work during the week before the festival. Both systems give the students extra experience and get them up for the festival.

Conclusion

Festivals do not just happen. The major factors contributing to their overall success are painstaking planning and careful problem solving. With these and a few years of experience, your festival should run smoothly and effectively.

21

Getting a Job

Your First Job as Stage Manager

There is no minimum number of college credits that qualifies an individual to become a professional stage manager. Outside of educational theater situations, no producer (or anyone else who hires stage managers) will ask to see your college diploma, your high school diploma, or any other kind of certificate. Producers might ask to see your résumé and will probably ask you about your past experience.

The two factors that count most heavily are your feeling of competence and your ability to sell yourself. If you have read this manual this far, understand it, and feel that you can apply everything in it, you are ready to stage manage. Now, can you convince someone else that you are ready?

In seeking your first job, my recommendation is that you apply immediately as stage manager at the theater closest to your home. If you are not accepted, ask if you may work as assistant stage manager, property person, assistant property person, or on the crew. Once working in any subordinate position, demonstrate your competence and tell the producer that you want to work your way up.

The frequent pattern is that if hired as props, no matter how competent you prove yourself, you will always be seen by that producer as props. So, with the experience you have, start applying to other theaters for positions of greater responsibility. Later, when you have worked at another theater as stage manager, the producer for whom you propped will welcome you back as stage manager.

The best time to get a paid stage management position is when you already have a job in community, educational, or showcase theater. This might mean taking a bread-and-butter daytime job while you work in community theater at night until you can get the experience and credits you need.

If you are considering going to college with a career in theater in mind, I suggest that you visit possible campuses and talk to the students who are in the theater program. It is too easy to be misled by advertisements and catalogues. From the students seek the answers to the following questions:

1. How many main stage and little theater productions are put on every year? Some colleges provide the opportunity to make theater happen. Others have very limited production opportunities even though they may have fine academic programs. Your concern is whether or not you will have a chance to work. In some schools where there are many productions every year, there may also be very large numbers of students. Will you be a small fish in a large pond? Perhaps it would be better to go to a smaller school where everyone works without waiting to be in the junior class. Ask the students about this; they know.

2. Does any one faculty member teach with passion? Well, if not passion, a point of view? Well, lacking a point of view, how about a sense of joy? You can't write to a prospective teacher and ask, "Will you light my fire?" But you can ask the students if they have found any faculty members they can endorse as enthusiastic. Again, the students generally know.

By the time you have discussed these two questions with prospective fellow students you will have a good idea if you will fit into their theater community just from the vibes you get.

There are many different atmospheres in which to study theater. Check around at junior colleges, private and state supported colleges and universities, and independent theater programs before making up your mind. Don't feel trapped if you don't find what you want the first semester; you can usually transfer credits to other institutions.

Résumés

A résumé is a letter of introduction that you write on behalf of yourself to a prospective employer.

Put yourself in her or his shoes. What does she or he want to know about you? Your past experience is most important. What have you done? Put your most recent credit at the top of the page. Whom did you work with? At what theaters? The faster the prospective employer can find the information she or he wants, the better (see Figure 21-1).

It's a good idea to list the names of a few prominent cast members along with your credits. It is name dropping in its most obvious and honest application.

CREDITS

PLAY	THEATRE	DIRECTOR(PROD)
*MI?DLE OF THE NIGHT (Jonas Rimson, Arlene Schwimmer)	JCA Center Playhouse	(Bill Miller)
*THE TUNNEL OF LOVE (Ron Doyle, Linda Priest)	Theatre Rapport	(Bob Cole)
· THE ANTHEM SPRINTERS (Patrick Burke, Gary Walberg)	Actors Studio West	Charles Rome Smith
*A MY NAME IS ALICE (Dina Babbitt, Wadsworth Taylor)	JCA Center Playhouse	(Bill Miller)
+THE GLASS MENAGERIE (Piper Laurie, Ann Sothern)	Huntington Hartford	George Keathley
−THE FANTASTICKS (Janice Hague, Michael McGiveney)	Immaculate Heart	Patricia Madsen
−THE VOYAGE (Ron Stevens, Wadsworth Taylor)	" "	R. Montgomery
*CRAWLING ARNOLD (Hal Adelson, Shirley-May Pilnick)	JCA Center Playhouse	(Bill Miller)
· AFFAIRS OF STATE (Joan Caulfield, John Himes)	Orange County Theatre	Reid Lowden
· FUNNY THING HAPPENED ON WAY TO FORUM (Sterling Holloway, Gil Lamb)	Fresno Music Circus	Jonathan Lucas
+FUNNY THING HAPPENED ON WAY TO FORUM (Danny Dee, Sherri Spilane)	Sacramento Mus. Circ.	" "
·SHOW BOAT (Alan Gilbert, Marvin Miller)	" " "	Milton Lyon
·GUYS AND DOLLS (Ed Ames, Joyce Jameson)	" " "	Jonathan Lucas
··TAKE ME ALONG (John Conte, Danny Lockin)	" " "	" "
+110 IN THE SHADE (John Davidson, Gaylea Byrne)	" " "	" "
+MUSIC MAN (Kathleen Freeman, Norwood Smith)	" " "	" "
+PAJAMA GAME (Wally Griffin, Patti Karr)	" " "	" "
+BYE BYE BIRDIE (Peter Marshall, Jess Pearson)	" " "	" "
+CAMELOT (Kenneth Nelson, Lyle Talbot)	" " "	" "
·NOBODY LOVES AN ALBATROSS (Frank Aletter, Kathleen Freeman)	Las Palmas	Alan DeWitt
·ONE FLEW OVER THE CUCKOO´S NEST (Warren Oates, William Smith)	Player´s Ring Gallery	John Erman
·ENTER LAUGHING (Lillian Adams, Arthur Peterson)	" " "	Harvey Korman
·THE TORCH BEARERS (Jeanne Arnold, Len Lesser)	Equity Library Theatre	" "
·THE EMPEROR (Henry Darrow, Bart Heyman)	Cahuenga Playhouse	Bill Wintersole

*director
−technical director
· stage manager
+assistant stage manager

resume January ´69
Lawrence Stern
Main P.O. Box 1901
Los Angeles 90053
(213) 55? 2424

Figure 21-1 Short Form Résumé Showing Varieties of Theatrical Management Experience

```
                           RESUME

            LAWRENCE STERN

            Main Post Office Box 1901        213/555-2424
            Los Angeles, California, 90053

            Single      6 feet      155 lbs.    Good health

CURRENTLY   Assistant Production Manager, Greek Theatre Assoc.

            Year round operation of Huntington Hartford
            Theatre (1,000 seats, legitimate local productions
            and touring companies) in Hollywood and summer
            operation of Greek Theatre (4,400 seats, outdoor
            amphitheater; popular attractions, musicals, opera,
            ballet, dance) in Los Angeles, as well as packa-
            ger of touring attractions for San Francisco,
            San Diego, Sacramento, Santa Barbara, and Hono-
            lulu.  Responsible for research of Broadway pro-
            ductions and touring attractions, cost analysis,
            and coordination with producers of incoming pro-
            ductions.

RECENT      Technical director, Immaculate Heart College
THEATER     for productions of THE VOYAGE and THE FANTASTICS,
EXPERIENCE  1966.  Responsible for construction of sets and
1963 - 1966 coordination with art department, as well as
            instruction of student crew.  Worked with di-
            rectors Ray Montgomery and Patricia Madsen.

            Production Stage Manager, Sacramento Music Circus
            (1,700 seat tent theater in the round) for
            CAMELOT, BYE BYE BIRDIE, PAJAMA GAME, 110 IN THE
            SHADE, TAKE ME ALONG, MUSIC MAN, GUYS AND DOLLS,
            SHOW BOAT, and A FUNNY THING HAPPENED ON THE
            WAY TO THE FORUM, 1965.  Worked with directors
            Jonathan Lucas and Milton Lyon.  Responsible for
            the coordination of department heads in produc-
            tion phase, management of the company in rehear-
            sals, and light, sound and music cues during
            performance.

            Since February 1963, stage managed Center
            Playhouse's THE CRUCIBLE directed by Frank
            Bessell, and PALACE OF A THOUSAND DREAMS
            (children's play) directed by George Werier.
            At Cahuenga Playhouse stage managed THE EMPEROR
            produced by Lou Rifkin, directed by William
            Wintersole.  Stage managed THE TORCH-BEARERS
            for director Harvey Korman at Equity Library
            Theatre West and ENTER LAUGHING (also directed
            by Mr. Korman) and ONE FLEW OVER THE CUCKOO'S
            NEST (directed by John Erman) at Paul Levitt's
            Players' Ring Gallery.  Last Hollywood assign-
            ment was stage managing Dorothy Roth's produc-
            tion of NOBODY LOVES AN ALBATROSS at the Las
            Palmas Theatre.  Have written, produced and
            directed parodies of plays I've worked on since
            high school days.
```

Figure 21-2   Long Form Résumé for a Theatrical Manager

A more formal résumé, including schooling, unrelated work experience, and biographical data might be desirable if you want the producer
to know more about you (see Figure 21-2). The problem with the long
form is getting the producer or administrator to read it. You should
assume that a producer is a very busy person who doesn't have time to

MILITARY   Commissioned second lieutenant through ROTC,
EXPERIENCE   June 1957, as <u>Station Manager</u>, Armed Forces Radio
1959 - 1963   and Television Service, Island of Crete, was
                responsible for producing 130 hours per week of
                radio and 70 hours per week of television. Pro-
                duced, directed, wrote, supervised a staff of 20
                military announcers and Greek national techni-
                cians, scheduled, surveyed, punched, floor
                managed, worked camera, reorganized film and
                record libraries, supervised a radio station in
                Athens, hosted frequent visitors to the only TV
                facility in Greece. Won three network awards for
                outstanding programs.

                Served as Wing Information Officer for 3rd
                Weather Wing, Offutt Air Force Base, headquarters
                Strategic Air Command (SAC). Responsible for
                nation-wide news releases and public information.
                Edited monthly newsletter to 100 subordinate
                units. Organized and directed base little theater
                group producing VISIT TO A SMALL PLANET, NIGHT
                MUST FALL, THE CURIOUS SAVAGE and THE SEVEN YEAR
                ITCH. Drama critic for base newspaper.

                Final Air Force assignment, Assistant Director,
                Candidate Advisory Service, United States Air
                Force Academy, Colorado. Traveled from state to
                state in public relations capacity bringing
                Academy to attention of educators. Arranged for
                displays at state and national educational con-
                ferences and presented slide briefings. Won
                first place in Academy's annual short story
                contest, 1962. Honorable discharge as first
                lieutenant, February 1963. No Reserve obligation.

EDUCATION   WESTERN RESERVE UNIVERSITY, Cleveland, Ohio.
1953 - 1958   Master of Arts in theater (direction, scene
                design, lighting, television production, play-
                writing). BA in English, 1957, minored in
                theater arts. Reported for school paper, debated,
                served as class and student council officer,
                wrote book and lyrics "Letter Girl" (annual
                college musical) in junior year. Cum laude
                graduate, elected to Omicron Delta Kappa, national
                honorary leadership fraternity. Worked way
                through college as nightshift lathe operator at
                Thompson Ramo Wooldridge, bakery hand for Fisher
                Brothers, page at Cleveland Public and Western
                Reserve University libraries, playground super-
                visor, counter boy at Lake Shore Country Club.

EARLY   <u>Grew up in Cleveland, Ohio</u>. Father was a
BACKGROUND   watchmaker. Attended public schools: Hazeldell
                Elementary, Patrick Henry Junior High, Glenville
                High School. Graduated January 1953 in upper 10
                percent of class. Active in high school dra-
                matics under Eugine C. Davis. Class officer.
                Held part-time jobs as machinist and library page.

REFERENCES   Personal references will be forward upon request.

Figure 21-2 *(Continued)*

read. Put the most important, earthshaking words at the top: HIS OR HER NAME, i.e., "Mr. or Ms. Wheeler-dealer, I want to work for you." This sentence, written legibly at the top of your résumé, besides informalizing and possibly getting his or her attention, also states your immediate goal.

The Harvard Business School recommends that an accurate statement of your goals be the first item in your résumé. However, in the case of the stage manager, a concise statement of goals might severely limit the application of your résumé. If you are a stage manager this week, you may want to work as a road manager for a music group, advance person for a circus, light designer for an ice show, or guest director for a resident theater next week.

Instead of printing your goal as part of your résumé, tailor each résumé to the specific prospective employer with a cover letter or a handwritten note. Tell him or her concisely how you think you can serve him or her best.

Your address and phone number(s) are essential.

Note that race, religion, national origin, and age are not included in the résumé.

Send your résumé out regularly to every theater in town, and if you're willing to travel, to selected theaters out of town. Every three months is not too often. It is absolutely impossible for you to know exactly when a theater will be in need of new personnel.

A résumé is usually worthless unless it is followed up with personal contact. Start with a phone call. Ask if your résumé arrived. Then ask if there are any openings now or if any are expected. Ask if you might drop by for a chat in the hopes of getting acquainted and being kept in mind for some future opening. At the very least, get the name of the person who actually hires the stage manager at that theater.

In your contact file keep a record of the theaters to which you've sent your résumé, and the names of the people to whom you've spoken in your follow-up phone conversations. Note their comments carefully. Who is the stage manager now? Could you work without salary on the crew until a paying slot opens up? During pre-opening rush, could you work with the crew just to get acquainted with their staff?

Hiring is usually done face to face, and personality may be a much more significant factor than experience. For the novice it is important to realize that although you may be the best stage manager in the world, there are directors, production managers, and producers who will not care to work with you because they feel that your personality will not mesh with theirs in what they consider to be the best interest of production. Over the years they have become able to make this evaluation instantaneously. It is something that does not lend itself to open expression in the interview process. If you are rejected and feel there is no reason other than the interviewer's feeling against you, try to trust his or her judgment and try someplace else.

When you have several credits, you may wish to have your name and capsule résumé published in the *Players' Guide*, an annual pictorial directory for stage, screen, radio and television, published by Paul L. Ross, 165 West 46th Street, New York City 10036, phone: (212) 869–3570. The section devoted exclusively to stage managers might bring your name to the attention of a prospective employer. The Guide is published annually in August. Deadline for submission of materials is the first week in February.

When your level of experience warrants it, you might also wish to submit your résumé to the Theatre Communications Group (TCG), 355 Lexington Ave., New York City 10017, phone: (212) 697–5230. TCG assists in the exchange of information among theater people nationwide. They have their own résumé format and will send you their form on request.

The trade papers rarely contain advertisements for stage managers. It is definitely a producers' market with supply exceeding demand in situations where the stage manager is paid. And yet, in community and little theaters where the stage manager is not paid, or is dreadfully underpaid, it is almost impossible to get competent people to serve as stage manager. This means that the novice can easily gain the valuable experience she or he needs if she or he wants to work up to the level of the professional stage manager.

Do not underestimate yourself. Send your résumés to theaters that you feel require greater experience than you possess. You might make a valuable contact that will pay off later. Or you may be hired for a slot far above what you're seeking by a producer who recognizes your potential.

When you are "at liberty," you will have plenty of time to send out résumés and to update your contact file so that you can get off your next round with far less effort. From your file you will be able to pull the addresses of the theaters, and you can send them out marked to the attention of the specific individual who does the hiring.

It is a Hollywood aphorism that "the best time to get a job is when you have one." Even if you are happily employed in what seems like a long-range situation, get out your résumé regularly and keep up your contacts.

Personal Mailing List

In addition to mailing out résumés to prospective employers, you may wish to keep up your contacts with people in the business by regularly sending them notes on your progress, invitations to shows you're doing, and programs of shows you've done (not to mention Christmas and New Year's greetings).

It takes very little effort and does not cost much in postage and stationery to let your theater acquaintances know what you're doing—and it can pay off in many pleasant ways.

Three months after your present show closes, ten members of your cast, staff, and crew may be working in ten different theater situations. Each represents a possible introduction for you to another set of directors and producers. But three months after you close you may run into an actor with whom you worked nightly, and he or she may not remember your name.

The theater scene is both fluid and forgetful. To exploit the former quality, you have to overcome the latter.

Your personal mailing list might consist of all of your cast lists with crew and staff members added.

I worked for many years outside of New York as a non-union stage manager. When I came to New York, I stage-managed showcases for about two years, getting paid next to nothing—working with Equity and non-Equity actors. One of the actors I worked with recommended me to a producer, and I got an interview. I know that the actor's recommendation helped, but I had to put myself on the line —let the producer know that I had the experience and the background that would make me an asset to his company. I got the job and the Equity contract. Once that job was over, I was back looking for paying work and stage-managing Equity showcases—to keep growing as a stage manager until I landed my next Equity job—and so it continued for the seven years I actively stage-managed as an Equity stage manager.

Martha R. Jacobs
Stage Manager
New York City

Martha's work as a stage manager led to her current administrative work in live theater.

Long-Range Goals

Where are you going, Stage Manager? Do you want to stage-manage for the rest of your life? Do you want to find some big, cushy theater with stable management and move in to stay—to sixty-five or senility, whichever comes first?

There seem to be too few career stage managers in the business. There are a lot of aspiring actors, aspiring directors, aspiring producers, and aspiring writers who call themselves stage managers. There are a lot of stage managers who are on their way out of the theater—on their way to law school, teaching English, programming a computer, or selling shoes. Stage management seems frequently to be a phase rather than a career.

If you make a career of it, you can hope for a salary of $350 per week. If you get to Broadway, your salary might go as high as $1140 per week as production stage manager for a musical. (These figures reflect the Equity contracts as of 1985. For more current information, call your local Equity office.)

But that's the optimistic viewpoint. You must expect feast and famine, periods of high pay and periods of unemployment.

A big-name visiting director at our school said that no one important he had ever met started out as a stage manager. I'm pushing to be the first.

> Jill Johnson
> Theater arts student
> Occidental College, California

Former stage managers don't wear minature gold clipboards around their necks. So sometimes it's hard to tell. Your visiting director had obviously not met Humphrey (*Casablanca*) Bogart, Dale (*Man of La Mancha*) Wasserman, or Gordon (*Mark Taper Forum*) Davidson. I'm sure these three (actor, writer, director) do not exhaust the list. Stage management is not a mandatory prerequisite for any other job in theater. But it is a potentially valuable way to enter the very competitive world of theater and meet others who can help you along the way.

I've come a long way since my last letter. I am an Equity stage manager, and have worked the past three years at the Mark Taper Forum (for, ironically, Gordon, who was indeed a stage manager and who consequently demands a great deal of his stage manager teams). My best advice is to start wherever you can, experience any and all aspects of theater, and make it known to those around you what your ultimate goals are. I began as an intern in the Taper casting office and told *everyone* that I wanted to stage-manage. That information reached someone who needed a production intern, a position which let me prove myself as well as learn the ways of professional theater. I was offered a year-long position as resident production assistant, which enabled me to work with various directors, designers, and stage managers. Then they needed a stage manager for *Moby Dick: Rehearsed*, and here I am, one year later, resident Production Stage Manager in a brand new four theatre complex.

> Jill Johnson
> Production Stage Manager
> Los Angeles Theatre Center
> Los Angeles, California

Unlike many careers, stage management does not offer regular promotions, hours, vacations, and retirement. A few benefits are provided
by union membership, but it is up to the individual to plan her or his
own career progress. Promotions are yours for the getting, the hustling,
and the self-promoting. If you plan to be a career stage manager, you
must evaluate your own aggressiveness as a very significant factor in
your potential career. If you are not aggressive, you will drift from one
union minimum situation to the next.

If stage management is just a phase for you, here is my best advice:
Get out just as soon as you can and do your thing. Stage management
demands too much of your organizational ability, energy, time, and
emotional juices for you to think of it as a bread-and-butter job to support
your real interest in life. When you have stage-managed three or four
shows in two or more theaters, you will have a fair understanding of
the job, and certainly adequate background for any related theater work.
It won't take you more than six months of steady work to know if you
want to make it a career. Then if you want to be an actor, director,
producer, writer, or shoe salesperson, get out and act, direct, produce,
write, or sell shoes.

But if you want to be a stage manager, give it all you've got. Be a
great stage manager!

Appendix

A Few Theater Stories

Knowing jokes is not a substitute for having a sense of humor. There are occasions, however, when a good theater anecdote can be helpful.

1. Fresh from grad school and the Actor's Studio, the young director's first assignment was with an old, established Yiddish theater company. On his first day with the group, he assembled the entire company on stage and delivered to them The Method.

He spoke eloquently for *five* hours(!): inner stress, remembered emotion, Stanislavsky, Vahktangov, Strasberg, everything. And when he was through, dripping with perspiration, he knew in his heart that he had just delivered the definitive lecture on The Method. He strode away triumphantly to let them think it over.

One old time Yiddish actor turned to another. "So how does he want, louder or softer?"

2. A hastily assembled and rehearsed cast of *Stalag 17* was in the hushed conspiracy sequence when the stage manager noticed that the dialogue on stage had decreased to an inaudible whisper. He prompted with a line that would lead the cast out of this sequence. There was only silence on stage. So the stage manager prompted again. Another silence. Finally an actor broke the silence with a harsh whisper: "We all know *what* the line is, but *who* says it?"

3. The wedding of the daughter of a very famous Hollywood character actor brought out many producers, directors, and agents. As the proud father escorted the bride down the aisle, this whisper was overheard: "Will you look who they got to play the father!"

4. The old circus worker came home drenched from a storm. For years and years his job had been to follow the elephants in the parades and clean up after them.

His wife pleaded with him. "Why do you do it?" You're past retirement age. It's bad for your health—out in all kinds of weather. Please, I beg you, retire."

"What," he answered, "and give up show biz!"

5.   The novice actor was elated by a call from his agent. It was just a one-line walk-on in an historical play, but it was work. The actor who was to do the part had been taken ill. They opened that night. The agent explained that he would get his costume and full particulars at the theater.

"By the way," said the agent, "your line is, 'Hark, I hear a cannon.' "

On the way to the theater the novice rehearsed his line: "**Hark**, I hear a cannon." "Hark **I** hear a cannon." "Hark, I hear a **cannon**." He was absolutely determined to deliver his one line well.

He got into his costume and the stage manager briefed him. His cue would be the firing of the cannon.

He went on stage. He waited. His moment was coming. He became more and more excited. Finally the cannon exploded.

And the novice delivered his line as follows: "What the hell was that?!!"

6.   The old stripper had been out of work for years. Her agent called to ask her if she would do a Seal Lodge in Draidel, North Dakota. She was desperate; she agreed.

Sure enough, it was popping-out-of-the-cake time, as the band played, on a table surrounded by aging Seals in their purple fezzes. But something happened. As she danced the men started to clap. Then they started pounding on the table. They rose out of their seats, banged harder and faster on the table, stamped on the floor, became excited and then frenzied. Some started jumping up onto the table. Then they started grabbing for her. She pushed them away. They grabbed some more. She pushed, fought, clawed, shoved, kicked and, fighting off their hands, somehow managed to escape to her dressing room. She slammed and bolted the door and turned to her agent, who was reading the trades with his feet sprawled over her makeup table. In an angry voice she asked, "Did you hear that band?"

7.   Following his debut at Carnegie Hall, the soloist was overwhelmed by the audience which rose as one man yelling, "Again, Again, Again."

The singer repeated his last number, and when he finished, his bow to the audience was again met with screams of "Again, Again, Again."

He repeated each number in his program until the audience had called him back for a total of twelve encores, and in total exhaustion tried to thank his audience for their enthusiastic reception: "I thank you, but I am simply too fatigued to continue."

Above the audience's chant of "Again, Again, Again," rose a single voice shouting, "You gonna keep on singing until you get it right."

8.   Cecil B. De Mille was about to shoot his greatest, most costly epic scene. He had stationed his three best cameramen strategically. In the scene a herd of elephants stampeded through a native village, an earthquake swallowed up half the village, a tidal wave covered everything else and, as the waters receded, a volcano erupted spewing hot lava and burning the remaining huts. Then the

Yugoslavian army on horseback, dressed as the hordes of Ghengis Khan, swept through the remains, raping and pillaging, only to be in turn swept off by a tornado.

Eighty-seven assistant directors and the headquarters staff of the Yugoslavian army held the thousands of extras in place. Three hundred and seventeen special effects men readied the wind machines, dynamite, and chicken feathers.

Then C.B. gave the command, "Lights, cameras, action."

And it all happened beautifully—the elephants, earthquake, tidal wave, lava, burning, the Yugoslavian army, raping, pillaging, and the tornado. And when the last chicken feather had settled to the ground, Cecil B. De Mille knew that he had produced the most incredible sequence ever captured on film.

"Did you get that, Dick?" he asked his ace cameraman.

"Gosh, C.B., I forget to take the lens cover off the camera."

"Never mind," said C.B. "Did you get that Roger?" he asked his second cameraman.

"Oh, boy, C.B. I forgot to load the film."

"Never mind," De Mille said and shouted up to the third cameraman on the dolly, "Did you get that, Arthur?"

Arthur shouted back, "I'm ready when you are, C.B."

9. The community theater in Frigidoria, Maine, was about to open when the prompter came down with pimples. Fortunately, the ingenue had a maiden aunt who lived only a few blocks from the theater. Hastily she was summoned and installed behind the scenery with a script and flashlight, and instructed to watch the lines. She was told to let the actors know if they gave the wrong ones.

All went smoothly until the third act. The leading man went up. There was silence on the stage. Then he repeated his last line, "Behold, the moon rises by yonder peak."

Nothing.

So he moved upstage to the flat which hid the ingenue's aunt, kicked the flat, and delivered his last line once again. "Behold, the moon rises by yonder peak."

And then he heard the ingenue's aunt whispering, "Wrong."

10. The Boy Scout saw a nun trying to cross a busy intersection near Broadway. He offered to help her.

"Oh, thank you, young man, but I can make it."

Please, sister, let me help," said the scout. "We're supposed to do good deeds."

When they had crossed, he said, "May I ask what order you're with so I can tell my scoutmaster?"

"Oh, for Pete's sake," she said, "I'm with *The Sound of Music*."

11. The last act of a college's production of *Hedda Gabler* was building to its melodramatic conclusion in which Hedda takes the pistols, which the playwright had so conspicuously planted, and exits into the library to shoot herself. After a shot is heard, Tesman crosses to the library door, peers offstage, and announces to the audience, "Shot herself. Shot herself in the temple. Fancy that."

The student actor playing Tesman waited for the shot. Finally he heard—

click, click. He crossed to the library door, peered offstage, and said, "Oh my God, she stabbed herself to death."

12.   We were rehearsing a play called *Golden Boy*. Charlie Lynch was playing the part of Tom, a prize fighter, and Dorothy Kilheffer was playing the part of Lorna. These two are in love. In the process of finding out that they are in love they have a violent quarrel. During this quarrel he says to her, "I wouldn't look at you twice if they hung you naked from a Christmas tree."

At this moment I heard a quite audible gasp from John Schaeffer (President of the College). I thought to myself, "Uh-uh, we may be going to get the blue pencil." But we went on without interruption.

At the end of the scene Dr. Schaeffer called Dotty to him and said something to her in a rather agitated whisper.

After rehearsal I asked Dotty what happened. He had said to her, "Dotty, that's a terrible thing for a man to say to a woman. That's the worst thing he can possibly say. Don't worry, Dotty, if they hung you naked from a Christmas tree, I'd look at you twice."—(Darrell D. Larsen, retiring after 35 years as director of theater for Franklin and Marshall College, *Alumnus Magazine*, July, 1962).

13.   Sammy Ginsburg had been in show biz for eighty years as a stunt man in a circus. His specialty was diving one hundred feet into a barrel of water. As he began his act, he addressed the crowd.

"Ladies and gentlemen, good evening. Tonight for the forty-seven thousandth, four hundred and fifty-third consecutive time you will see me climb up on this one hundred foot ladder and dive into this barrel of water."

A hush fell over the audience. The drums started to roll.

"Of course," Sammy continued, "it's not like in the old days. I've been doing this same stunt for sixty-five years, and I'm a little slower now—my arthritis."

He reached for the ladder and moaned. "Also a little bursitis I have it in my right arm. But I have to go on with the show because I'm the sole support of a family of fourteen."

He slowly pulled himself up on the second rung and groaned low again.

The crowd became apprehensive at the sight of this old man groaning up the ladder. "Don't jump," shouted a member of the audience. Soon several others joined in and it became a chant, "Don't jump, Sammy, don't jump." Finally the whole audience was standing up, chanting, shouting, imploring Sammy not to go through with it.

"Okay, okay already," said Sammy, stopping his climb and addressing the audience. "The next performance is at 10:30."

14.   Edward G. Robinson once said that you could always tell if he was a good guy or a bad guy in a movie by the angle of the brim of his hat. If it was up, he was usually a detective, and if it was down, he was the heavy. While filming a flick in which he was a terrible villain, his hat brim suddenly popped up.

"What did you do?" asked a friend.

"What could I do?" replied Robinson. "Why I arrested myself, of course."

15. A local high school interviewer asked John Barrymore if he thought Romeo and Juliet had been sexually intimate. "Well," replied Barrymore, "in the Chicago company they were."

16. When Cecil B. De Mille arrived at the Pearly Gates, St. Peter asked him to produce a film.

C.B. said no.

"But you can use all the greatest talent we have here," St. Peter persisted. "Directors: Stanislavsky, Eisenstein, Griffith. . . . "

"No," said C.B.

"Actors: Barrymore, Gable, Cooper, Bogart. . . . "

"No," said C.B.

"Composers: Beethoven, Tschaikovsky, Mozart, Gershwin, Hammerstein. . . . "

"Well," said C.B.

"Writers: Shakespeare, Shaw, O'Neil, anyone you want."

"Okay," said C.B., "with talent like that, how can I refuse. I can start this afternoon."

"Great," said St. Peter, "but first I'd like you to read this girl I know. She sings."

17. Dustin Hoffman was scheduled to shoot a scene from the movie *The Marathon Man.* He arrived on set looking totally bedraggled. Sir Laurence Olivier asked what had happened. Hoffman explained that in order to prepare for his scene as a runner, he had stayed up all night running. "My dear young man," asked Olivier, "have you thought of acting?"

18. A lovely Hollywood lady was complaining to her friend that she couldn't sing. The friend sympathized. "And I can't dance." The friend sympathized. "And worst of all, I can't act."

"Why don't you give up show business?" her friend asked.

"I can't quit. I'm a star."

19. The rabbi was running late when he arrived at the funeral. Flustered, he tried in vain to find the notes that would help him to personalize his eulogy. "He was so loved by his brothers. Although they all live far from here, they have gathered with us to pay their last respects. His brother . . . "

"Arthur," someone whispered.

" . . . his brother Arthur," continued the rabbi, "is from . . . "

"a doctor in Cleveland," the same person whispered.

"Cleveland," continued the rabbi. "where he's a doctor. And his brother . . . "

"Leonard," came the whisper.

"His brother Leonard is . . . "

"an accountant in Kansas City," whispered.

" . . . here from Kansas City where he's an accountant. And his brother . . . "

"Sam," whispered.

" . . . and his brother Sam, who . . . "

"An agent in Hollywood," whispered.

"Sam enchanted evening, you will meet a stranger. . . . "

20.   An American Black actor strode into the rehearsal hall of the British National Company where Sir John Gielgud was casting *Hamlet.*

"Hey, Blood. What it is?"

"May I help you, sir?"

"Yeah, man, I wants to read."

"I beg your pardon. This is an audition for Shakespeare's *Hamlet.*"

"Yeah, I dig. Slip me a script and let's get on down."

"You wish to audition? . . . For which part?"

"The main man, Jive."

"You're going to read for Hamlet? And with which scene did you wish to audition?"

"The solo gig."

"The soliloquy? I see. Very well. The stage is yours."

The Black actor took center stage and then took several moments to get into character. Slowly, and very obviously in complete control, he began to speak. "To be, or not to be: that is the question: whether . . . "

His projected voice was eloquent. His enunciation was crisp. His interpretation was electrifying. Every subtle nuance of meaning was reflected in his eyes and facial expression. Every gesture, every moment, said "Prince of Denmark." Without benefit of makeup, lighting, or scenery, he was totally Hamlet. It was a truly sensational reading. When he finished there was rapt silence from the other auditioning actors. Then loud applause. The Black actor jumped down from the stage and strode over to Gielgud.

"Man, you didn't think I could do it."

Gielgud replied, "I have never . . . In my years in the . . . that was the most. . . . How do you do that?"

"That's actin', man."

21.   Phillip runs into his old friend Elliot, an actor on Broadway.

"How are you, Elliot?"

"Terrific. Couldn't be better. I've been running over at the Helen Hayes Theatre for the last three months and it looks like we'll run forever. Before that I shot a spaghetti Western in Yugoslavia. My TV series is in reruns nationally. I've been selected as spokesperson for Campbell Soups and my last three commercials are all still running. And Neil Simon wants me to do the lead in his next play. But enough about me. How about you? How did *you* like my last movie?"

22.   The late Ruth Gordon was performing in a play. The phone on the set rang and she knew it was her cue, but she went up on her lines. She picked up the phone, turned to the actress standing next to her, and said, "It's for you."

23.   A director dies and goes to heaven. On his very first day there he is delighted by St. Peter's tour of Heavenly Civic Theatre. The actors in rehearsal are first rate. The facilities are without equal—state of the art lighting, sound, and stage equipment. "This is terrific!" exclaims the director, "I can't imagine what hell must be like."

With a snap of his finger St. Peter transfers the director to the Satanic Civic Theatre. The director is equally impressed—from the chandeliers in the lobby to the ornate barber chairs in the makeup room, the facilities are equal. "I can't see any difference," protests the director.

"No," says St. Peter knowingly, "but in Heaven the critics aren't allowed at opening night."

24. A producer and writer are on their way to Palm Springs for a weekend of work on a script when their car breaks down in the desert. They walk and then crawl across the burning sands. Finally, almost totally dehydrated, they come upon a tiny stream of cool water. The writer scoops up some water in his hands and is about to bring it to his lips when the producer throws some desert sand into the water in the writer's hands. "Why did you do that?" shouts the writer.

The producer answers, "Just trying to help you fix it up a little."

25. An actor returns home to find his home burnt to the ground. He asks his neighbor what happened. The neighbor says, "Sorry to tell you, but your agent came to your home, beat up your wife and kids, locked them in the basement, stole your TV and VCR, and torched your house."

"What," stammers the actor incredulously, "my agent came to my home?!!!"

26. Two guys are sitting in a bar. One asks, "What's your I.Q?"

"One eighty-five," replies the second.

"How do you feel current sub-particle quantum research will impact on Einstein's theory?" They chat for a while.

In another part of the bar two others are talking. "What's your I.Q?" asks the first.

"It's 120," answers the second.

"Did you catch the Dodgers game last night?"

They chat.

In a dimly lit corner two others are talking. "What's your I.Q?" asks the first.

"About 39," replies the second.

"Have you read any good scripts lately?"

I love old theater stories. If you have any that you'd like to contribute to future editions of *Stage Management*, please see the last page of this manual for my address.

Glossary

The terms compiled in this glossary are the special vocabulary of the stage manager.

Abstract set   Nonrepresentational set that suggests rather than simulates appropriate surroundings.

Accent   Emphasis placed on an action or phase of a play by lighting or staging technique.

Achromatic lens   A lens that transmits light without separating it into its spectral colors. Lenses should be achromatic.

Acoustics   The qualities of sound transmission within a theater.

Act curtain   See Curtain.

Acting area   That part of the stage used by actors during the performance; may be extended to aisles or elsewhere if the action of the play takes place there.

Ad-lib   (1) Anything said by actors on stage other than the lines of the script, (2) to extemporize in a performance or interpolate impromptu remarks possibly because of a lapse of memory, as a reaction to an unplanned incident, or to cover a late entrance.

Adaptor   Short length of cable with a different type of plug on each end (i.e., twistlock to pin, or pin to stage plug); also, a plug inserted into a socket so that it will accept a different type of lamp base.

AEA   Actors Equity Association. Union for stage actors and stage managers.

AFTRA   American Federation of Television and Radio Artists. Radio and TV entertainers' union.

AGVA   American Guild of Variety Artists. Nightclub entertainers' union.

Amateur   Anyone whose work in or for the theater is without financial reward.

Amber   A popular yellowish-orange color.

Ampere   Unit of electric current; one ampere is the amount of current sent by one volt through a resistance of one ohm.

Amphitheater   An oval or circular building with rising tiers of seats about an open space.

Anchor   To fasten to the floor.

Angel   One who invests money in a production.

Antagonist   Adversary of the hero or protagonist.

Anti-pros   Lighting instruments hung in front of the proscenium.

Anticipate   React to a cue that has not yet occurred (i.e., actor falls before shot is fired; actor turns to door before knock, etc.).

Antique   To make props or set pieces appear old.

Appliqué   Ornamentation cut from one material and applied to another.

Apprentice   Individual who works in the theater for the learning experience, usually not paid.

Apron   The part of the stage in front of the proscenium.

Arbor   Metal frame supporting counterweights in system for flying scenery.

Arc spotlight   Spotlight in which the source of light is an arc of electric current jumping a small gap between two carbon sticks; the carbon sticks are either hand-adjusted or driven electrically to remain a constant distance apart; an iris shutter is used to control the size of the beam or to shut it off completely.

Arena theater   A theater having the acting area in the center of the auditorium with the audience seated on all sides.

Arm   A batten supporting a curtain; usually a short batten used for wings.

Asbestos curtain   Fireproof curtain located immediately in front of the front curtain. In some areas it is required by law that this curtain be raised and lowered in sight of the audience during a performance. Also called fire curtain and fireproof curtain.

Aside   Dramatic device in which the character speaks directly to the audience while other characters on stage supposedly do not hear him or her.

At liberty   Euphemism for unemployed.

ATPAM   Association of Theatrical Press Agents and Managers. Union for theater publicists and house managers.

Audition   Tryout performance before producers, directors, casting directors, or others for the purpose of obtaining a part in a production; may be acting, singing or dancing.

Auditorium lights   See House lights.

Baby spot   Small spotlight, usually 100, 250, or 400 watts; lens is ordinarily 5", 4 1/2", or smaller in diameter.

Backlight   To focus lighting instruments on the backs (shoulders) of actors to produce emphasis or separation from background.

Backdrop   A large area of painted canvas fastened to a batten and used for a background which hangs straight, i.e., sky drop, woodland drop, lake drop, etc. Contrast to Cyclorama which is not painted but lighted.

Backing light   Illumination behind a set used to give a lighting effect on a backdrop.

Backing unit   Any piece or pieces of scenery placed behind an opening (door, window, etc.) to limit the view from the audience of the offstage areas.

Backstage   (1) The entire area behind the curtain line: stage, dressing rooms, green room, etc., (2) any part of the stage outside of the acting area during a performance.

Baffle   Metal or wood screen used to prevent light spill.

Balcony front spotlights   Spotlights that are mounted on the front of the balcony or related locations to light the acting area.

Barndoor   A metal shutter with doors to control light spill.

Batten (1) A length of rigid material, usually wood, fastened to the top and bottom of a drop or leg, (2) the 1″ × 3″ lumber used to construct scenery, (3) the wood or pipe on a set of lines to which scenery or lights are fastened.

Beam, Ceiling Beam in ceiling of an auditorium in which spotlights are concealed.

Beam front spots Spotlights mounted high in the beams (or prepared slots) of the auditorium ceiling for the purpose of lighting the acting area from above.

Belaying pin A hardwood pin or pipe used in pin rails to tie ropes from gridiron.

Bit part Small role in a production, rarely with more than two or three lines. See Walk on.

Black light Light that causes certain colors and materials to glow in the dark.

Blackout Closing of a scene, act, or the play itself, usually on a particularly effective line, by a sudden extinguishing of the lights. Used frequently in musical revues.

Blacks Black draperies or curtains.

Bleed When a prior color is seen through a subsequent coat, it is said to bleed.

Block A pulley or pulleys in a frame, part of counterweight flying system.

Blocking Movement of actors in the acting area.

Blocking notation Written description of actors' movement.

Boards The stage. "To walk the boards" means to appear on stage.

Bobbinet Transparent curtain of silken texture. See Scrim.

Book Play manuscript. In musical productions, the libretto without the music.

Boomerang Color wheel. A box attached to a lighting instrument to hold color frames. Makes color changes convenient. See Color box.

Border *Scenery*: An abbreviated drop at the top of the set, which masks the flies from the audience. May represent sky, foliage, etc. *Lighting*: row of overhead lights on stage. First row behind the proscenium arch is called the concert border, X-Ray border, or first border. Others are numbered from down- to upstage: second border, third border, etc.

Border lights Strips of lights mounted in a metal trough divided into compartments with individual color frame holders. Instruments are normally wired into three or four different circuits and are used for general lighting in the stage area.

Bottle Slang for bulb or lamp that is used in a stage lighting instrument.

Box set Traditional set of three walls.

Brace cleat A small metal plate attached to the frame of a flat. A stage brace is hooked into it to brace a flat.

Brace, Stage An adjustable device made of two lengths of 1″ × 1″ wood held between clamps, used to support scenery from behind. A forked iron hook fastened to one end of the brace is twist-hooked into a brace cleat attached to the unit requiring support, and an iron foot at the other end of the brace is secured to the floor by means of a stage screw.

"Break a leg" Traditional wish of good luck exchanged between theatrical people prior to opening night curtain instead of "good luck."

Breakaway Scenery or props that disappear, break, or change form in full view of the audience.

Break character To say or do anything, as an actor, during a rehearsal or performance, which is not consistent with what the character portrayed would say or do.

Bridge A long, narrow platform hung from the grid immediately adjacent to a light pipe or attached to it, for the purpose of allowing a technician access to lighting instruments.

Bridge lights Those lights that are mounted on the bridge.

Bridge, Paint A long narrow platform hung from the grid at the back wall, upstage from which a scenic artist may paint scenery or drops attached to a frame on the wall.

Bring up To increase the intensity of the lights. See Dim in.

Build Accumulation and gradual acceleration of tempo, emotional intensity, and action by dramatist, actors, or director at any point in a play, but particularly in the approach to the climax.

Bump it To hit the floor forcefully with flown scenery in order to trim the scenery.

Bump up To bring up as fast as possible.

Burn in The first red flow emitted by the filament of a lighting instrument before full intensity light is emitted.

Bury the show To strike sets, costumes, and props after the final performance.

Cable Flexible wire for conducting current from dimmers to lighting units or effects equipment.

Cage Wire enclosure used to separate lighting equipment or sound equipment from the stage.

Call (1) Notice to actors backstage announcing the amount of time before the curtain, normally half hour call, fifteen minute call, and five minute call, (2) notice of rehearsal or performance placed on the call board and reiterated by the stage manager.

Call board Bulletin board for actors.

Call boy Individual who gives calls to the actors. It is advised that the stage manager do this her- or himself.

Candlepower Illuminating capacity of an instrument.

Carpenter Stagehand responsible for handling scenery, building and repairing the set.

Cast (1) Players in a play, (2) to select actors to play roles.

Caster A small wheel used to make movable scenery.

Ceiling A large horizontal canvas-covered frame hung on two or more sets of lines, used to close in the top of an interior set. *Book ceiling*: built in two pieces which fold together at the middle (book-like) parallel to the footlights, to permit flying. *Roll ceiling*: canvas is attached to front and back battens and rolled around them for storing and transportation.

Ceiling plate A plate for bolting together and hanging a ceiling piece.

Center stage The area in the center of the acting area.

Central staging Placing the audience area on all four sides of the acting area.

Chalk line A long length of string rubbed with chalk which is snapped to transfer straight chalk to floor or flat.

Characterization Delineation by dramatist of a role in a play or portrayal by an actor of a role on stage.

Cheesecloth An open-weave cotton cloth sometimes used as scrim.

Chew the scenery To rant and rave on stage.

Cinemoid A colored plastic sheet used for producing color in light.

Clamp Most lighting instruments come with a C-type clamp to fasten them to a pipe. There is a similar cable clamp used to hold heavy quantities of cable to a light batten, but this is most frequently done with tape.

Claque   Paid members of an audience hired to applaud.

Clavilux   An instrument invented by Thomas Wilfred for throwing upon a screen varying patterns of light and color which permit combinations analogous to the successive phrases and themes of music.

Clear please   (1) Order to strike props or get out of the way, (2) warning that the curtain is going up.

Cleat   Metal hardware used for securing flat.

Clew   A metal plate that holds several lines so that they can be handled by a single line.

Climax   That part of the central action, usually near the close, in which tensions are greatest and in which the theme is finally and fully revealed.

Clincheplate   A metal plate used to back clout nails.

Clipboard   A board with a metal clamp on the top for holding plots, cue sheets, etc.

Clip cues   To speak one's lines before the preceding actor has had time to finish the cue phrase. This usually destroys the meaning or effectiveness of the final words.

Clout nails   A type of nail used in scenery construction, which bends to hold materials together when it strikes the clincheplate.

Color box   A metal container of six color frames that may be attached to the front of a spotlight for color changes. Some of these are controlled remotely from a switchboard or from the spotlight. See Boomerang.

Color frame   A metal, wood, or cardboard holder for the color medium in the front of a lighting instrument. More frequently called a Gel frame.

Color medium   A transparent material such as glass, gelatine, or cinemoid, which is placed in front of lighting instruments to produce color.

Color wheel   A device to make color changes. A large cumbersome, wheel mounted on the front of a spotlight, that has four to six openings for different colored gelatines. It may be manually operated by the spotlight operator or it may be motor driven.

Come down   To move toward the downstage area, or toward the audience. See Downstage.

Comedy   (1) Style of drama characterized by the humorous and amiable, (2) a play in which the protagonist fights a winning battle.

Composite   (1) Several pictures showing an actor in various costumes and poses, (2) part of an actor's résumé.

Concert border   Lights mounted on the first pipe upstage of the proscenium.

Connector   A device for connecting two cables together or a cable to a switchboard or unit. Each connector consists of two parts, a female or receiving part and a male which has studs or prongs which fit into the female. Multiple connectors are female connectors to which more than one male connector may be fastened. A number of units may be attached to one cable easily by use of branch-offs or multiple connectors.

Contour curtain   A curtain that is gathered up in scallops.

Conversation piece   A comedy in which there is much talk and little action.

Corner iron   Right-angle iron strap or L-shaped plate used for support or reinforcement.

Corner plate   A triangle of 3/16" or 1/4" plywood used to reinforce corners of flats in scenery construction.

Counterweight system   Mechanical use of weights to help balance heavy flow scenery, curtains, etc.

Crash box   A box filled with broken glass or small metal parts used for sound effects.

Crisis   Turning point in a play.

Crosspiece   Horizontal batten in a flat.

Cue   A signal in dialogue, action, or music for an actor's action or speech or a technician's duty backstage.

Cue sheet   A list of the exact cues for the execution of specific duties by the crew.

Curtain   A hanging drapery that conceals the stage or scene from the audience. It may rise, part, fold, drape, or sink. Also called Front curtain, Main curtain, Act curtain, House curtain, Flag, and Rag.

Curtain line   (1) An imaginary line across the stage that marks the position of the front curtain when it is closed, (2) the last line of a scene or act which is the cue for the curtain to close.

Cut   (1) To remove a line or lines from a script, (2) order to stop rehearsal.

Cut drop   A drop that has pieces cut out or is edged to represent leaves, foliage, or other decoration.

Cut line   A trip line that is cut to release the asbestos curtain in case of fire.

Cutout   See Groundrow.

Cutting list   A list of the pieces of wood with their dimensions needed for scenery and set pieces.

Cyclorama (CYC)   A huge, seamless backing sheet of material, usually white, which may be lit to indicate sky. Sometimes it is hung in a semicircle with the sides coming well downstage to enclose the acting area.

Cyclorama lights   High-powered individual reflector-type border lights mounted on a castered frame (or hung from a light batten) to light the cyclorama.

Dark night(s)   Period when theater is not open to the public.

Dead spot   Area in acting area that is insufficiently lit.

Diffused light   Nearly shadowless light.

Dim   To decrease the intensity of the light on the stage by means of rheostats or dimmers. Also called Take down.

Dim in   To increase the intensity of the light. Also called Dim up or Bring up.

Dimmer   An electrical device used in a switchboard to regulate current. Types: Resistance, Slide, Plate, Transformer Vacuum, Remote control, Silicon rectifier.

Dip in intensity   Unplanned lowering in intensity of stage lighting.

Direct beam   Lenseless projection equipment used to cast shadow or project translucency on a screen, cyc, or flat.

Discovered at rise   On stage when the curtain goes up.

Distemper   Paint made by mixing dry pigment with size. Scene paint.

Dolly   A low truck with casters used for moving scenery, set pieces, or theatrical equipment.

Dome   A permanent plaster cyclorama.

Dope   Glue used for attaching canvas flats.

Douser   Cutoff device in arc light or follow spot.

Downstage Toward the footlights (or if no footlights, toward the pit, apron, or audience).

Draw curtain A type of curtain suspended from an overhead track that opens from center to each side. Also called a traveler curtain.

Dress parade On stage, under the lights (preferably before appropriate flats) check of costumes to be worn by each character.

Dress rehearsal Final rehearsal before opening.

Dressing a set Adding minor decorations to the set, usually the ornamental touches as opposed to functional props that must be on the set for use of actors.

Drop See Backdrop.

Drop curtain A curtain that rolls up from the bottom.

Duck Strong cotton material.

Dutchman A strip of material, usually muslin, about three inches wide, which is used to cover cracks where flats meet. Masking tape is sometimes called Instant Dutchman.

Duvetyn Velvety cotton fabric.

Effect The impression given to an audience of a particular thing by a technical achievement: a rainbow produced by lights, wind produced by a wind machine, etc.

Electrician The operator of the control board and lighting instruments. Not necessarily an electrician in the non-theater meaning of the word. Also called Boardman, Lighting Technician, or Tech.

Elevations (1) Working drawings of the flats of a setting, (2) risers, platforms, etc., that give variety to the stage level.

Elevator stage A section or sections of the stage floor that may be lowered and raised by hydraulic process.

Entr'acte (1) Intermission, (2) short scenes performed before the curtain.

Entrance Actor's appearance on stage.

Epilogue A scene that follows the end of the play.

Equity See AEA.

Expressionism From a school of thought that developed in Germany in the late 19th Century. Really an extension of Impressionism and opposed to Realism and Naturalism. Expressionists are concerned with producing an inner emotional, sensuous, or intellectual reaction. It is this inner emotion that they try to express, and they maintain that it does not necessarily bear a relation to the outer aspect of life.

Exteriors Settings painted to represent outdoor scenes.

Facing Decorative trim, painted or applied around doors, windows, flats, etc.

Fade in Gradual dim up of light or sound.

Fade out Gradual dim out of light or sound.

Fall Rope used with block and tackle.

False blackout A blackout that occurs within a scene but does not call for a scenery or prop change. Usually denotes passage of time. See Blackout.

False proscenium An inner frame especially built for a production to close down a large proscenium, to mask lighting equipment or to give special design to the production. See Proscenium.

Fantasy Play unrestricted by literal and realistic conventions of the theater and usually distinguished by imaginative uses of the supernatural and the mythological.

Farce Play designed only for entertainment and laughter; there is no serious or sincere attempt to depict character nor is there genuine concern with probabilities or realities.

Farce-Comedy A form halfway between farce and comedy which contains elements of both.

Feedback Undesirable noise in sound system; sometimes caused by mike being too close to speaker.

Filament image Projection of filament from spot, to be corrected by adjustment of spot or diffusion.

Fill light Addition of light to blend areas or reduce shadows.

Fire curtain See Asbestos curtain.

Fireplace unit A fireplace frame made to fit a flat opening.

Fireproof curtain See Asbestos curtain.

First border See Border.

Flag See Curtain.

Flaking Paint coming off of flat that needs to be refinished.

Flameproofing Solution sprayed or brushed on flats or fabrics to retard flames.

Flash pot A box device in which a smoke or flash effect is created, also called flash box.

Flat A wooden frame covered with canvas used as a scenic unit. It may be from 10 to 20 feet in height and vary in widths. The widest flat is usually 5′9″ so that it will go through the 6′ openings in freight cars. This one is called a "six" or full flat. Other flats are named by their conventional widths.

Flat paint Paint that absorbs light, opposed to glossy, which you would not want to use generally for scene paint.

Flies The space above the stage occupied by sets of lines and hanging scenery.

Flipper A small piece of scenery hinged to a larger flat.

Float To lower a covered flat by placing the foot against the bottom rail and allow it to float down so it is lying flat on the floor. The flat will fall slowly because of air resistance.

Floodlights Light units that give a general diffused light. Also called Olivette.

Floor cloth Canvas or duck covering for the stage floor. Also called Ground cloth.

Floor plan A scale drawing of a stage setting showing the position on the floor of the walls, windows, openings, etc.

Floor plate Metal plate with ring used by tying lines to the floor.

Floor pocket An opening in the stage floor that contains a receptacle for large stage electrical plugs and is metal covered.

Flown Term applied to condition of scenery that has been raised into the flies.

Fly To lift scenery above the level of the stage floor, out of view of the audience by means of lines from the gridiron.

Fly curtain A curtain that is raised and lowered.

Fly gallery A narrow bridge or gallery running along the side of the stage, well above the floor, from which are operated ropes secured to the pin rail.

Fly man Name applied to any stagehand who is to fly scenery.

Fly rope See Lines, Fly rope.

Follow spot A spotlight on a movable joint, operated so as to follow a player on the stage with a beam of light.

Foot To apply the foot to the bottom rail of a flat or the base of a ladder so that another stagehand may raise it.

Foot-candle A unit for measuring the illumination given by an instrument: it is equal to the amount of direct light thrown by one international candle on a square foot of surface, every part of which is one foot away.

Foot iron A steel brace bolted to the bottom of a piece of scenery or set piece so that it may be fastened to the stage floor by means of a stage screw.

Footlights Strip lights, a source of illumination for the acting area, which may be portable, permanent, open-trough type or disappearing. Being used less and less in modern theaters.

Fortuny System Indirect lighting, using spotlights focused on colored silk fabrics. The silk redirects the light to the stage. It is shadowless, diffuse, and allows for subtle color changes but is impractical because of expense and space required.

Foul To cause scenery or lights hung in the flies to become entangled with each other.

Fourfold Four flats hinged together.

Fourth wall Name given to the hypothetical wall of separation between the stage and the audience in a proscenium theater.

Foyer Entrance hall into a theater.

French scene The division of an act in which the number of characters is constant. Entrance or exit of character(s) marks the beginning of the next French scene.

Fresnel Type of spotlight using a Fresnel lens or step lens. Lens is named for French physicist Fresnel who developed it for lighthouse beacons. The Fresnel produces an even field with soft edges.

Front curtain See Curtain.

Frost Translucent gel used to diffuse light.

Full Maximum intensity of lighting or sound.

Full stage The entire area of the stage that can be used as the acting area.

Funnel A cylinder of cardboard or thin sheet metal fastened perpendicularly to a square of the same material. Also called Snoot, and Highhat.

Fuse A strip of metal with a low melting point, usually in an insulated fireproof container, which breaks when the current becomes too strong.

Gaffer Stage crew head.

Gagging Slang for unauthorized improvisation or revision of lines by an actor.

Gain Volume control on an amplifier.

Gallery Highest balcony in a theater.

Gang (1) To hook together, (2) to move two dimmers together.

Gelatin (Gel) Thin, transparent sheet of material for producing colored light.

Gel frame A metal, wood, or cardboard holder for the color medium which is placed in front of a lighting instrument. Also called Color frame.

Ghost A streak of light that leaks from some light source and falls where it is not wanted. See Spill.

Ghost Load An offstage lighting instrument used to load a resistance dimmer so that it will dim out an onstage instrument properly.

Gimp tacks Small roundheaded tacks used for furniture upholstery.

Gimp tape A decorative upholstery tape used as a finish strip on the edges of furniture.

Give stage To move on stage so that the center of interest will be thrown to another actor.

Glare Light reflection too uncomfortable for the audience.

Glass crash   See Crash box.

Glue burn   Stain on flats caused by glue.

Glue gun   Small, hand-held electrical device for heating and applying glue.

Go   Order to take a cue, execute an effect.

Go on   To enter on the stage.

Go up   To forget one's lines and to be unable to resume without assistance.

Gobo   (1) Metal plate with pattern used in lighting instrument to project pattern on cyc or lighting effect on flat, (2) a louver, usually of metal, used to prevent spill from lighting instrument.

Good theater   Any piece of business that clicks with the audience, or that communicates surely and easily with the audience.

Gopher (Gofer)   A production assistant who gets his or her title from the fact that he or she is frequently sent to "go fer" something.

Grand drape   Curtain extending width of the stage opening, which is hung just back of the proscenium and in front of the front curtain. It can be lowered to cut the height of the stage opening.

Grand valance   The first drapery border in front of the main act curtain usually of the same material.

Green room   Waiting or reception room, behind, near, or under the stage, used by authors, directors, actors, to meet their public. So called because the first "retiring" room in Covent Garden Theater in London was all in green. Most professional theaters do not have green rooms today, but many little community and university theaters provide such meeting places.

Gridiron (Grid)   The framework of steel or wooden beams above the stage, which supports the rigging used in flying scenery.

Grip   A stagehand who assists the master carpenter in moving settings.

Grommet   Metal eyehole, usually found at the top of drapes and through which ties are run.

Ground cloth   See Floor cloth.

Ground plans   Layout of the stage showing location of set, properties, and lights for a production. See Floor plan.

Ground row   (1) A row of lights on the floor to light lower area of a cyc or drop, (2) a low profile of scenery designed to represent rocks, earth, skyline, etc., that stands self-supported on the ground, usually in front of the cyc, and is used to conceal the base of the cyc, the lighting equipment and cables, as well as to help give the illusion of depth and/or horizon.

Grouping   Placing the cast about the stage.

Guy line   Rope or wire from high scenery to floor used to steady or strengthen.

Half hour   Warning by the stage manager a half hour before the curtain goes up.

Ham   An actor who is bad or pretentious, or both.

Handle   A word that an actor adds to the beginning of a line, that was not originally written in the script: Oh, gee, gosh, well, but, etc.

Hand prop   Any property that is handled by the actor during the course of the play, but particularly those props that the actor carries onto the stage as opposed to those that are discovered. See Properties.

Hanger iron   Hardware for hanging scenery. It has a ring attached to one end of a steel plate which is bolted to the scenery.

Hanging the show   Putting up the sets of a play: flats, doorways, lights, etc.

So called because originally the show was set with wings and backdrops that had to be hung from the grid. Also called Mounting.

Head block Three or more pulley blocks framed together and placed on the gridiron above the outer edge of the fly floor. The ropes from three or more loft blocks come together at the head block and pass down to the pin rail. Also called Lead block.

Heads up Order to watch for moving scenery.

Highhat See Funnel.

Hold (1) To sustain an effect for audience response, (2) to pause in delivering a line so that audience may react.

(To) Hold Book To prompt, take blocking notation, and make notes on line changes and cues during rehearsals.

Hood See Funnel.

Horseshoe stage A stage that is surrounded on three sides by the audience.

House The auditorium and front of the theater, as contrasted with the stage and backstage areas. Also used to refer to the size of the audience, as in "How's the house?"

House lights Electrical fixtures that provide light for the audience. Sometimes called Auditorium lights.

Hung up Condition of being unable to continue one's lines or business because another actor is ad-libbing or because another actor has already taken the position you were to take.

IATSE International Alliance of Theatrical and Stage Employees. Union for stagehands.

Impressionism Theory that productions should be concerned with artistic interpretation rather than with reality. Strives for psychological reaction by use of color and line.

Ingenue Young girl in a play, usually providing the love interest.

Inner proscenium See False proscenium.

In one, two, three "In one" is the area on stage just upstage of the curtain line five or six feet. "In two" is the first area plus the next five or six feet upstage. "In three" adds the next five or six feet upstage or full stage.

Inset A small scene set inside a large one.

Interiors Sets representing indoor scenes.

Iris shutter A manually operated shutter for varying the size of a light beam emitted from a lighting instrument.

Jack A triangular device made of wood that is hinged to the back of a ground row or other set piece for the purpose of bracing it from behind.

Jackknife stage Two portable stages with narrow ends parallel to foots, and on pivots. When one stage has been used, it is swung offstage into the wings. From the wings on the other side of the stage the second stage is swung into position on the acting area. The jackknife stage permits quick changes of scenery, as do elevator and revolving stages.

Jog A narrow flat.

Juicer Electrician.

Juvenile Player of youthful male roles.

Keep alive To store scenery or properties so that they will be readily available.

Keyboard A switchboard, usually with slide controls.

Key light The main source of light.

Keystone A small piece of 3/16″ or 1/4″ plywood cut in the wedge shape of a keystone and used to reinforce joints in scenery.

Kill (1) To take an article off a set, (2) to extinguish lights or stop sound effects or other effects.

Klieglight Trade name for spotlights.

Lamp Source of light. See Bottle.

Lamp dip Lamp coloring lacquer that gives a durable transparent color tint.

Lash To bind two flats together with a lash line.

Lash cleat A small metal hook on the frame of a flat, behind which a lash line is thrown to bind the flat to the edge of another flat.

Lash line Length of #8 sash cord fastened to the back of a flat and used to lash flats together.

Lash line eye The metal eye to which the lash line is secured.

Lead Principal role in a play, or actor or actress playing the role.

Lead block See Head block.

Leg drop A drop from which the entire center portion has been omitted.

Left stage The area on stage at the actor's left as he or she stands center stage facing the audience. Stage left.

Legit Popular abbreviation for the legitimate stage, live theater as opposed to movies.

Leko Once a brand name, now a generic term for any ellipsoidal reflector spotlight. (Compare to Fresnel and P.C.)

Lekolite Trade name for spotlight.

Lens Glass cut for the purpose of condensing and concentrating the rays of light from lamp source and reflector.

Levels (1) A platform, set of steps, or ramp that raises the playing space above the level of the stage (also called Risers, Elevators, and Platforms), (2) an imaginary line drawn across the stage at any distance from the curtain line but parallel to it.

Lid Top of platform or ceiling.

Light batten A pipe or batten to which lighting instruments are clamped and along which lighting cables are run.

Light plot Sequence of light changes from beginning to end of the play, with lines or business that immediately precede each change. Each change is described.

Light towers Poles mounted at the sides of the stage or audience area to mount lighting instruments. Also called Light trees.

Light tree Tower of pipe or wood used to hang lighting instruments in the wings.

Line, Lines Speech or speeches in a play.

Line (of business) Type of role or roles in which an actor specializes.

Line drawings Blueprints from which sets and set pieces may be constructed without reference to any other drawings or specifications.

Lines, Fly Rope The ropes from the grid that raise and lower scenery. One end is attached to the batten and the other is secured on the fly gallery. Three ropes are usually used on each batten. The nearest one to the gallery is called the short line. The one in the middle is the center line. The farthest is the long line.

Linnebach projector A large metal box with concentrated light source for projecting pictures from a gelatin or glass slide.

Lintel   Horizontal crosspiece over door, window, or arch.

Live weight   Weight of moving body as opposed to weight of inert body.

Load, Electrical   (1) Amount of current used in a circuit, (2) electrical equipment to be connected to a line.

Load in   Process of moving all of a company's equipment (scenery, props, costumes, etc.) into a theater.

Load out   Process of moving all of a company's equipment out of a theater.

Lobby   That part of the theater between the entrance and the last row of seats, usually separated by a wall and doors.

Lobster-Scope   A spotlight effect machine producing a flicker of light.

Loft block   A pulley block in the gridiron through which a line may be run.

Louvers   (1) Concentric rings of thin metal strips fitted to the front of a projector to cut off all but the straight beam of light (also called Spill Rings and Baffles), (2) parallel strips of wood or metal used to mask a light source from the audience.

Make fast   To tie off securely or fasten any line.

Manager   There are various types other than stage manager. *Producers* are sometimes called managers. *House Manager*: responsible for all details in management of the theater building. *Business Manager*: handles money, payrolls, accounts, contracts, etc. *Company Manager*: responsible for the company, usually on the road. *Personal Manager*: acts as a representative for an author or actor.

Manuscript (ms)   Written or typed play, or the book of a musical. Usually used in rehearsal.

Mark it   Order to record level of intensity of light or sound cue.

Martingale   A two-fer or branchoff connector. Two lines with female plugs spliced into one line with a male plug used to connect two instruments to one cable. (I have heard this term pronounced "Martin-dale" in supply houses on the West Coast. If any reader knows the origin or correct spelling of this term, please let me know. Thanks.)

Mask   (1) To hide from sight, or to conceal from the audience, (2) any sort of cardboard or sheet metal slide to be placed in the guides of a spotlight to restrict the light to various shapes. Also called a Mat.

Masking (Piece)   A piece of scenery used to conceal backstage from the audience.

Mat   See Mask.

M.C.   Master of ceremonies, introducer of acts or participants in a variety program.

Medium   See Color medium.

Melodrama   An exaggerated, romantic, exciting, and improbable play. Incident and situation are important, characterization is not.

Mezzanine   (1) Sometimes the first balcony of a theater having more than one; (2) the first few rows of the balcony and separated from the balcony proper.

Milk it dry   To squeeze the maximum laughs out of a line, bit of business, or situation.

Mopboard   Baseboard.

Motivation   Reason behind all stage action and speech. Skill with which the director and actors find the motivation for characters and incidents will determine the quality of the play.

Mounting   See Hanging.

Movement Passing of actors from place to place on stage. See Blocking.

Mugging Excessive facial contortions during a performance.

Mule block A block with pulley used to change the horizontal direction of a line.

Mullion Slender vertical bar between windows.

Multiple pin connector A female receptacle that accepts three male pin connectors.

Muslin Material frequently used for covering flats.

Naturalism Same in external form as Realism but emphasizes the natural function in life as opposed to Realism which is more selective.

Newel Post that supports handrails of steps, also called newel post.

Notices Reviews, dramatic criticism.

Offstage Area backstage, outside of the acting area.

Ohm Unit of electrical resistance.

Olio A mixture, medley, miscellaneous collection. Usually variety acts following an old-fashioned melodrama.

Olio curtain A curtain that rolls up from the bottom. Also called Drop Curtain.

Olivette See Floodlight.

Onstage Inside the acting area.

O.P. Opposite prompt, usually the left side backstage.

Open cold To give the first public performance for critics without out-of-town tryouts or invitational previews.

Orchestra Lower floor of the auditorium.

Organic blocking Process of blocking in which the director allows the actors to move at will and then uses their movement as the basis for his blocking.

Out front (1) The part of a theater that is beyond the front curtain—lobby, box office, seats, etc., (2) any area occupied by members of the audience.

Outlet box Heavy metal fireproof box containing two to four female receptacles, porcelain insulated.

Overture and beginners, please The British equivalent of Places, please.

P.A. System Public address system. Microphone and loudspeakers, or any sound amplification equipment.

Pace To the theater what tempo is to music. The timing of lines and business. Not to be confused with speed.

Paper tech A crew-only technical rehearsal to iron out the mechanical bugs.

Parallel A collapsible frame support for a stage platform.

Part (1) Character assigned to an actor in a play, (2) typewritten portion of a play that pertains to an actor's scenes and contains all of his or her lines and cues. See Side.

Patch panel A plugging panel used to interconnect dimmers and outlets, also called plugging panel.

Pay out Order to allow rope to pass through hands.

P.C. Plano convex spotlight. Compare to Leko and Fresnel.

Peephole stage Stage with definite division between acting area and audience, such as a proscenium arch. Also called a Picture frame stage. Compare to Central staging and Horseshoe stage.

Periactus A three-sided revolving apparatus painted with scenery.

Period plays Costume plays of other eras.

Perspective drawing Rendering of floor plan and elevations to perspective of audience.

Phantom load Added resistance to a dimmer so that it will dim out a spot too small to dim ordinarily.

Picture frame stage See Peephole stage.

Pigtail See Martingale.

Pilot light Dim light used by stage manager to follow prompt script.

Pin rail A rail with holes in it, into which wooden pins are placed to secure lines. See Fly gallery.

Pipe batten See Batten.

Pipe clamp An adjustable metal jaw for mounting lighting instrument on pipe battens.

Pit Sunken space in front of stage, usually where orchestra performs.

Pivot stage See Jackknife stage.

Places, please Signal given by stage manager to the cast for taking their respective positions preparatory to the rise of the curtain.

Plano-Convex Type of lens or type of spotlight using that type of lens.

Plant (1) Member of the acting company who is placed in the audience for the purpose of fostering the illusion that the audience is taking part in the performance, (2) a prop on stage at curtain rise, particularly one concealed from the audience.

Platform A collapsible and portable unit used to add levels to the stage, or to provide an additional acting area.

Playing space Stage space, inside or outside the set, visible to the audience and used for acting during the play.

Plot (1) List of what is required of each technical department in order to make a play work (light plot, sound plot, property plot, costume plot, special effects plot, etc.), (2) planned action or intrigue of a play.

Plug (1) A scenic unit placed in or in front of another piece of scenery to change it. For example, an arch for one act may be changed for the next act by placing it in a window plug, a fountain plug, etc., (2) a male connector with insulated handle, with two strips of copper along the side to make contact with similar strips in the outlet box.

Plugging box Portable outlet box.

Position An actor's place on the stage as set by the director.

Practical Something that is usable. For example, a pair of French doors might be constructed so that only one opens. The one that does open is the practical one.

Preset To place props, costumes, or any materials in position prior to curtain or prior to use.

Pre-set (or Pre-select) switchboard A switchboard where one or more complete changes can be set up in advance without interfering with the lighting of the scene in progress.

Preview Performance given prior to formal opening.

Principals Actors who carry major roles in a production.

Problem play Play built around a difficulty of society. Its characters personify the various forces and their conflict is the subject matter of the play.

Producer The individual (amateur or professional) who accepts the responsibility for obtaining the personnel and the materials to make theater happen.

Profile board Plywood, 3/16" or 1/4", used to edge a flat.

Projector Directional floodlight, using a metal parabolic reflector to project parallel light rays.

Promptbook   Book of the play including all business, action, plans, and plots needed for the production. Also called Prompt script.

Prompt script   See Promptbook.

Prompt side (P.S.)   Side of the stage from which the stage manager runs the show, usually the right side.

Prompter   One who stands in the wings or out of sight of the audience, and assists actors with their lines and cues. Usually utters only the first few words of a line that an actor forgets, or significant words of the line.

Prop box   Box kept offstage in which props are stored.

Properties (Props)   Articles used for a play—hand props, trim props, and set props.

Prop table   Table offstage where props are set prior to the curtain. Actors are conditioned to obtain their hand props from the same place on the table at each performance, and return their props there if they carry them offstage.

Proscenium   The wall dividing the auditorium from the stage.

Proscenium arch   The edge of the opening of the proscenium.

Proscenium opening   The opening in the proscenium through which the audience views the play.

Protagonist   Hero of a play or the character who carries its principal idea.

Put together   A rehearsal at which all elements of the production are brought together in their appropriate sequence.

Quartz-Iodine   A long-life lamp used in lighting instruments.

Quick study   Hurried and technical memorization of a part and its business by an actor, usually in an emergency when a part must be learned at a moment's notice. Also refers to an actor whose memorization comes easily to him or her.

Quiet please   Order for silence.

Rag   See Curtain.

Rail   The top or bottom board in the frame of a flat.

Raked stage   A stage slanted down toward the audience.

Raking   (1) Placing the side walls of a set at an angle to improve the sight lines, (2) slanting stage area, platform, or audience seating area to improve sight lines.

Ramp   Inclined platform.

Rant   To deliver lines in a shouting, melodramatic and extravagant manner.

Readthrough   Rehearsal at which the script is read from beginning to end.

Realism   Fidelity to nature or real life. Representation without idealization. Adherence to actual fact.

Reflectors   Shiny metal surfaces used in spotlights and projectors in back of the light source to intensify the light and give it direction: spherical, ellipsoidal, and parabolic.

Rehearsal   Repetition of scene or practice of a production in private, preliminary to public performance, and for the perfection of that performance.

Rep company   Company playing repertory.

Repertory   Collection of plays, operas, or parts that may be readily performed because of familiarity with them on the part of a cast or actor. A repertory company is one in which, instead of performing one play continuously, there are several productions ready and they are varied each night or week. Usually the same actors have parts in several productions.

Reprise   Repeat of a musical number.

Resistance dimmer   A type of stage dimmer used to decrease intensity of lighting instruments.

Return piece   A flat set at right angles to the downstage corner of a set. It is parallel with the footlights or curtain and runs offstage to mask the wings.

Reveal   See Thickness.

Revolving stage   One or more circular stages (mounted on top of the permanent stage) electrically or manually revolved to effect scene changes or special effects.

Right stage   The area on stage at the actor's right as he stands center stage facing the audience. Stage right.

Ring down   To drop the front curtain on the last scene or act. Based on an old theatrical custom of ringing a bell to denote the closing of the show.

Risers   See Levels.

Road irons   Angle irons placed at corners of flats to protect them when they must be moved frequently as on tour.

Road show   A theatrical production that tours several cities and towns.

Rococo   Overelaborate style of decoration.

Roll curtain   A curtain that rolls up from the bottom. Also called Olio curtain and Drop curtain.

Rondel   See Roundel.

Rosin box   A box, large enough to stand in, containing rosin used by actors or dancers to rosin shoes or slippers.

Roundels   Circular heat-resisting glass color media.

Royalty   Compensation to authors and composers paid for permission to perform their works.

Run   Length of a stage engagement or the total number of performances.

Runway   Extension of stage into audience area.

Saddle iron   A narrow strip of iron used to brace the bottom of a door flat. Also called Door iron and Sill iron.

Safety factor   Safe percentage by which load on ropes, cables, and dimmers may be exceeded.

SAG   Screen Actors Guild. A union for actors working in filmed entertainment.

Sandbags   Canvas bags filled with sand used to weight lines or the jacks behind scenery.

Satire   A form of comedy in which sharp derision is aimed at an idea or individual.

Scene   (1) Setting of an action, (2) division of an act or play.

Scene dock   A storage area for flats and other scenic units, usually located in either wing area of the stage.

Scioptican   Device used to create moving effects such as clouds, flames, waves, etc.

Scrim   A finely woven material through which light may or may not be seen, depending on how it is lit. Also called Theatrical gauze and Bobbinet.

Selvage   The edge on either side of a woven or flat-knitted fabric, so finished as to prevent raveling.

Set   To prepare the stage for the scene that is to be performed.

Set dressing   Props arranged to decorate the set. Also called Trim props.

Set of lines   A unit group of ropes hanging from the gridiron used to fly scenery. There are usually three or four lines in a set.

Set piece A unit of scenery standing alone.

Set props Props that stand on the stage floor, or other props not carried on by the actors. Compare to Hand props.

Set up To erect a set and install related equipment.

Shift To change scenery and properties from one setting to another.

Shoe A block of wood enforcing the joint between toggle and stile.

Showcase theater A theater whose main purpose is to obtain paid work for members of the cast.

Show curtain A drop or curtain behind the front curtain that is painted to give atmosphere to the particular play being presented.

Shtick Slang: business, usually comedy business.

Shutter An apparatus mounted on the front of a spotlight, or designed into it, which cuts entirely, or in part, the rays of light. There are iris, combination, funnel, and slide shutters. Also called Cut-Off.

Side Page of an actor's part. Usually half the size of a standard typewritten sheet. When bound together, called sides.

Sight lines Lines, painted or imagined, that divide area the audience can see from area the audience cannot see.

Sitting on their hands Phrase used to describe an unresponsive audience.

Situation Relationship of characters to one another or to a condition. A play may have a series of situations. The basic situation refers to that one problem that is central to the play.

Size water A thin solution of glue and water used in mixing scene paint.

Sky drop A drop painted blue to represent the sky.

Smoke pocket Steel channels on each side of the proscenium arch that guide the ends of the asbestos curtain.

Snatch To hook or unhook flown scenery during a scene change.

Snatch lines Adjustable ropes or chains used to fasten scenery to a counterweighted batten.

Sneak To bring in a light or sound cue imperceptibly.

Snoot See Funnel.

Snow cradle Device for making snow effect.

Soft light Diffused light with little or no shadow.

Soubrette A minor female part in comedies whose characterization calls for pertness, coyness, coquetry, intrigue, etc., and is frequently a show part.

Sound effects Sounds performed offstage in relation to stage action.

Space stage Method of staging plays with lights focused on actors so that no setting is necessary.

Spelvin, George Fictitious name used on a program by an actor whose real name already appears in the program. George Spelvin was first used by a minor actor who doubled in the cast of *Brewster's Millions* in 1907. The play was so successful that its author, Winchell Smith, continued to have George Spelvin listed in the rest of his productions for luck. Harry Selby is another name that is similarly used.

Spike To mark the position of a set piece on the stage floor, usually with tape.

Spike marks Those marks, colored crayon, luminous paint, or tape used to help stage crew position set pieces. Infrequently used to help actors determine where they should be.

Spill Unwanted light due to a poorly focused or shuttered spotlight. Sometimes spill is unavoidable because it is emitted from a lighting instrument that cannot be shuttered.

Split stage Two or more scenes placed on stage simultaneously.

Spotlight Lighting instrument designed to produce a concentrated beam of light.

Spot line A single rope specifically rigged from the gridiron to fly a piece of scenery that cannot be handled by the regular lines.

S.R.O. Standing Room Only.

Stage Entire floor space behind the proscenium arch.

Stage brace See Brace.

Stage call Meeting of the cast and director on stage to discuss problems before a performance or rehearsal.

Stage directions Instructions in the script concerning movements and arrangements on the stage.

Stagehand An individual who is always present backstage when an actress or actor has to make a quick change in the wings.

Stage manager The individual who accepts responsibility for the smooth running of the production on stage and backstage in pre-rehearsal, rehearsal, performance, and post-performance phases.

Stage pocket Outlet box distributed about the stage, usually sunken into floor and equipped with a self-closing slotted cover.

Stage screw (Peg) A large, tapered screw with a handle used to secure stage braces to the floor.

Stage wait Period of time when there is no dialogue or action on stage, usually an undesirable situation caused by a late entrance or a dropped line.

Stage whisper A stage convention in which one actor whispers loud enough for the entire audience to hear, but is assumed to be heard only by those to whom he or she is whispering and not by other actors on stage.

Stand by An order to be alert for a cue.

Standby Understudy

Stands Metal devices for holding and mounting spotlights, floodlights, and projectors.

Star Leading actor or actress.

Stile The vertical piece of wood that forms the slide in the frame of a flat.

Stock Resident company of players performing one play nightly for a week and rehearsing another play for the following week.

Stock scenery Flats and other scene units kept on hand for repeated use.

Straight Refers to a role or performance that is natural, normal, and uncolored by eccentricities.

Strap hinge A hinge with long tapered flaps used for hanging windows and doors.

Strike To clear the stage of scenery, props, etc.

Strip light A long, troughlike reflector with sockets for lamps of small wattage, or a row of individual reflectors housed in a rigid sheet-metal structure. Used to produce general illumination.

Stroboscope An instrument for producing the illusion of motion by a series of pictures viewed in rapid succession.

Subtext Meaning underlying the lines.

Supernumerary (Super) An extra or walk-on in a production. A person who merely appears in a mob scene or in the background, and who has no individual lines of her or his own to speak.

Swatch　Sample of material or paint.

Sweep　A method used for setting up and cutting circles or arches.

Switchboard　A combination of switches, dimmer plates, and fuses for controlling light. Also called Dimmerboard.

Tab　A sheet of canvas or other material, framed or unframed, narrower than a drop but suspended like a drop, used chiefly for masking offstage spaces. Also called a Leg.

Tableau curtain　A curtain that is gathered up in an ornamental arch. See Curtain.

Tag　Term for the final speech of a scene, act, or play, serving as a cue for the curtain.

Takedown　See Dim.

Take-in　Process of moving all of the sets and set pieces for the forthcoming production to the acting area for the first time and setting it all up as it is supposed to play.

Take it out　Order to raise scenery.

Take stage　To move into an area of greater prominence on the stage with other actors yielding focus.

Teaser　(1) Scenery border suspended form the grid just back of the front curtain used to mask from the audience anything in the flies, edge of a ceiling piece, etc. It can be raised or lowered to change the height of the stage curtain. It is often used in place of a grand drape, (2) any short drop suspended above to mask.

Technical director　Individual responsible for construction of scenery and set pieces.

Technical rehearsal (Tech)　A rehearsal at which the technical aspects of the production are integrated.

Technician (Tech)　An individual who runs lights, sound, or special effects equipment.

Template　A pattern made of cardboard or plastic—most useful to the stage manager are those for furniture and lighting instruments.

Template table　(1) A special type of workbench used in the construction of flats, (2) a pattern.

Theatrical guide　See Scrim.

Thickness　A width of lumber or other material attached to the edge of an opening—doorway, arch, window—to give the edge the effect of depth or thickness. Also called Reveal or Return.

Three-dimensional scenery　Scenery that will be seen from all sides and is therefore finished on all sides.

Three fold　Three flats hinged together.

Throw　Distance between lighting instrument and surface to be lit.

Throw it away　To give no particular emphasis or expression to a speech or line in a play.

Thrust stage　Acting area of stage that extends into the audience, or the audience is seated on three sides of the apron.

Tie off　To secure lines to hardware or the pin rail.

Time sheet　Record kept by stage manager of exact times of each act, scene, and scene change.

Title role Character whose name appears in the title of the play, usually the most important role.

Toggle (Bar) The crosspiece in the frame of a flat.

Top it To build or increase the volume or emotional intensity of a line to a greater level than the previous line.

Tormentor Long, narrow curtains or flats, upstage on either side of the proscenium arch, used to mask the wings. See Leg.

Tormentor lights A number of spotlights mounted on a vertical pipe batten on either side of the stage, just behind the tormentors.

Trades Newspapers and magazines devoted to the theater, or any other special interest.

Tragedy Drama in which the protagonist fights a losing battle.

Translucency A sheet of treated, thin material. When backlighted, may be used to produce silhouette effects.

Traps Trapdoors which open into the basement trap room and permit the use of sunken stairways, scenery, or actors rising from or sinking into the ground.

Traveler A curtain that opens to the sides.

Treadmill stage Machine device consisting of belts running on the stage floor, on which scenery or actors may give the illusion of traveling over a distance.

Trim To hang and adjust drops or borders so that the lower edge is parallel to the floor.

Trim props Those properties that are placed within the set or hung on the walls of the set for ornamentation.

Trip To elevate the bottom of a drop or other flown scenery, with an auxiliary set of lines, in such a way as to make it occupy a space approximately half its height. Tripping is used on a stage where there is not enough fly space to get a unit out of sight by taking it straight up with one set of lines.

Trip line A line or lines to a batten used to adjust its position.

Truck A dolly.

Tungsten-Halogen Long-life lamps used in lighting equipment.

Turkey A show that is a failure. The term originated when bad shows were opened on Thanksgiving Day to clear expenses and make a little money in the two or three holiday performances. Any badly cast or badly produced show.

Turntable Moving stage, revolving stage.

Twist lock Electrical connectors that have to be twisted into place and therefore cannot easily be withdrawn. They are especially useful where cords must lie on the stage floor and are in danger of being kicked out of an outlet.

Two fold Two flats hinged together. Also called a Wing.

Twofor Two-fer or martingale or multiple connector. Two female plugs spliced into one male plug in order to plug two lighting instruments into a single cable.

Typecasting Selecting actors for roles because they resemble in real life the characters they will portray.

Ultraviolet light See Black light.

Understudy An actor who must be perfect in a given role, know all the lines and businesses, but who appears only when the person playing that role is taken ill or for some other reason cannot appear.

Unit set Set built of scenic units that can be used together in various combinations to form different settings.

Upstage (1) Away from the footlights or audience, (2) to move upstage of another cast member and thereby compel that cast member to turn his back to the audience if he wishes to speak to the "upstager."

Valance Teaser or border.

Vampire trap Double-faced section of a flat that revolves on a pivot for fast escapes or disappearance of props.

Velours Curtains used to dress a stage, made of velour, usually consisting of a backdrop with wing curtains for side masking.

Velveteen Imitation velvet material used for draperies.

Voltage The measurement of the force needed for the flow of electricity.

Wagon (Stage) A low platform on wheels or casters on which a set may be placed and then moved quickly into place.

Walk-on A very small part, with or without lines.

Walk the curtain To walk behind the curtain as it closes to insure that it closes properly.

Walk-through A rehearsal in which actors get out of their chairs and walk through their movements on stage.

Walk up To raise a flat from the floor to a vertical position, by hand.

Wardrobe (1) Costumes and all articles of dress of a play or production, (2) room in which costumes are stored or fitted.

Wardrobe person The person in charge of costumes and their upkeep.

Warn A signal that a cue is due within a short time, usually within a minute.

Watt A unit of electric power equal to a current of one ampere under one volt of pressure.

Wing See Two fold.

Wings (1) Space outside the acting area, at the right and left of stage, (2) draperies that hang at the sides of the stage to mask the offstage areas.

Working drawings Blueprints made from the designer's drawings. See Line drawings.

Work light Light for the stage area used during rehearsals, scene shifts, and construction. Work lights are usually controlled by a wall switch instead of from the dimmerboard.

Yoke The metal, U-shaped support that holds a lighting instrument.

Zip cord Lightweight household electrical wire that should not be used for stage lighting, except for practical lights on the set.

Reader's Comments Form

Does this book meet your needs?

Did you find it easy to read and understand?

Was it organized for convenient use and application?

Was it complete?

Was it well illustrated?

Was it suitable for your theater?

The name of your theater:

   Type (circle one): professional—educational—community—show-case—children's—religious

Your name and job title:

Did you use this book (check appropriate lines):
☐ As an introduction to the subject?
☐ For advanced guidance on the subject?
☐ As an instructor?
☐ As a student?

Your comments:

☐ I wish to make reference to Chapter_____:
I feel additional information or examples should be included in the area of_____:

Please use the reverse side or attach additional pages for your comments if necessary.

Perhaps in your work you have discovered a management procedure, a method, or a technique that would be of help to the future stage managers. Insights into the peculiarities of dance, ballet, opera, ice shows, theme park, dinner theater, puppetry, magic, variety shows, and festivals would be especially appreciated. Your comments or additions could help to improve the next edition of this manual.

Send to: THE STAGE MANAGER
          P.O. Box 480273
          Los Angeles, California 90048

Index